REVOLUTIONARY ᴵ

A BOOK IN THE SERIES

BICENTENNIAL REFLECTIONS ON THE FRENCH REVOLUTION

General Editors: Keith Michael Baker, Stanford University
Steven Laurence Kaplan, Cornell University

REVOLUTIONARY NEWS
THE PRESS IN FRANCE,
1789–1799

Jeremy D. Popkin

DUKE UNIVERSITY PRESS

Durham and London

1990

© 1990 Duke University Press
All rights reserved
Printed in the United States of America
on acid-free paper ∞
Library of Congress Cataloging-in-Publication data
appear on the last page of this book.

To Gabriel and Alexander

CONTENTS

ACKNOWLEDGMENTS

This book draws on fifteen years of research on the press during the era of the French Revolution, during which I have been fortunate to enjoy the encouragement of many friends and colleagues and support from a variety of sources. I would like to thank series editors Keith Baker and Steven Kaplan for their helpful comments on the manuscript; my friends Sarah Maza and Mark Summers also offered useful observations on the work as a whole, and Lynn Hunt critiqued the section on the *Père Duchêne*. The idea for this project grew out of an essay on the press during the Revolution that Robert Darnton invited me to prepare, and I am grateful for his encouragement. The influence Pierre Rétat's insights into the nature of the press have had on me can be seen in many places in this book. Above all, I owe special thanks to my good friend and fellow press historian Jack Censer, who continued, as he has for many years, to find the time in a busy schedule to offer me the benefit of his close reading of my work.

Over the years my research has been aided by the staffs of the Bibliothèque nationale, the Archives nationales, the Newberry Library, the Harvard College (Widener) Library, and the M. I. King Library of the University of Kentucky. I enjoyed fellowship support for my work from the National Endowment for the Humanities, the Newberry Library, the American Philosophical Society, and the University of Kentucky Research Foundation, to all of whom I express my thanks. Some material in this book appeared earlier in my book *The Right-Wing Press in France, 1792–1800* (1980), and in my contribution to Robert Darnton and Daniel Roche, eds., *Revolution in Print: The Press in France, 1775–1800* (1989): I am grateful to the University of North Carolina Press and the University of California Press, respectively, for permission to reuse it here in modified form.

This book is dedicated to my sons Gabriel and Alexander, in the hope that whatever they decide to do when they grow up, they will enjoy their work as much as I have enjoyed researching and writing about this subject.

EDITORS' INTRODUCTION

I N PARIS, IN THIS SYMBOLIC NIGHT OF 14 JULY, NIGHT
of fervor and of joy, at the foot of the timeless obelisk, in this
Place de la Concorde that has never been more worthy of the
name, [a] great and immense voice . . . will cast to the four winds
of history the song expressing the ideal of the five hundred Mar-
seillais of 1792." The words, so redolent in language and tone of
the instructions for the great public festivals of the French Revolution, are those of Jack Lang, French Minister of Culture, Communications, Great Public Works, and the Bicentennial. The text
is that of the program for the grandiose opera-parade presenting "a
Marseillaise for the World," the internationally televised spectacle
from Paris crowning the official celebration of the bicentennial of
the French Revolution.

The minister's language was aptly fashioned to the occasion. It
was well chosen to celebrate Paris as world-historical city—joyous
birthplace of the modern principles of democracy and human
rights—and the Revolution of 1789 as the momentous assertion
of those universal human aspirations to freedom and dignity that
have transformed, and are still transforming, an entire world. It
was no less well chosen to leap over the events of the Revolution
from its beginning to its end, affirming that the political passions

engendered by its momentous struggles had finally ceased to divide the French one from another.

The spectacle on the Place de la Concorde exemplified the unavowed motto of the official bicentennial celebration: "The Revolution is over." Opting for a celebration consonant with the predominantly centrist, consensualist mood of the French in the late 1980s, the presidential mission charged with the organization of the bicentennial celebrations focused on the values which the vast majority of French citizens of all political persuasions underwrite—the ideals exalted in the Declaration of the Rights of Man. It offered the nation—and the world—the image of a France finally at peace with itself: a people secure in the tranquil enjoyment of the human rights that constitute France's true revolutionary patrimony, confident in the maturity of French institutions and their readiness to meet the challenges and opportunities of a new European order, firm in the country's dedication to securing universal respect for the democratic creed it claims as its most fundamental contribution to the world of nations. No hint of subsequent radicalization, no echo of social conflict, no shadow of the Terror could mar this season of commemoration. It followed that the traditional protagonists and proxies in the great debate over the Revolution's character and purposes, Danton and Robespierre, were to be set aside. The hero for 1989 was Condorcet: savant, philosopher, reformer, "moderate" revolutionary, victim of the Revolution he failed to perfect and control.

But the Revolution—ambiguous, complex, subversive as it remains, even after two hundred years—still proved refractory to domestication. Not even the solemn bicentennial spectacle on the night of 14 July was sheltered from certain treacherous counterpoints. Spectators watching the stirring parade unfold down the Champs-Élysées toward the Place de la Concorde already knew that this same route would shortly be followed by participants in a counterrevolutionary commemoration returning a simulacrum of the guillotine to its most notorious revolutionary site. These spectators were moved by the poignant march of Chinese youths pushing their bicycles in evocation of the recent massacre in Tienanmen Square, even as this brutal silencing of demands for human rights was being justified in Beijing as reluctant defense of the Revolution against dangerous counterrevolutionary elements. The spectators were stirred by Jessye Norman's heroic rendition of the *Marseillaise,* even as it reminded all who cared to attend to its words that this now universal chant of liberation was also a ferocious war song calling for the letting of the "impure blood" of the enemy. On the very day of the parade a politely exasperated Margaret Thatcher, publicly contesting the French claim to the paternity of the Rights of Man and insisting on the identity of Revolution with Terror, reminded the world of the jolting equation, $1789 = 1793$. For their part, the performers sent by the USSR to march in the parade, garbed in dress more Russian than Soviet, raised questions about the socialist axiom that the Russian Revolution was the necessary conclusion to the French. As men and women throughout the communist world rallied for human rights, was it any longer possible to see 1917 as the authentic future of 1789?

The tensions and contradictions of commemoration have their own political and cultural dynamic, but they are nourished by the tensions and contradictions of historical interpretation. If the Revolution has been declared over in France, its history is far from terminated—either there or elsewhere. Indeed, the bicentennial of the French Revolution has reopened passionate historiographical debates over its meaning that began with the Revolution itself. As early as September 1789, readers of the *Révolutions de Paris*— one of the earliest and most widely read of the newspapers that were to play so powerful a role in shaping the revolutionary consciousness—were demanding "a historical and political picture of everything that has happened in France since the first Assembly of Notables," to be offered as a means of explaining the nature of "the astonishing revolution that has just taken place." Observers and participants alike sought from the outset to grasp the causes, nature, and effects of these remarkable events. And if they con-

curred on the momentous character of the Revolution, they differed vehemently on its necessity, its means, its fundamental
mission. Burke and Paine, Barnave and de Maistre, Condorcet and
Hegel were only among the first in a dazzling succession of
thinkers who have responded to the need to plumb the historical
identity and significance of a phenomenon that has seemed from
its very beginning to demand, yet defy, historical comprehension.

This rich tradition of political-philosophical history of the
Revolution, which resounded throughout the nineteenth century,
was muted and profoundly modified in the wake of the centennial
celebrations. In France, 1889 inaugurated a new age in revolutionary historiography dedicated to that marriage between republicanism and positivism that underlay the very creation of the
Third Republic. This marriage gave birth, within the university,
to the new Chair in the History of the French Revolution at the
Sorbonne to which Alphonse Aulard was elected in 1891. From
this position, occupied for more than thirty years, Aulard directed
the first scholarly journal devoted to the study of the Revolution,
presided over the preparation and publication of the great official
collections of revolutionary documents, and formed students to
spread the republican-positivist gospel. He established and institutionalized within the university system an official, putatively
scientific history: a history dedicated to discovering and justifying, in the history of the Revolution, the creation of those republican, parliamentary institutions whose promise was now finally
being secured in more felicitous circumstances. Danton, the patriot determined in 1793 to institute the emergency government
of the Terror to save the Republic in danger, but opposed in 1794
to continuing it once that danger had eased, became the hero of
Aulard's French Revolution.

Given his institutional authority, his posture as scientific historian, and his engaged republicanism, Aulard was able to margin-
alize conservative interpretations of the Revolution, ridiculing the
amateurism of Hippolyte Taine's frightened account of its origins
in the philosophic spirit and culmination in the horrors of mass

violence, and dismissing, as little more than reactionary ideology, Augustin Cochin's analysis of the genesis and implications of Jacobin sociability. Within the university, the revolutionary heritage became a patrimony to be managed, rather than merely a creed to be inculcated. But this did not preclude bitter divisions over the manner in which that patrimony was to be managed, or its now sacred resources deployed. Aulard's most talented student, Albert Mathiez, became his most virulent critic. The rift was more than an oedipal conflict over the republican mother, Marianne. Mathiez questioned Aulard's scientific methods; but above all, he detested his mentor's Dantonist moderation. As an alternative to an opportunistic, demagogic, and traitorous Danton, he offered an Incorruptible, Robespierre, around whom he crafted a popular, socialist, and Leninist reading of the Revolution. The Bolshevik experience reinforced his Robespierrism, investing it with a millennial hue, and stimulated him to undertake his most original work on the "social movement" of the Terror. Thereafter the relationship between the Russian Revolution and the French Revolution, between 1917 and 1793, haunted the Marxianized republican interpretation to which Mathiez devoted his career.

Although Mathiez was denied Aulard's coveted chair, he taught in the same university until his early death. His exact contemporary, Georges Lefebvre, shared much of his political sensibility and his interest in history from below, and succeeded him as president of the Society for Robespierrist Studies. Lefebvre's election to the Sorbonne chair in 1937 proved decisive for the consolidation, and indeed the triumph, of a social interpretation of the French Revolution based on the principles of historical materialism. More sociological than Mathiez in his approach, and more nuanced in his judgments, he broke fresh ground with his monumental work on the peasants (whose autonomy and individuality he restituted) and his subsequent studies of social structure; and he rescued important issues from vain polemics. His rigor, his pedagogical talent, and the muted quality of his Marxism—most effectively embodied in the celebrated study of 1789 he published for the sesquicentennial of the French Revolution in 1939—earned him, his chair, and the interpretation he promoted worldwide prestige. After 1945, and until his death in 1959, he presided over international research in the field as director of his Institute for the History of the French Revolution at the Sorbonne. Under Lefebvre's aegis, the Marxianized republican interpretation of the French Revolution became the dominant paradigm of revolutionary historiography in France following the Second World War; and it was largely adopted, from the French leaders in the field, by the growing number of historians specializing in the subject who became so striking a feature of postwar academic expansion, particularly in English-speaking countries.

Lefebvre conveyed his mantle of leadership to his student, Albert Soboul, who succeeded to the Sorbonne chair in 1967. Soboul owed his scholarly fame above all to his pioneering thesis on the Parisian sansculottes, a work recently subjected to severe criticism of its sociological and ideological analyses, its understanding of the world of work, and its often teleological and tautological methods. But his influence far transcended this acclaimed monograph. A highly placed member of the French Communist party as well as director of the Institute for the History of the French Revolution, Soboul saw himself as both a "scientific" and a "communist-revolutionary" historian. Tireless, ubiquitous, and prolific, he tenaciously rehearsed the Marxist account of the French Revolution as a bourgeois revolution inscribed in the logic of the necessary transition from feudalism to capitalism. But his relish for confrontation, and his assertive defense of an increasingly rigid orthodoxy, eventually invited— and made him the chief target of—the revisionist assault on the dominant interpretation of the Revolution as mechanistic, reductive, and erroneous.

Challenges to the hegemony of the Sorbonne version of the history of the French Revolution were offered in the late 1950s and early 1960s by Robert Palmer's attempt to shift attention toward the democratic politics of an Atlantic Revolution and, more

fundamentally, by Alfred Cobban's frontal assault on the method-
ological and political assumptions of the Marxist interpretation.
But such was the power of the scholarly consensus that, condemned more or less blithely in Paris, these works drew relatively
little immediate support. Not until the late 1960s and early
1970s did the revisionist current acquire an indigenous French
base, both intellectual and institutional. The charge was led by
François Furet, who left the Communist party in 1956 and has
subsequently gravitated toward the liberal political center. One of
the first French historians to become intimately familiar with
Anglo-American scholarship (and with American life more generally), Furet served as the third president of the École des Hautes
Études en Sciences Sociales, accelerating its development into one
of Europe's leading centers for research in the social sciences and
humanities—and a formidable institutional rival to the Sorbonne. Disenchanted with Marxism, he also turned away from the
Annales tradition of quantitative social and cultural history vigorously espoused in his earlier work. For the past fifteen years he
has sustained a devastating critique of the Jacobin-Leninist "cate-
chism," redirecting scholarly attention to the dynamics of the
Revolution as an essentially political and cultural phenomenon; to
the logic, contradictions, and pathos of its invention of democratic sociability; to its fecundity as a problem for the political and
philosophical inquiries of the nineteenth century upon whose
inspiration he insists historians must draw.

It is one of the great ironies of revolutionary historiography,
then, that whereas the centennial of the Revolution inaugurated
the consolidation of the official republican exegesis, so the bicentennial has marked the distintegration of its Marxist descendant.
The field of inquiry is now more open, more fluid, more exciting
than it has been for many decades. By the same token, it is also
shaped by concerns and sensibilities deriving from recent changes
and experiences. These latter are many and varied. Any comprehensive list would have to include the eclipse of Marxism as an
intellectual and political force; the dramatic decline in the for-

tunes of communism, especially in France; the resurgence of liberalism in the West, with its rehabilitation of the market as model and morality, asserting the intrinsic connection between political liberty and laissez-faire; the dramatic shifts in the East from Gulag to glasnost and perestroika, from Maoism to Westernization, with their oblique and overt avowals of communist failure and ignominy extending from Warsaw to Moscow to Beijing. But such a list could not omit the memory of the Holocaust and the traumas of decolonization among colonized and colonizers alike, from the Algerian War to the sanguinary horrors of Polpotism. It would have to include the stunning triumph and the subsequent exhaustion of the *Annales* paradigm, with its metaphor of levels of determination privileging a long-run perspective and quantitative techniques; the emergence of a new cultural history, pluralistic and aggressive, fueled by diverse disciplinary and counterdisciplinary energies; the striking development of the École des Hautes Études en Sciences Sociales as counterweight to the traditional French university; and the efflorescence of a tradition of French historical studies outside France whose challenge to Parisian hegemony in the field can no longer be ignored. Neither could it neglect the dramatic eruption of the revolutionary imagination in the events of 1968, and the new radical politics of race, sex, and gender that have become so profound a preoccupation in subsequent decades.

The implications of this new situation for the study of the French Revolution are profound. Many fundamental assumptions, not only about the Revolution itself but about how to study it, have been called into question. Though the Revolution is better known today than ever before, the collapse of the hegemonic structure of learning and interpretation has revealed egregious blindspots in what has hitherto counted for knowledge and understanding. While the republican-Marxist view innovated in certain areas, it sterilized research in many others. Today it is no longer possible to evoke complaisantly the bourgeois character of the Revolution, either in terms of causes or effects; the roles, indeed the very definition, of other social actors need to be reexamined. A rehabilitated political approach is avidly reoccupying the ground of a social interpretation in serious need of reformulation. Questions of ideology, discourse, gender, and cultural practices have surged to the forefront in fresh ways. Fewer and fewer historians are willing to accept or reject the Revolution "en bloc," while more and more are concerned with the need to fathom and connect its multiple and contradictory components. The Terror has lost the benefit of its relative immunity and isolation. And despite extravagant and often pathetic hyperbole, the Right has won its point that the Vendée in particular—and the counterrevolutionary experience in general—require more probing and balanced treatment, as do the post-Thermidorian terrors. Finally, there is a widespread sense that the narrow periodization of Revolutionary studies must be substantially broadened.

When the bicentennial dust settles, there will therefore be much for historians of the French Revolution to do. Many questions will require genuinely critical research and discussion, searching reassessment, vigorous and original synthesis. Our ambition in editing these Bicentennial Reflections on the French Revolution is to contribute to this endeavor. In organizing the series, which will comprise twelve volumes, we have sought to identify fundamental issues and problems—problems that have hitherto been treated in fragmentary fashion; issues around which conventional wisdom has disintegrated in the course of current debates—which will be crucial to any new account of the French Revolution. And we have turned to some of the finest historians in what has become an increasingly international field of study, asking them to reassess their own understanding of these matters in the light of their personal research and that of others, and to present the results of their reflections to a wider audience in relatively short, synthetic works that will also offer a critical point of departure for further work in the field. The authors share with us the belief that the time is ripe for a fundamental rethinking. They will of course proceed with this rethinking in their own particular fashion.

The events that began to unfold in France in 1789 have, for two hundred years, occupied a privileged historical site. The bicentennial has served as a dramatic reminder that not only our modern notions of revolution and human rights, but the entire range of our political discourse derives from them. The French Revolution has been to the modern world what Greece and Rome were to the Renaissance and its heirs: a condensed world of acts and events, passions and struggles, meanings and symbols, constantly reconsidered and reimagined in the attempt to frame—and implement—an understanding of the nature, conditions, and possibilities of human action in their relation to politics, culture, and social process. To those who would change the world, the Revolution still offers a script continuously elaborated and extended—in parliaments and prisons; in newspapers and manifestoes; in revolutions and repressions; in families, armies, and encounter groups. . . . To those who would interpret the world, it still presents the inexhaustible challenge of comprehending the nature of the extraordinary mutation that gave birth to the modern world.

"Great year! You will be the *regenerating year,* and you will be known by that name. History will extol your great deeds," wrote Louis-Sébastien Mercier, literary anatomist of eighteenth-century Paris, in a rhapsodic *Farewell to the Year 1789.* "You have changed *my Paris,* it is true. It is completely different today. . . . For thirty years I have had a secret presentiment that I would not die without witnessing a great political event. I nourished my spirit on it: there is *something new* for my pen. If *my Tableau* must be *redone,* at least it will be said one day: In this year Parisians . . . stirred, and this impulse has been communicated to France and the rest of Europe." Historians of the French Revolution may not bid farewell to the bicentennial year in Mercier's rapturous tones. But they will echo at least one of his sentiments. Our tableau must be redone; there is something new for our pens.

Keith Michael Baker and Steven Laurence Kaplan
26 August 1989

REVOLUTIONARY NEWS

INTRODUCTION

O N THE NIGHT OF 21 SEPTEMBER 1792, EARLY IN
the fourth year of the French Revolution, in an old
building on the narrow rue Saint-André des Arcs, a few
hundred yards from the Seine, several hand-operated wooden
printing presses creaked as printers sweated to produce the next
day's edition of the *Journal de Perlet*. Like all other Parisians, these
workers had just lived through an extraordinary month and a half.
Six weeks earlier, in the insurrection of 10 August 1792, the
Parisian revolutionary militants, the *sans-culottes*, had stormed the
royal palace of the Tuileries, a short walk across the Seine from the
Journal de Perlet's printing shop, and had forced the deposition of
King Louis XVI. The king was in prison now, but that had not
stopped the Austrian and Prussian invasion of France. As the
enemy had moved closer to the French capital, fear and political
agitation had led to the "September massacres" of suspected counterrevolutionaries in the Paris prisons. For three days an improvised tribunal had handed down sentences at the Abbey prison,
a few blocks from the *Journal de Perlet's* offices. In the midst of
revolution, war, and violence, however, the employees of the
Journal de Perlet continued to report to their jobs. And now, on 21
September 1792, they produced a small eight-page newspaper
informing readers in Paris and all over the country that the
inaugural session of the new National Convention, France's third

law-making body in less than four years, had proclaimed France a republic.

The popularly elected assembly that took this step was the central institution of a new political culture created since the meeting of the Estates-General three years earlier.[1] Its members drew inspiration from the great orators of the classical city-republics, but they were all too conscious of the fact that late-eighteenth-century France was no Athens or Rome. The anonymous author of a pamphlet entitled *Ways to Communicate Directly with the People*, published in 1789, who offered drawings of a giant megaphone, a mobile sonic reflector, and other devices by which an orator could address a populace many times the size of the citizenry of the ancient city-states, was responding to a widespread fear that the size of modern countries would make participatory government in the classical sense impossible.[2] But it was not the elaborate machines proposed by the anonymous inventor of 1789 that conveyed to the mass of the French people in September 1792 the news that its representatives had proclaimed a republic: it was the *Journal de Perlet* and its many competitors. The newspaper press was an indispensable link between government and public: it was at the heart of the new political culture of publicity and openness that was meant to ensure that the rulers truly reflected the will of the people.

The French Revolution was part of the series of great modern revolutions that have made popular consent the sole basis on which a government in the Western world can claim legitimacy. But the French revolutionaries went further than any others in their insistence that all politics had to be carried on in public to be legitimate. The American Revolution's Continental Congress and the Philadelphia Constitutional Convention of 1787 had met behind closed doors, and the United States Senate did not admit reporters until 1795. In 1917 Lenin and the Bolsheviks dismissed revolutionary Russia's elected assembly and inaugurated a tradition of secret decision making that is only now being challenged in the name of *glasnost*. But in France from the time the Estates-

General convened in 1789 until Napoleon made himself dictator in all but name in 1799, lawmaking was conducted in public assemblies, and this openness to the public was seen as essential to the entire revolutionary project. "Publicity is the people's safeguard," Jean-Sylvain Bailly, the revolutionary mayor of Paris, proclaimed in August 1789; secrecy was inherently counterrevolutionary. [3]

To symbolize the importance of this public lawmaking, the revolutionary assemblies had opened their galleries to spectators in 1789. But the coverage of their debates in the press was even more important: only the newspapers could make it at least theoretically possible for the 600,000 citizens of the capital and the 28 million people of France to "virtually be present at the sessions of this august Senate, as if they were attending in person," as one editor put it. [4] There were a host of other media by which aspects of the revolutionary message were made public: caricatures, songs, pamphlets, plays, public festivals. [5] But contemporaries already recognized that the periodical press was uniquely important in public life. In the remarkable "Analytic essay on the different means for the communication of ideas among men in society" that he published in 1796, the revolutionary politician and journalist Pierre-Louis Roederer pointed out the special qualities that distinguished the periodical press from all other media. Newspapers contained only the latest and most pressing news; they had more readers than books or other forms of printed matter that customers had to seek out in bookstores, because, thanks to hawkers and postmen, newspapers sought out their audience. Journals had a greater social impact than other media because they were read by all classes and because they reached their audience "every day, at the same time . . . in all public places," and because they were "the almost obligatory diet of daily conversation." Consequently, Roederer concluded, "they act more powerfully than any other form of writing." [6]

Roederer's claim was based on a sociological analysis of the press and its readership; he was among the pioneers in using data on newspaper subscriptions to provide a quantitative measure of public opinion.[7] But the periodical press was important not merely because of the actual number of its readers and its special form of impact on them. Alone among the revolutionary media, it served as a symbol and a stand-in for "the people" in whose name all political acts were now carried out, but which could not assemble and speak in any concrete manner. According to the revolutionaries' constitutional theory, articulated in the Declaration of Rights in 1789 and the succession of revolutionary constitutions that followed, the people were to choose representatives and confer on them the power to make laws, which would be binding on the electorate because they were the outcome of the people's own expression of its will. But the national elections held during the 1790s were hardly convincing expressions of the public will. In every election the definition of the electorate was different; participation was very low; in the absence of organized political parties, local conflicts tended to overshadow national political issues; and throughout the Revolution, circumstances changed so quickly that the representatives found themselves dealing with issues that had not been dreamed of when they were elected.

Under these conditions, the political press was an indispensable symbol of the public opinion of a people that lacked the means to speak for itself. The newspaper was always active; it could react quickly to changing events. Without the press, there would have been no continuing link between the public and its representatives during the Revolution and no way for the deputies to maintain that their actions represented the popular will. Already in the last decades of the Old Regime, both the monarch and his opponents had come to invoke the supposed blessing of "the public" to legitimate their political claims. The censored press of the Old Regime had been unable to present itself as the voice of this public, but the theoretically unregulated press of the Revolution was able to do so: public opinion ceased to be an abstract "conceptual entity," as Keith Baker has termed it,[8] and became something definite, tangible, manifested on a daily basis in the newspapers.

The press was thus indispensable to give legitimacy to the new lawmaking of the Revolution by making that process public. It was equally indispensable to the process by which the French transformed themselves from passive subjects to active citizens. *"Les grands ne nous paraissent grands que parce que nous sommes à genoux. Levons-nous!"* read the epigraph that appeared on the first page of every issue of the *Révolutions de Paris*: its call for readers to "stand up" was a weekly exhortation to the French people to make themselves "new men" who determined their own fate.[9] Newspapers were powerful tools of agitation and propaganda in favor of this new participatory citizenship, and they broadcast the news of activists such as the Paris *sans-culottes* to the wider nation. It was the press that molded the dispersed and fragmentary events that made up each of the revolutionary *journées* into intelligible form, labeled them, and validated their results by presenting them as public manifestations of the people's will.

Paradoxically, however, the same newspaper press that provided the public dimension and the means of communication required by the Revolution's new style of politics was also one of the driving forces behind the divisions and conflicts of the revolutionary decade. In the abstract, the press was the vehicle by which politics was made public and therefore legitimate: concretely, the newspapers provided a babble of voices, some applauding each turn of revolutionary events, others condemning it. Opponents of the Revolution used the press just as effectively as its supporters did. Each journalist put together his own picture of the Revolution; each challenged the claims of the political figures and movements he reported on; each denied the legitimacy of competing newspapers that depicted events differently. By publicizing and, indeed, amplifying the confrontations that destroyed the Revolution's claim to express a general will that, by its very definition, had to be unified, the press was as powerful a force in undermining the legitimacy of each successive set of revolutionary leaders' claims to speak for the people as it was in making the assertion of those claims possible. The goal of all revolutionary leaders from the summer of 1789 onward, to stabilize the achievements of the Revolution and bring it to an end, could only be accomplished when the press was brought under firm control. [10]

These large claims for the importance of the press during the Revolution are hard to reconcile with the humble appearance of a printed text like the copy of the *Journal de Perlet* that eventually, almost two centuries later, found its way into the University of Kentucky library, where some 700 issues of that paper, bound together in tidy volumes early in the nineteenth century at the expense of a certain "M. Jobon, watchmaker, rue St. André des Arts no. 57 à Paris," now repose. The paper's small octavo format, the absence of headlines, illustrations, and other common features of modern newspapers, and the hasty printing, riddled with typographical errors and done on bad paper, make it appear insignificant. In its columns, the resounding phrases of the revolutionary orators are buried in the midst of the banalities of parliamentary procedure and the details of long-forgotten legislation. As one turns the pages of a bound volume of this obscure newspaper, one hardly feels oneself in the presence of a great historical force. But this mute survivor of the French Revolution still has much to tell us about that extraordinary event, if we know how to read it attentively.

The newspapers of the French Revolution were products of the ongoing news story to which they devoted most of their space: they were much more closely tied to the events they reported than were the newspapers of other times and places. The title page of the *Journal de Perlet* reflected this connection. On 22 September 1792, the opening day of the National Convention, the paper began a new series, and its full title read *Suite du Journal de Perlet. Convention nationale, Corps administratifs, et nouvelles politiques et littéraires de l'Europe*. The issue of 22 September 1792 also carried the heading "L'An IV de la liberté et de l'égalité" to establish beyond a doubt the paper's adherence to the great principles of the French Revolution. But the symbols of the Revolution were constantly changing, and on 23 September 1792 the paper replaced its reference to the fourth year of liberty and equality, which summoned up memories of the storming of the Bastille and the Revolution's constitutional-monarchist phase from 1789 to 1792, with a heading that read "L'An Premier de la République," in deference to the Convention's decision the day before to declare the French monarchy abolished and to proclaim this action as the true start of the new era.

Not only did the *Journal de Perlet* proclaim the new era that the Convention asserted it had begun, it also conveyed the sense of urgency that characterized the Revolution. Like most of the important newspapers of the decade, it appeared every day and delivered its account of events the morning after they had happened: indeed, when the sessions of the Convention ran late into the evening, as they often did, the paper had to break off its summary of them in the middle. This daily rhythm of publication and the breathless quality of the paper's news stories conveyed the sense that every day of the Revolution was important, that "time . . . was a succession of turning points, of choices between slavery and freedom, disaster and success," as the French scholar Pierre Rétat has written.[11] This sense of being in the middle of dramatic events was quite different from the leisurely tone of the prerevolutionary news press, which appeared once or twice a week and frequently printed dispatches that were already ten days old before they reached their audience.

Naturally, readers of the newly retitled *Journal de Perlet* wanted to know where the paper stood on the great issues of the Revolution. The opening of the National Convention and the beginning of a new series of the newspaper's issues was an opportunity for the paper to set out a program, in the form of a "Notice to Our Readers." On 22 September 1792 the crush of news was too great to leave place for such a notice, but the next day's issue included one. The paper promised that it would not only record the news, but that it would take an active part in politics. It would "oppose agitators of all factions, enlighten our fellow-citizens about their true interests, and defend liberty and equality whose triumph must now be assured." These phrases sound trite and uncontroversial today, but to revolutionary readers they were code words with a definite meaning in the context of the heated struggles of the Revolution. A warning against false friends of the people "who constantly talk to it about its interests, but only think of their own," was aimed at a faction the paper's authors detested, the radical Jacobin followers of Robespierre; a promise to "eschew calumny and seditious declamations that dishonor both a man and a journalist" was a reference to a rival journalistic text, that of the most celebrated of the radical writers, Jean-Paul Marat.

From the *Journal de Perlet's* statement of purpose an experienced revolutionary newspaper reader could quickly conclude that he would find in the paper news coverage favorable to the general course of the Revolution, but critical of those who wanted to push the movement for change even further than it had gone by the fall of 1792. It was a program calculated to appeal to two kinds of readers: those who supported the Revolution out of conviction, but who feared the sort of violence that had surfaced during the September massacres, and those who secretly opposed the Revolution, but could no longer purchase an overtly counterrevolutionary newspaper now that the royalist and moderate press had been silenced. The *Journal de Perlet's* prospectus demonstrated that politics and calculations of marketability were rarely separated in the revolutionary press.

Modern-day newspaper readers, whether French or American, would find the *Journal de Perlet's* presentation of the news primitive. There were no headlines over individual stories. Under the paper's logo, there was a paragraph set in italic type summarizing the day's news and intended to guide the hawkers who cried the paper aloud in the streets. But the publisher made no effort to put the most sensational news first in this list, and indeed the summary paragraph rarely gave much of an indication of the paper's content. Sometimes the anonymous compiler of the paper's legislative news began with a paragraph of general reflections or comment; on other days he simply started where the Assembly had started and followed the meandering course of the debates. Unlike modern journalists, the *Journal de Perlet*'s reporter did not explicitly highlight important discussions or omit trivial ones. This manner of reporting the news gave the impression that the journalist was simply transcribing events, without coloring his story in any way, but in fact the *Journal de Perlet*'s reports were highly selective. Forced to compress hours of debate into a summary that could be read aloud in perhaps thirty minutes, the paper's reporter had to extract what he considered the main point from lengthy speeches, and he left out many interventions altogether.

Modern research libraries like the one in which I read the *Journal de Perlet* have many books about the French Revolution that are better documented and more easily assimilated than the undigested mass of information in that two-century-old newspaper. In their periodical rooms, modern libraries offer a selection of current newspapers that strike us as much better at conveying the most essential and exciting news about the world around them. Only a few specialists in the history of the French Revolution now read the newspapers published in France in the 1790s. When the ink on their pages was fresh, however, those same papers were eagerly sought after. Once upon a time they were among the first reports French readers could obtain about the great events going on around them. The aim of this book is to bring to life the newspaper press in France during the ten years of the French Revolution, from 1789 to 1799. I will explain both the characteristics of the press of the Revolution that make it different from the modern press and the ways in which that press influenced the course of the first of the great modern revolutions. In doing so I have tried to convey as effectively as I can how the newspapers of the period operated and what it was like to publish one, to write one, and to read one.

The task of writing the history of the French press during the Revolution is a daunting one. The Bibliothèque nationale in Paris has collections of over thirteen hundred titles published in France in the years from 1789 to 1799, and other libraries contain numerous periodicals not represented in its holdings. No book, least of all one as limited in length as this one, can hope to describe all these papers. Nor is it easy to single out a few newspapers from this mass of source material and argue that they were uniquely important or uniquely representative of the press in this tumultuous period, or that their story fairly typifies the larger history of the press as a whole. Historians who have tried to be comprehensive in their treatment of the press during the Revolution have followed a pattern established by the great nineteenth-century French bibliographer Eugène Hatin in his still-valuable *Histoire politique et littéraire de la presse en France*, published more than a century ago. They have given a history of the Revolution's major political events, together with dozens of thumbnail sketches of the publications most closely associated with each. Important for the historian of the French Revolution who wants to know which newspapers represented which political currents at any particular time, works such as those of Jacques Godechot and Hugh Gough have been less successful in analyzing the role of the press in revolutionary political culture: they have tended to present the newspapers as simple reflections of politics, rather than as one of the forces shaping the course of the Revolution. [12]

Whereas even the best scholars of the press during the Revolution have been too overwhelmed by the volume of sources to do much more than give a descriptive survey of it, the historians of the French Revolution have often shown a curious indifference to the periodical press. In the 1830s Thomas Carlyle wrote of the "thousand wagon-loads of this Pamphleteering and Newspaper matter . . . rotting slowly in the Public Libraries of our Europe," of interest only to "bibliomaniac pearl-divers." [13] By the time collectors began to take an interest in them, all copies of some revolutionary-era titles had disappeared, and even some of the more prominent papers have survived only by a fluke. The physical disappearance of the revolutionary newspapers suggested that the press of the 1790s had truly been an ephemeral phenomenon, like the papier-mâché statues erected for the revolutionary festivals.

Carlyle himself knew, however, that these forgotten newspapers had once been a great historical force. As he evoked the atmosphere of the Revolution, he spoke of the flood of publications that "circulate on street and highway, universally; with results! A Fourth Estate, of Able Editors, springs up; increases and multiplies; irrepressible, incalculable." [14] Like historians of the Revolution ever since, however, he in fact used the newspapers only as a means to the end of constructing his own narrative of the Revolution. Mined by the nineteenth-century scholars of the Revolution as source material, the newspapers themselves largely disappeared from the revolutionary story. With the advent of Rankean "scientific" history and its preference for archival materials, the press of the Revolution lost its status as a privileged witness to the past. Alphonse Aulard and Albert Mathiez, the great pioneers of modern archivally based revolutionary historiography, both produced, as offshoots of their other projects, important articles about the governmental subsidies to the press, [15] but their findings only served to underline the fact that the newspapers were anything but neutral reporters of events. Historians of the Revolution resorted to newspapers as sources only when they could not find anything better. And despite continued lip service to the importance of the press during the Revolution, scholars treated it as a screen to be pushed aside so that they could observe the "real" forces of the past: the social classes whose conflicts supposedly determined its outcome, or the political groupings whose struggles provided its dramatic structure. [16]

It is ironic that the modern historian most identified with the social approach to the French Revolution should also have provided a graphic demonstration of the impossibility of disentangling social reality from its journalistic manifestations. In the 1950s Albert Soboul undertook to emulate his master Georges Lefebvre's epoch-making study of the French peasantry in his own work on the Parisian *sans-culottes*. In the best tradition of scientific history he drew on archival sources, above all on revolutionary police records, to identify the *sans-culotte* militants and classify them by age and occupation. But Soboul aspired to bring his subjects to life, and in his endeavor to understand the thoughts of these individuals who left no writings of their own, he fell back on the press: on Hébert's *Père Duchêne*, which is cited more than eighty times in the index to his great work, and on the publications of the *enragé* journalists Leclerc de Lyon and Jacques Roux. True to his Marxist view that culture must ultimately be a by-product of social reality, however, he concluded that the *sans-culotte* movement "grew from the great masses of the people." In his paper, Hébert had perhaps "defined slogans, suggested methods of action," but "he was following the popular thrust more than leading it." Hence the *Père Duchêne* was in and of itself a secondary topic.[17] Soboul's bluff confidence in his ability to distinguish between the true views of the *sans-culottes* that these journalists articulated and the personal opinions and bourgeois political ideas that they also expressed has been challenged by subsequent scholars. As Jacques Guilhaumou has written, for Soboul, "journalistic discourse is . . . a system of *illusion-allusion* whose referents are 'real actions'. . . . It is admitted that behavior and discourse may diverge, but these discourses are not granted any materiality, any level of significance."[18] Nevertheless, his *Les Sans-culottes parisiens de l'An II*, often taken as an example of pure social history of a voiceless underclass, proves in fact to be in good part a dialogue between the historian and a revolutionary journalist; social reality proves to be inseparable from its representation in the press.

Guilhaumou's critique of Soboul reflects the recent shift in historical thinking from treating language as a secondary phenomenon to recognizing that we cannot disentangle our knowledge of the past from its language and other forms of cultural expression. Three major books—Mona Ozouf's analysis of the Revolution's public festivals, François Furet's polemic against the social approach to the French Revolution and in favor of a serious study of revolutionary discourse, and Lynn Hunt's imaginative approach to its political culture through its language and its visual imagery—have put this approach in the center of current historiographical debates about the French Revolution. None of these historians has shown any particular interest in the press, however. Furet, who acknowledges the importance of the "specialists" who rose to power by their expertise in manipulating the language of the Revolution, "those who produced it and so became the custodians of its legitimacy and its meaning," nevertheless discusses only the orators of the assemblies and clubs.[19] Lynn Hunt, whose *Politics, Culture, and Class in the French Revolution* has made the term *political culture* central to all recent scholarly writing about the Revolution, grants this political culture autonomy from the underlying social structure. She asserts that "revolutionary language . . . was itself transformed into an instrument of political and social change" and that it "helped shape the perception of interests and hence the development of ideologies." But she explicitly limits her definition of that culture to "symbolic practices, such as language, imagery, and gestures," and she separates the content of revolutionary language from the media through which it was expressed. Because newspapers existed in other countries at the time of the French Revolution, she concludes that "the large number of newspapers and clubs, however dramatic the contrast with pre-revolutionary times, did not make the politics of the Revolution revolutionary."[20]

Hunt's effort to separate message from medium in revolutionary political culture seems as artificial as Soboul's effort to find a social reality independent of all cultural representation. Just as the revolutionaries created new language and new images to replace the words and symbols of the Old Regime, they created a new press that functioned very differently from its Old Regime predecessor. As the West German scholar Rolf Reichardt has concluded, the "new form of publicness and its communication system—a network of assemblies and clubs, newspapers, pamphlets, broadsides, songs and other media . . . that had never before existed in such numbers, and never been so closely and intensely tied to events" was in itself a central part of the "democratic culture" of the Revolution.[21] The new form that the press took on after 1789 was in itself one of the major signs of the Revolution: the medium was in itself part of the revolutionary message.

But is the newspaper press merely to be considered part of a larger "revolutionary culture," indistinguishable in its effects from pamphlets, plays, caricatures, and songs? In a suggestive essay on revolutionary oratory and theater, Marc-Eli Blanchard has argued convincingly that not all revolutionary media were created equal. Parliamentary oratory, "as privileged and prestigious as it was," never equaled the force that the resources of "natural-sounding language, gestures and costumes" gave to the theatrical reenactments of revolutionary events: Blanchard concludes that the theater became a revolutionary medium in a way that the tribune could not.[22] By its comprehensiveness, its continuous coverage of the ongoing Revolution, and its ability to keep pace with fast-moving events, the newspaper press was not just one medium among others, but a uniquely important part of revolutionary reality. Pierre Rétat, the most original of the current French scholars of the press, has argued that the consciousness of the Revolution as a new age, different from what went before, is inseparable from the appearance of its press: "the birth of the [revolutionary] newspaper coincides with that of a new era; it has the vocation of measuring it and defining its rhythm." And insofar as the Revolution is a matter of "forms of language" that "carry the revolutionary message and symbols," the press "is one of the strongholds of this new language, full of meaning."[23]

In this book, I will demonstrate the central importance of newspapers through an approach that looks at the structure and the political impact of the press as a whole and treats it as a body of closely interrelated texts. After a chapter describing the press in France before the Revolution and the emergence of the first revolutionary news periodicals in mid-1789, I turn to an analysis of three groups who shaped this vital medium for the communication of political news and ideas: the journalists, the newspaper publishers, and the audience. The following section looks at the journalistic texts themselves, describing the ways in which they were presented, their interaction with revolutionary politics, and their role in the mobilization of a democratic movement. The final chapter describes the disintegration of the unique press system that had emerged in 1789 and then assesses its role in the political culture of the Revolution and its place in the broader history of modern journalism. My hope is that this approach will serve both readers interested in the history of the French Revolution and those concerned with the development of the modern media.

1. FROM THE PRESS OF THE OLD REGIME TO THE PRESS OF THE REVOLUTION

T HE SCENE WAS THE PALAIS-ROYAL, THE COMPLEX of cafés, shops, and promenades that served as the center of Parisian political discussion before and during the Revolution; the time was 1788, in the midst of the crisis that would soon topple the French monarchy. Nothing was more natural for a playwright than to have one character ask another whether he would like to see the most recent newspaper. And so Isabelle de Charrière, the Dutch-born dramatist who was one of the leading female French-language writers of the time, began one of her short sketches for the stage with the following line: "Would you be interested in reading the latest *Gazette de Leyde*?"[1] The well-informed gentleman in her play chose to offer his acquaintance news about France published in the Dutch city of Leiden because he knew that the newspapers published inside the country were tightly controlled by the French government and contained little news of political substance. But he also knew that these domestic newspapers were not the only journals available to those who wanted to keep up with important French events. Periodicals published outside France's borders but intended for a French audience, such as the *Gazette de Leyde*, were a major feature of the journalistic scene, and no self-respecting café in the Palais-Royal would have been without them.

The situation that Isabelle de Charrière dramatized in 1788 had existed in France for almost a century. Ever since the expulsion of the Huguenots under Louis XIV, the French press had been divided into two sectors: a domestic press, licensed and censored by the government, and an extraterritorial press, created by private entrepreneurs and covertly tolerated by the same authorities who controlled the domestic papers. Initially, the extraterritorial papers had been the outlets of Huguenot hostility to the regime that had expelled them, but over time they had been toned down and established a de facto right to circulate in France. Like many other features of the Old Regime in France, this seemingly illogical arrangement actually served to satisfy the needs of both the French government and of the educated and sophisticated social elite that made France the center of the European Enlightenment.

The censored domestic press, which included by 1788 not only the venerable *Gazette de France*, founded in 1631, but also several other national papers and about forty provincial publications, functioned in accordance with the principles of royal absolutism according to which France was theoretically governed. According to absolutist doctrines, it was up to the ruler to determine what information was fit for his subjects to have and to provide it for them. It went without saying that the news provided by such a press would be favorable to the government. By granting licenses or *privilèges* to selected publishers, the French government was able to leave the running of the press to private entrepreneurs but still ensure that the domestic papers were in reliable hands. A *privilège* was a valuable property: it not only gave the publisher permission to put out a journal, but also theoretically guaranteed him against competition. The holders of *privilèges* for prerevolutionary newspapers therefore had a very real stake in the Old Regime's system of press regulation. In addition to controlling the press through the granting of *privilèges*, the French monarchy had a censorship system that required newspaper publishers to obtain prior approval for every item they printed. This censorship system, easily flouted by the publishers of books and pamphlets, was more effective in controlling periodicals because they were dependent on the royal mails for the delivery of most of their copies and because a periodical, which depended on the regular flow of payments from its subscribers, could not easily be published without a return address, as books and pamphlets often were. The combination of licensing, censorship, and dependence on the postal system ensured that the domestic press printed only what the king's ministers wanted it to print.

Although the French domestic press was under the government's thumb, it was not as rigidly controlled as the press in modern totalitarian countries has been. As a part of a paternalistic governing apparatus meant to satisfy the needs of the French king's subjects, the press was allowed and even encouraged to provide a variety of news and information. From Versailles, French ministers reminded the king's ambassadors that their duties included sending regular reports so that the *Gazette de France* could provide a reasonably accurate picture of foreign affairs. In an age when the king was the one true public person in the kingdom, the *Gazette*'s description of the royal routine and of the elaborate court ceremonies that punctuated it interested readers much as the details of the lives of presidents and celebrities appeal to them today. Eager to promote economic prosperity, French authorities patronized Parisian and provincial advertising periodicals; convinced that the development of culture and the progress of knowledge contributed to the glory and power of the state, they allowed publications devoted to literature, the sciences, and the practical arts.

Especially after 1750, any would-be journalist who was willing to promise to eschew religious and political controversies and any would-be publisher with influential connections who could argue that he had found some segment of the reading public not yet served by a periodical could usually wangle permission to launch a new title. The 252 new enterprises begun between 1751 and 1788 show the vitality of the press.[2] There were periodicals for women, for improving landlords, for army officers, for poets, for aficionados of sensational courtroom dramas, for theatergoers, and for a host of other special-interest groups.[3] Most of these publications were closer to modern magazines than to newspapers, but by the 1780s the *Gazette de France*'s theoretical monopoly on the publication of foreign and political news had been broken by several competitors, such as the *Journal de Bruxelles*, the news supplement to the popular weekly literary journal *Mercure de France*, and the country's first daily newspaper, the *Journal de Paris*, founded in 1777. Despite licensing and censorship, the press in prerevolutionary France was anything but dull.

French readers responded enthusiastically to the variety of available journals, and the political newspapers, despite being censored, were among the most successful of all. The *Gazette de France* had 12,260 subscribers in 1780, when interest in the American War of Independence had boosted newspaper circulation all over Europe, and it still had almost 7,000 in 1784. None of the British newspapers of the period had a press run of over 4,500, although the total circulation of all the London papers combined was certainly greater than that of the French political press. The weekly *Mercure de France* with its political supplement, the *Journal de Bruxelles*, was even more successful, reaching a peak circulation of around 20,000 copies in the mid-1780s.[4] This degree of success was exceptional, of course, and many French periodicals limped along with sales of a few hundred copies per issue.[5] But the market for periodicals was sufficiently lucrative to attract numerous publishers, who found it less risky than printing books. In the 1770s and 1780s France's leading publisher, Charles-Joseph Panckoucke, built the first modern journalistic empire, acquiring a virtual monopoly on the domestic political press and buying out numerous competitors to consolidate the success of his publications.[6]

For all its variety, however, the French domestic press remained limited in one crucial area. It could not report honestly and openly on the country's political life. In an increasingly prosperous country in which royal decisions affected the interests of more and more subjects, it was officially forbidden to discuss the pros and cons of government policies. In a political system where day-to-day power was exercised by powerful and often contentious personalities, it was officially forbidden to discuss the rivalries of ministers. The French government, increasingly willing to allow periodicals that stimulated public discussion in every other area of life, balked at officially permitting any honest discussion of its own doings. It suppressed the news of private court intrigues and also of events known to everyone in the kingdom, such as the clashes between the ministers and the sovereign law courts, the *parlements*, that shook the country from 1750 to 1774.

Kept in the dark by their domestic periodicals, the French reading public turned to a variety of other forms of journalism to find out what was really going on in the king's antechambers and the bureaus of the ministers. The wealthy subscribed to manuscript newsletters, which relayed a variety of behind-the-scenes rumors. Political crises generated pamphlets, one-shot publications that were sometimes genuinely unauthorized and sometimes secretly tolerated or even encouraged by the police. Political caricatures and topical political songs could reach even those who were not literate. Newsletters, pamphlets, cartoons and songs all offered political news and opinions that never found their way into the official periodical press, but these media were not sufficient to structure a regular "public space" in which political issues could be discussed intelligently. Except for the newsletters, these media appeared only sporadically and unpredictably. Lacking continuity, they could not amplify or correct themselves, and they could not form a connection among their readers, a forum in which views could be exchanged. Well suited to evading the French government's controls, these media were less adapted to fulfilling functions such as the regular dissemination of information and the formation of public opinion that are required in any political system depending on some degree of public acquiescence to rulers' policies.

It was the foreign-based periodical press that came closest to filling this gap in the prerevolutionary French press system. The numerous newspapers and magazines published outside France's borders, but written in the French language, served as an outlet for news and thoughts that were barred from the domestic press. Newspapers published in Leiden, Cologne, Avignon, or London came to French readers bearing the promise of uncensored news: they were the complement of the *Gazette de France*, revealing what French subjects assumed their domestic press was bound to conceal. And indeed the columns of newspapers such as the *Gazette de Leyde* and the *Courier du Bas-Rhin* were filled with items that never appeared in the domestic French press, such as the *parlements'* vociferous denunciations of arbitrary authority and the details of events like the Lyon silkworkers' uprising of 1786. In the *Gazette de France*, the French king appeared to rule unassisted; in the foreign gazettes, his ministers were depicted as the real movers behind French government policy.[7]

To all but the best-informed readers, the foreign gazettes appeared to be free and unrestrained sources of news. Those in the know realized that the situation was more complex. Not licensed by the French government and not subject to prior censorship, these publications were kept in line by a variety of other mechanisms. The French government could bribe these papers' editors, harass their Paris correspondents, complain to their host governments about their contents, and above all, prevent them from sending their copies through the French royal mails. After bitter experience the American revolutionary envoy and future president, John Adams, complained that "all these papers . . . discover a perpetual complaisance for the French ministry, because . . . if an offensive paragraph appears, the entrance and distribution of the gazette may be stopped by an order from court, by which the gazetteer loses the sale of his paper in France, which is a great pecuniary object."[8]

Indirectly controlled by the French government, these extraterritorial papers nevertheless enjoyed considerably more freedom than the French domestic press did. It was much easier for the French government to tolerate responsible newspapers whose editors and publishers were known and could be pressured than it was to put up with completely uncontrolled pamphleteers and caricaturists. At times, as when it needed to float loans or release diplomatic trial balloons, the French government even benefited from the existence of newspapers with a reputation for independence; they could further its policies in ways that the domestic press could not. But to give the foreign gazettes credibility, the French ministry needed to let the foreign papers appear to be uncensored, and this could only be achieved by letting them publish news that was suppressed in the domestic press. Hence they were routinely allowed to print reports about opposition to the ministry from the *parlements* and other traditional corporatist institutions, as well as reports about popular violence in France and reports from other capitals contesting the official French view of international affairs. In this way French readers of the foreign-based press got a much broader and more realistic picture of their country's political life than they could find in the licensed domestic press, although it was still a more sober and less complete panorama than British newspaper readers could find in the uninhibited but notoriously corrupt London papers. Despite their high cost compared to the domestic press—a year's subscription to most of these papers cost thirty-six livres or more, whereas the *Gazette de France* cost only twelve livres in 1774 and fifteen livres in 1785—the foreign-based papers were quite successful by pre-revolutionary standards. The *Gazette de Leyde* had sales of over 2,500 in France during the American war, and its regular readers were said to include the king himself; the cheaper *Courrier d'Avignon* had a circulation of about 4,000 in 1778. The foreign-based gazettes provided a middle ground between the French government's natural tendency to want to control the news completely and the French public's desire for uncensored information; their content was the measure of what it was permissible to discuss openly in France.

Although the foreign-based gazettes were considerably more informative than the censored domestic press, by the end of the Old Regime they were no longer sufficient to satisfy the French reading public. As the French monarchy staggered from one political crisis to another in the years after 1750, readers craved more than the limited but accurate news reports that the gazettes provided. They wanted commentary and behind-the-scenes stories that would help them make sense of what was happening. The traumatic crisis of 1771–74, when Louis XV's determined justice minister René Maupeou tried to crush the *parlements* and make the government's claims to absolute power effective, was especially important in stimulating a thirst for new forms of political journalism that went beyond mere reporting. The Maupeou "coup" gave rise to a number of printed works that purported to offer the same completely uninhibited reporting as the manuscript newsletters, and in the more relaxed years after Maupeou's fall in 1774, multivolume works bearing titles such as the *Espion anglois* and the *Mémoires secrets* that revealed the inner workings of the Maupeou ministry and then of the court under the new king Louis XVI became best-sellers. These gossipy chronicles borrowed from the libelous techniques of the British press and anticipated some features of the French revolutionary newspapers. They never achieved regular periodical publication, however, and they came out months or years after the events they described. Although they were models of what a truly uninhibited press might look like, they were not yet real newspapers.[9]

The *Mémoires secrets* and similar publications showed French readers what would happen if all restraints were taken off the publication of inside political information; the *Annales politiques, civiles et littéraires du dix-huitième siècle* that the former lawyer and pro-Maupeou publicist Simon-Nicolas-Henri Linguet launched from London in 1777 demonstrated the impact that an impassioned journalist determined to propagate his personal views could have. During a tumultuous career in the 1760s and early 1770s, Linguet had managed to make enemies of the French *philosophes*, the judges of the *parlements*, his fellow lawyers, and most of French officialdom: he then used his journal to pay them back. But he conducted his crusade in vigorous and colorful language that made his publication a tremendous public success.

Readers responded to the spectacle of a journalist lambasting respectable judges, lawyers, and academicians, and Linguet managed to avoid French government retaliation thanks to the protection of the king and queen and to the fact that he made his furious attacks in the name of defending absolute authority and traditional religion. His ideas were often conservative, but Linguet's direct and violent way of expressing them and his insistence that France was on the brink of an apocalyptic crisis were revolutionary, and his style of journalism had a direct influence on many of the writers who later became famous in France during the Revolution.[10]

The audience for the variety of domestic and foreign periodicals circulating in France had been growing steadily since the middle of the eighteenth century, but it was still limited. Even though more than half of the adult men in the kingdom could read by 1789—literacy among women was somewhat lower—an annual subscription to most magazines or newspapers was still far beyond the means of most of the population. True, the growing number of reading rooms and circulating libraries in France's towns allowed readers who could not afford individual subscriptions to have some access to journals, but these institutions also charged fees. There is little doubt that most readers of periodicals came from the aristocracy, the clergy, and the well-to-do bourgeoisie. Journalists could count on their readers having a fairly good education: they could refer to the Latin classics and to the celebrated authors of the seventeenth and eighteenth centuries and be sure of being understood. Few prerevolutionary journalists made any attempt to adapt their language to a genuinely popular audience of people who could read but lacked formal education. The prerevolutionary press in France was thus reading material for a limited but sophisticated audience of cultured men and women, connoisseurs who knew how to interpret the nuances and silences of the journalistic texts they read. Their journals kept them abreast of what was new and allowed them to appear well informed, but these periodicals were not meant to stir them to action.

The new political world that came into being with the fall of the Bastille in July 1789 brought with it a very different kind of press. The transformation from the press of the Old Regime to a new kind of journalism had begun before 14 July 1789. The restrictions on press freedom had started to crumble more than a year earlier. On 8 May 1788 the royal ministers Etienne-Charles Loménie de Brienne and Chrétien-François Lamoignon de Basville, desperate to remove the obstacles to new taxes that were needed to meet the government's fiscal crisis, had tried to abolish the *parlements*, the law courts that had refused to approve revenue-raising reforms. Like the Maupeou "coup" of 1771, this attempted reform had unleashed a flood of antiministerial pamphlets and pro-*parlement* agitation. The force of this opposition drove the ministers to take a gamble that put the whole of the Old Regime at stake. On 5 July 1788 they announced the first summoning of the kingdom's traditional representative assembly, the Estates-General, in 175 years. The Estates-General—made up of deputies chosen by members of France's three traditional orders: the clergy, the nobility, and the commoners or Third Estate—would undercut the *parlements'* claim to represent the interests of the nation; if it approved new taxes, there could be no further opposition to them. And in what may have been a frantic bid to counter the hostile pamphlets, Brienne lifted the censorship restrictions and encouraged all authors to publish their ideas about how the Estates-General should proceed.[11]

The combined impact of the measures against the *parlements* and the summoning of the Estates-General was to launch a national political debate on a scale that France had never seen before. In August 1788 bankruptcy forced Brienne out of office and in the following month the *parlements* were recalled, but preparations for the Estates-General continued, and so did the nationwide excitement. At least 767 pamphlets were issued between 8 May and 25 September 1788, with an additional 752 between 25 September and 31 December of that year, but this was only a prelude to the 2,639 titles that appeared during the election of the deputies to the Estates-General in the first four months of 1789.[12] Many of these pamphlets, such as the abbé Sieyès's *Qu'est-ce que le Tiers Etat?* were printed in multiple editions, and the total number of copies of pamphlets circulated in France in the year before the Estates-General finally convened in May 1789 probably exceeded 10 million.

The prerevolutionary crisis converted the traditional political pamphlet into a mass medium. But the pamphlet was by its very nature an irregular, episodic form of publication that appeared at moments of crisis and then ceased when the crisis was over. Periodicals had been less significant during the crisis of 1788, and the government had had greater success in keeping control over them: three weeks after the decree of 5 July 1788 turning the pamphleteers loose, the ministry had temporarily banned the *Gazette de Leyde*, the most influential newspaper circulating in the country, for its support of the *parlements*.[13] Still, it was obvious both to the government and to would-be journalists and imaginative publishers that the convening of the Estates-General would create a demand for political news and ideas that could hardly be satisfied by pamphlets alone. In the province of Brittany, where conflicts between the nobles and the Third Estate had already reached a violent pitch in the fall of 1788, the future deputy C. F. Volney put out five issues of a *Sentinelle du peuple* that foreshadowed many of the techniques of the revolutionary polemical press in its attacks on the privileged orders; it can be regarded as the first truly revolutionary journal, even though there is a strong suspicion that it was covertly funded by the royal ministry to fan divisions among its Breton opponents.[14]

While Volney's paper was providing a foretaste of what the revolutionary polemical press would look like, the royal authorities were bombarded with requests for permission to publish accounts of the proceedings of the upcoming Estates-General. This was not in itself a revolutionary idea: wherever representative institutions similar to the Estates-General existed in Europe, their meetings were routinely reported in the press. The royal officials who had to deal with the stream of requests for privileges to cover the upcoming Estates-General assumed that some arrangement would be worked out, although they refused to grant an authorization to any of the eager applicants besieging them.[15] While royal bureaucrats and ambitious journalists were making plans for coverage of the Estates-General, the king's subjects were also thinking about freedom of the press. The *cahiers de doléances* that the electoral assemblies for the three estates drew up when they chose their deputies frequently called for the abolition of censorship. A number of the clergy had hesitations, fearing a flood of irreligious publications, but the *cahiers* of both the nobles and the Third Estate voiced overwhelming support for freedom of the press. At the same time, however, these *cahiers* stopped short of endorsing completely unfettered freedom of publication, something that had never been permitted anywhere in the civilized world. For the most part, when the French called for freedom of the press in 1789, they were thinking of a system like that in England, where prior censorship and licensing had been abolished, but where authors and publishers could be prosecuted for libel, blasphemy, and obscenity.[16] Furthermore, the discussions of freedom of the press in the *cahiers* dealt with the issue in the abstract; they did not differentiate between books and newspapers. The *cahiers* did not specifically address the role the press might play in a reformed French monarchy. If there was to be a new press for the new era that was dawning in France, it would be shaped by the initiatives of journalists, publishers, and politicians, not by the wishes of the population at large.

Just as the Estates-General was convened at the government's initiative but quickly asserted its independence, the French government's plan for a press that would publish "what prudence will allow to be authorized"[17] rapidly broke down. The unexpected course taken by the Estates-General owed much to the preparations of a small group of political activists, inspired by the ideas of the Enlightenment and other currents of thought critical of the status quo and by the example of the American Revolution, who were determined to seize the opportunity to make fundamental constitutional reforms in France. Some of these men, many of whom had formed informal clubs and groupings to discuss ideas during the prerevolutionary crisis, had already begun planning to create a political press that would further their aims. As the Estates-General opened its sessions in the first week of May 1789, two of them—Jacques-Pierre Brissot and Honoré-Gabriel Riqueti, comte de Mirabeau—issued the first numbers of their unauthorized newspapers.

Brissot and Mirabeau were both veteran campaigners for major reforms in France. Both knew how powerful the press had become in English and American politics. Both were experienced in pamphlet journalism and both had worked on periodical publications before the Revolution. And both had an exalted vision of what the periodical press could contribute to the drastic political changes they wanted to promote. Brissot and Mirabeau both argued that only free, uncensored newspapers could institutionalize the kind of open debate that the prerevolutionary pamphlets had generated and make possible a genuinely representative government in a country as large as France. Newspapers "propagate instruction and reflect its influence, they unite all good spirits and all dedicated citizens; they establish communications that cannot fail to produce a harmony of sentiments, of opinions, of plans and of actions that constitutes the real public force, the safeguard of the constitution," Mirabeau exclaimed in the prospectus for his planned journal. Brissot echoed the same ideas in a pamphlet, pointing out that whereas books reached only a small audience, through newspapers "one can teach the same truth at the same moment to millions of men; through the press, they can discuss it without tumult, decide calmly and give their opinion."[18]

Brissot and Mirabeau voiced a utopian vision of a press that would serve France as a modern version of the agora of Athens, a public space in which all the citizens had assembled to participate in political decisions. Both ignored such obvious limitations on the power of the press as the fact that a good part of the French population could not read. But both were aware that newspapers were not simply a transparent channel of communication between citizens and their government. They were business enterprises, subject to the pressures of the marketplace: Mirabeau counted on making profits from his planned paper to pay his always staggering debts.[19] Brissot, for his part, considered the cheapness of newspapers as one of their great advantages because it allowed them to reach a broad audience, but he also counted on the force of economic competition to compel newspapers to print what the people wanted them to publish. Both men warned the public against the possibility that newspapers might be influenced by hidden subsidies, like the corrupt English press. To guard against the possibility of unpatriotic newspapers, Brissot explicitly conceded to the Estates-General the right to punish journalists who offended it, as the British Parliament punished them for breach of privilege.[20] The visionaries who launched the revolutionary press thus called for papers that were free from censorship but not free of charge to readers, and their demands for press freedom were mixed with a concern that the press could be corrupted and even turned against the Revolution.

Whatever the royal government had had in mind for the press, it had not simply intended to allow anyone who pleased to create his own newspaper. As soon as the first issues of Brissot's *Patriote françois* and Mirabeau's *Etats-Généraux* appeared, at the start of May 1789, they were both banned. Brissot gave in; the next number of his paper did not appear until after the fall of the Bastille. But Mirabeau, who unlike Brissot was a deputy to the Estates-General, refused to be cowed so easily. The ministers might not allow him to publish a newspaper, but they could not stop a deputy from communicating with those who had elected him. Mirabeau retitled his enterprise *Lettres du Comte de Mirabeau à ses commettans* and continued publication; the government quickly found itself unable to stop him. Several other deputies adopted the same procedure, often arranging for the publication of their reports on the Estates-General's sessions to be published in their native province rather than, as Mirabeau did, printing them in Paris for a national audience.[21] On 19 May 1789 the government gave up the fight against this form of journalism and granted permission for all comers to report on the Estates-General. So long as that body remained in session, parliamentary journalism would be permitted in France. But this concession, whose duration depended on the outcome of the Estates-General's meeting, was still far from establishing complete press freedom.

The bulletins of the Estates-General that began to appear after Mirabeau had opened the way were primitive compared to the long-established extraterritorial newspapers of the Old Regime. Their first numbers often lacked titles and were generally undated; they gave no address for subscriptions and no price. Mirabeau's first issues reflected the irascible count's rhetorical and political skills: they were more a commentary on the assembly debates than a summary of its proceedings. But most of the other journalists who took up covering the Estates-General as it was turning itself into the National Assembly were simple reporters, and their first issues were usually dry summaries of the proceedings. Lacking any system of stenography, the journalists could not take down the actual words of the deputies. Some of these chroniclers of the National Assembly nevertheless established themselves with both the public and the deputies as reliable sources of information. Bertrand Barère's *Point du Jour*, which unlike Mirabeau's paper gave only a summary of the proceedings without a personalized commentary, was concise, accurate, and highly respected. These bulletins were rudimentary compared to the work of the established chroniclers who worked for the foreign-based papers, however: until after the fall of the Bastille, none of the new French papers provided as thorough an account of the assembly's debates as the *Gazette de Leyde* did. Secure in its position as the European world's newspaper of record, that journal informed its readers that they could spare themselves the trouble of procuring the new Paris papers, because all they did was "give false impressions of everything that has happened," while another of the prerevolutionary extraterritorial papers, the *Courrier d'Avignon*, announced that its subscribers would continue to find in it "everything of interest that the Estates-General does, for less money, in a more organized fashion, than in any other printed work, and above all than those that typographical speculators are putting out in profusion."[22] As yet it was by no means clear that the printed bulletins of the Estates-General would displace the well-established pillars of the Old Regime's press system.

It was the fall of the Bastille that prompted the creation of a genuinely revolutionary press that really replaced the newspapers of the Old Regime. In Paris, all over France, and throughout the rest of the world, the public wanted the details of this first great revolutionary *journée*. The existing periodical press was poorly prepared to respond to this demand. The regular correspondents for already existing periodicals were fully occupied following the National Assembly in Versailles. In Leiden the editor of the continent's most respected newspaper could not believe the first reports he received. He withheld all details until his next issue, dated 24 July, which would have arrived back in Paris nearly two weeks after the uprising. In Paris the authorized periodicals were completely uninformative. The new papers that had been set up to cover the National Assembly also gave little news about the Bastille. Barère's *Point du Jour* focused on the National Assembly, and Mirabeau, otherwise occupied, interrupted the publication of his paper from the ninth to the twenty-fourth of July.

For news of the storming of the Bastille, readers had to turn to hastily improvised sources. Jacques Beffroy de Reigny, a popular dramatist and author of comic sketches, was one of those who turned himself into a newsman under the pressure of circumstances: he rushed to the Hotel de Ville, Paris's city hall, to find the leaders of the crowd and quickly composed an *Exact Summary of the Capture of the Bastille, Written under the Eyes of the Principal Actors who Played a Part in this Enterprise, and Read the same Day at the Hotel de Ville*. Within a few days so many "persons who claimed their part of the glory of the heroes to whom France owes this accomplishment" had visited him at home that he had the material for a second pamphlet.[23] The *Révolutions de Paris*, soon to be one of France's most important revolutionary journals, started out similarly as an improvised response to the Bastille crisis: a Paris printer had found someone to write up a hurried summary of events for him on the evening of 14 July and had rushed it into print. Only after this pamphlet had been copied by another printer and five editions had sold out did it occur to the author and this second publisher to announce that they would make their enterprise a periodical.[24] A sheet bearing the title *Relation of what took place at Rennes in Brittany on the arrival of the news of Necker's dismissal*, hastily set up in large letters by a Paris printer and bearing the unusually precise dateline "Rennes, 16 July, 3:30 PM," must be typical of the hundreds of ephemeral bulletins that appeared in Paris and all over the country as France plunged into a revolutionary crisis.

The impulse that had driven the Paris crowd to seize the Bastille and set up a revolutionary government in the capital swept through all of France in July and August 1789. A "municipal revolution" in France's provincial cities replaced royally appointed officials with popularly chosen magistrates; the rural movement known as the Great Fear led peasants to attack their *seigneurs*. Everywhere, the authority of the old government dissolved. Taxes went uncollected, a newly formed citizen militia— the National Guard—replaced the army and the police in maintaining order, and the system of censorship and privileges for printers, already in disarray before 14 July, disintegrated altogether. The door was now open for the growth of a virtually unregulated revolutionary press.

Journalists and printers rushed to take advantage of the revolutionary situation. Most of the papers hastily thrown together in the hectic weeks following the storming of the Bastille lasted only a few issues, but some were destined to be among the most important of the revolutionary titles. Brissot, who had retreated after the edict banning his paper in May, relaunched his *Patriote françois* on 28 July 1789. The weekly *Révolutions de Paris* began as a pamphlet on 20 July 1789; within a few days its author and publisher had decided to make it a periodical. The *Chronique de Paris* issued its first number on 24 August; Jean-Paul Marat began his *Publiciste parisien*, soon renamed the *Ami du Peuple*, on 12 September. Jean-Louis Carra and Louis-Sébastien Mercier combined to launch their *Annales patriotiques* on 1 October. November 24 was the birthdate of the Revolution's most important journal of record, the *Gazette nationale, ou Moniteur universel*, more commonly known simply as the *Moniteur*, a creation of the Old Regime press baron Charles-Joseph Panckoucke. The *Gazette universelle*, outstanding for its coverage of foreign news, was born a week later. Altogether, 140 new periodicals were started in Paris during 1789; thirty-four of these lasted at least one year.[25]

In the provinces, many of the prerevolutionary *affiches* added political news to the advertisements and literary features they were accustomed to carry; often they changed their titles and began publishing more frequently to satisfy the new demand for the latest reports.[26] "When we promised, at the time the Estates-General opened, to report all its actions, we did not foresee where this promise was going to lead us," the editor of the *Journal de Lyon* remarked at the end of the year, as he surveyed the change the Revolution had wrought in his enterprise. "This paper has ceased to be the journal of Lyon, to become, like all the other public papers, almost exclusively the journal of the National Assembly."[27]

By the end of the year 1789, not only the *Journal de Lyon* but the entire French press system had been altered almost beyond recognition. French readers had a choice of several dozen newspapers, representing a wide variety of political viewpoints and many different styles of journalism. The new papers covered the debates of the National Assembly, as the early newssheets of May and June had. But they also offered pointed commentary on what the legislators were doing, as well as news reports from Paris, from the French provinces, and sometimes from abroad; they quarreled with each other; and they faithfully reflected the excitement generated by the revolutionary process. Within six months of the fall of the Bastille, the combination of news, commentary, and invective and the variety of opinions that would make the press of the Revolution distinctive had already become established.

2. WRITERS, PUBLISHERS, AND READERS: THE WORLD OF THE PRESS

L ET US IMAGINE OURSELVES TRANSPORTED BACK IN
time to the Palais-Royal in Paris in 1791. The arcades and
the gardens where agitated crowds had gathered to hear
the news from Versailles in the summer of 1789 are somewhat
calmer now, but this complex of cafés, restaurants, gambling
dens, and shops is still one of the centers of Parisian gossip. Its
walks swarm with vendors crying their wares and prostitutes
stalking customers, but we are intent on other business: we are
making our way to the Cabinet Littéraire National of Madame
Vaufleury, opposite the café du Caveau, one of the most celebrated
gathering places of politicians in the city. In the café, we could
well encounter some of the leading journalists of the day. And at
Madame Vaufleury's, for the price of six sous, we will have at our
disposal one of the broadest selections of their products available
in France: what better vantage point to see what has become of the
press born in the troubled summer of 1789?[1]

The Cabinet Littéraire National offers us no less than twenty-
seven daily newspapers published in Paris, together with seven
other Paris publications that appear less frequently. The good
proprietress, a protégée of the duc d'Orléans who already ran a
reading room before 1789, has kept up the old custom of providing the foreign French-language papers as well, six of them, and
she promises us "many other periodical works, which it would
take too long to list here," a category that may include some of the

leading provincial journals. If we had been away from Paris since the beginning of the Revolution, we would be rather disoriented: only four of the Parisian titles she has on display for readers existed before June 1789, and even these papers have been transformed beyond recognition: the *Journal général de France*, which was once primarily an advertising sheet, is now a highly polemical outlet for counterrevolutionary propaganda. Madame Vaufleury's establishment offers a number of newspapers that concentrate on giving a detailed summary of the debates in the National Assembly, such as the *Moniteur*, the *Logographe*, and the *Bulletin de l'Assemblee Nationale*. But if we want more than just summaries of the legislative debates, we have a range of more polemical journals at our disposal: we may not want to sully our hands with Marat's incendiary *Ami du Peuple*, but it is there, together with the equally violent *Orateur du Peuple* and the revolutionary weeklies, the *Révolutions de Paris* and Camille Desmoulins's *Révolutions de France et de Brabant*. These little pamphlet-journals are the most radical of the revolutionary periodicals, but Madame Vaufleury also has the larger-sized quarto-format papers that back the Revolution: Brissot's *Patriote françois*, the *Chronique de Paris*, the *Annales politiques*, and several others.

The good woman respects the right of her customers to adopt whatever political opinion they please, however: as we sit and read Brissot or Desmoulins, we may be rubbing elbows with someone perusing the abbé Royou's counterrevolutionary *Ami du Roi* or the *Gazette de Paris*, for the Cabinet Littéraire National takes nearly as many right-wing papers as it does left-wing titles. The only sector of the press entirely missing from her list of offerings is the vulgar popular pamphlet press that has begun to flourish in 1790, of which the rival versions of the *Père Duchêne* are the best-known examples. The most scurrilous of the royalist papers, the *Actes des Apôtres*, is also absent. But respectable readers like ourselves, who are able to afford the comforts of Madame Vaufleury's establishment, probably do not miss these papers, and if we want them, they are available for a few sous from the ubiquitous colporteurs who cry their wares around the Palais-Royal and other gathering places.

The selection of papers available at Madame Vaufleury's Cabinet Littéraire National offers us a good introduction to the major features of the revolutionary press as it became institutionalized after 1789. As her list indicates, the newspapers were numerous. The exact number of titles appearing at any given moment is difficult to estimate, but it was certainly large. As late as the beginning of 1798, when the feverish excitement of the early revolutionary years was only a memory, the Paris police enumerated 107 publications they classified as "journaux politiques." At this date there were also about sixty papers in the French provinces.[2] To be sure, many of these papers were ephemeral enterprises that disappeared after a few issues. But revolutionary France sustained a respectable number of successful papers. The thirty-four Parisian titles on Madame Vaufleury's list were all, with one or two exceptions, solid enterprises whose titles would have been as familiar to well-informed readers in 1791 as they are to historians today, and there were several other successful papers, such as the *Journal de Perlet*, which did not appear on the reading room's list. Paris always had by far the most papers, but the larger provincial cities also spawned many competing titles, usually reflecting different political viewpoints.[3] This multiplicity of competing papers characterized the French press throughout the Revolution, even during periods like the Terror when political controls were tightest. It took the highly developed repressive apparatus of the Napoleonic government to stamp out the hardy newspapers that spread like weeds after 1789.

The list of newspapers available at the Cabinet Littéraire National demonstrates not only the sheer number of competing publications available in revolutionary Paris but also their tremendous diversity. To be sure, the different papers resembled each other in typographical appearance: with the exception of the *Moniteur* and the *Logographe*, which used a folio format copied from the English daily papers, all of Madame Vaufleury's chosen titles were either pamphlet-journals in octavo format or two-column quarto publications. None had headlines or illustrations incorporated into the text, and all used classical Roman-style body type. But out of these common ingredients, the journalists of the revolutionary decade assembled an astounding variety of approaches to the news. There were newspapers that were editorial pages without news content, like Camille Desmoulins's *Révolutions de France et de Brabant*, and newspapers that gave the news without discernible editorial commentary, such as the *Journal du Soir*. There were evening papers and morning ones, informational papers and satirical ones, prorevolutionary and counterrevolutionary papers.

The readers who paid their six sous to pass a few hours with Madame Vaufleury's selection of newpapers in 1791 were already accustomed to this profusion of newspapers and the wide range of journalistic styles featured in them. The multiplicity of papers reflected the virtual absence of government controls on entry into the press market, a situation radically different from that prevailing before 1789 or after Napoleon came to power. More than anything else, however, it reflected the lack of political consensus in revolutionary France. In 1789 revolutionary leaders like Mirabeau and Brissot had confidently predicted that the lifting of restrictions would create a press that would unify public opinion: instead, from the earliest moments of the Revolution, the newfledged newspapers made public the nation's irremediable divisions.

Only during the few months of the Great Terror in the summer of 1794 was the French press truly reduced to propagating a single political point of view. The width of the spectrum of viewpoints it represented did vary with the political situation: after a period of maximum diversity in 1789–92, the range of opinion in the press was steadily narrowed with the exclusion of overtly counterrevolutionary papers and then papers identified with defeated revolutionary factions until the dictatorship of the Committee of Public Safety produced a virtually monotone press in mid-1794. But this period was brief: after thermidor, the suppressed bands of the spectrum could be detected again, even if the most royalist and radical of them glowed only faintly. The coup d'état of 18 fructidor V (4 September 1797) brought renewed government interference with the press, but it was never as effective as the policies of the year II, and the collapse of the fructidorian Directory in the spring of 1799 unleashed the full panoply of political colors in one last brief display, before Napoleon put a final end to the revolutionary press system.

The dazzlingly diverse array of newspapers in Madame Vaufleury's *cabinet de lecture* and in the streets around it, so much more varied and opinionated than the press of the Old Regime, was thus one of the most tangible signs of the changes wrought by the Revolution. Like the other features of the new political culture born in 1789, this press was the collective creation of a society searching for new ways to govern itself. The readers who crowded the tables of the *cabinets de lecture* and paid their sous to the colporteurs outside were helping to create the press they read. The publishers who arranged for the printing and distribution of the newspapers were also vital to the workings of the revolutionary press system. And of course, the journalists, some famous, some obscure, who put together the words that were printed in the many papers published during the ten years of the Revolution were major participants in the making of this new medium.

The Journalists

The journalists of the revolutionary decade were well aware that theirs was a demanding and even dangerous trade. "It is not enough, when you want to put out a journal, to simply take up the pen and write," one revolutionary-era newsman told his readers in 1797. "I won't discuss my talent, that would be unbecoming, but it also takes, more than one might think, patience, persistence, prudence, resignation, and, I dare say, courage."[4] This editor and his colleagues worked harder and faster than newsmen ever had

The Patriot Journalists: An engraving from Camille Desmoulins's *Révolutions de France et de Brabant*, in May 1791. Leading prorevolutionary journalists including Brissot, Gorsas, Condorcet, and Prudhomme are shown with their papers. A hand rising from the ground represents Marat in the subterranean refuge he had fled to to escape the threat of arrest. The seated figure at lower right may represent the engraver. Source: The Newberry Library, Chicago.

before, and they enjoyed greater power and larger salaries than any of their predecessors. But as they exploited the new possibilities the Revolution had opened up for masters of the written word, these journalists also faced risks their predecessors had rarely confronted.

Eighteenth-century France had already made celebrities of its famous writers, but none had ever become so notorious and so politically influential in such short time as the journalists of the Revolution. The names of Camille Desmoulins, Jacques-Pierre Brissot, and the abbé Thomas-Marie Royou, all virtually unknown in 1789, quickly became better known than those of the vast majority of the National Assembly deputies they commented on. In 1793 eulogists compared the assassinated Jean-Paul Marat to Jesus and created a quasi-religious cult around him.[5] The world had seen a handful of famous journalists before 1789—England's notorious John Wilkes in the 1760s, Linguet on the European continent in the 1770s and 1780s—but their fame was completely overshadowed by that of their Parisian successors between 1789 and 1799.

These journalists were an extremely diverse group. They differed greatly in the degree of their involvement in the profession: the term *journalist* covers writers and editors who devoted all their working time to the business and made a living from it as well as occasional contributors whose contributions were unpaid and whose main concerns were elsewhere. Even those who were paid professionals were a varied lot. The stars were the great editorialists: Marat, Brissot, Desmoulins, Jean-Thomas Richer-Sérizy. They were less collectors of news than commentators upon it, political essayists working on a daily or weekly schedule. But the more numerous rank and file of the profession was made up of distinctly less glamorous "news workers," like the largely anonymous notetakers who recorded the speeches made at the legislative assemblies and the Jacobin club and the equally obscure Parisian and provincial editors who assembled news bulletins from foreign capitals, summaries of the latest debates, and the scrawlings of their more famous colleagues the commentators, if they were lucky enough to have one on their paper. A few papers, like Marat's *Ami du Peuple*, may have been true one-man operations, but most publications had at least two editorial employees, typically a writer who might also assemble provincial and foreign news by clipping out-of-town papers and a reporter responsible primarily for the coverage of the legislature.

The editorialist was usually the person publicly identified with the paper. It was rare for a single publication to house more than one of these journalistic celebrities. Louis-Sébastien Mercier and Jean-Louis Carra shared the editorship of the *Annales patriotiques*, but this was an unusual arrangement and Carra certainly overshadowed his colleague in the public's mind. Only a few papers had a team of identified contributors, as most of the great Paris dailies of the nineteenth century would. But most were in fact the product of editorial teamwork, and the total number of journalists active in Paris was therefore considerably higher than the number of papers, perhaps as many as three hundred to four hundred at any one time.

Statistics on journalists active in Paris in 1790–91 and in the period from thermidor to brumaire show that these writers came from a variety of backgrounds. The profession attracted men of every age between 20 and 60, but it was preeminently a younger man's occupation. The median age for revolutionary journalists was about 35 or 36, as compared to a median age of 53 for all known published authors in 1784;[6] the age distribution of journalists did not change significantly between the early revolutionary years and the Directory period (see table 1). The majority of early revolutionary journalists were from bourgeois backgrounds, but in general these writers' families, even if well-to-do, were rather obscure and their sons had always known that they would have to make their way in the world on the basis of their own abilities. One-fifth of those whose fathers' occupations are known were from families categorized either as artisans or simply as

Table 1. Ages of Journalists, 1790–91 and 1794–99

Age Range	1790–91	1794–99
43—	21%	20%
33–42	26%	20%
23–32	25%	27%
Under 23	3%	4%
Unknown	25%	29%
Sample size	122	193

Note. Tables 1–3 are based on data for journalists identified as active on one or more newspapers in Paris during the periods 1790–91 and 9 thermidor II-18 brumaire VIII, respectively. For the first group, journalists were identified primarily from the listings for papers published in Paris in the *Catalogue de la Révolution française* of Martin and Walter, and biographical data were drawn from standard biographical dictionaries. The sample certainly underrepresents the humbler and more anonymous members of the profession. More journalists can be identified for the later period thanks to the wider range of sources, including police records and memoirs; the larger size of the group also reflects the longer period studied. For a more detailed study of this group, see Jeremy D. Popkin, "The Journalists of the Directory Period: An Opinion-Making Elite," *Proceedings of the Consortium on Revolutionary Europe* (1980): 1: 3–12. Ages in table 1 are measured as of 1791 for the first group and as of 1796 for the second.

"poor"; these men were thrown on their own resources even more. For the Directory period, the percentage of journalists who can be identified as coming from such humble backgrounds was lower, and the proportion of nobles was higher than in 1790–91, but the proportion of writers in this sample whose social origins are unknown is very large (see table 2).

In both periods, the previous occupations that journalists were most likely to have exercised were the vaguely defined career of *gens de lettres* and the law—23 percent and 18 percent respectively

Table 2. Family Backgrounds of Journalists

Family Background	1790–91	1794–99
Nobles	12%	31%
Legal professions	29%	18%
Government	3%	9%
Medicine	2%	7%
Other educated professions	14%	4%
Commerce	19%	4%
Artisans	10%	7%
Peasants	—	4%
"Poor"	10%	11%
Miscellaneous	—	5%
Sample size	58	55

of the 1790–91 group and 19 percent and 12 percent of the Directory newsmen. Ten percent of the 1790–91 journalists had been clergy, as had 8 percent of their successors under the Directory (see table 3). This pattern was not very different from that for prerevolutionary journalists: in the period 1775–89, 21 percent of these had been *gens de lettres*, 15 percent had been lawyers or government officials whose posts implied the possession of legal training, and 7 percent had been clergy.[7] A similar pattern still prevailed in the mid-nineteenth century, although journalists who had previously been academics had taken the place of the eighteenth century's free-lance *gens de lettres* and clergy.[8] Although 1789–99 was an exceptional period in the history of French journalism, the recruitment pattern for journalists thus seems to have been roughly the same during the Revolution as it was before and afterward. From the time it emerged as a profession in the mid-eighteenth century to the end of the Second Empire, journalism attracted young men from families that had been able to provide them with some advanced schooling, but who usually

Table 3. Previous Occupations of Journalists[1]

Occupation	1790–91	1794–99
Gens de lettres	23%[2]	19%[3]
Legal professions	18%	12%
Clergy	10%	8%
Military	2%	4%
Other educated professions	8%	1%
Commerce	9%	4%
Artisans	1%	2%
Students	2%	3%
Unknown	27%	44%
Sample size	89	108

1. Based on samples of 89/122 (1790–91) and 108/193 (1794–99).
2. Fifteen percent of the journalists active in 1790–91 were definitely active as journalists before 1789.
3. At least 20 percent of this group had been active as journalists in 1789–92.

lacked the connections and resources that would have guaranteed them easy access to France's governing elites. Throughout this period, journalism was one of the few careers in which talent alone was enough to make success possible. Particularly during the Revolution, journalists were men who had made their own way, self-confident individualists practicing one of the rare occupations in France that lacked any collective institutions and had no professional hierarchy. Whatever their political views, they lived in a world structured according to principles of free and unrestricted competition like those that the liberal reformers of 1789 had tried to impose on all areas of French life.

The statistical data in tables 1–3 only partially reveal the diversity of backgrounds among the journalists of the revolutionary period. Some were "marginal men" of the Old Regime, not established in any fixed career before 1789, such as Desmoulins,

Carra, or Brissot, whereas others were well-known Old Regime men of letters, such as the marquis de Condorcet, Jean-François Laharpe, or J. B. A. Suard. Of the prerevolutionary men of letters, some had been Old Regime journalists, such as Pascal Boyer, the prerevolutionary Paris correspondent to the *Gazette de Leyde*, and Brissot, who had contributed to a number of periodicals, while others had been aspiring poets, such as Louis Fontanes, or playwrights, such as Joseph Fiévée. There were a few women journalists, like Louise de Kéralio of the radical *Mercure national* early in the Revolution and Caroline Wuiet, editor of several short-lived papers during the Directory, whose lives obstinately refused to follow the pattern of the men's.

The journalists of the revolutionary era did have a few things in common. Although no specific educational qualifications were necessary to become a journalist, the field required a degree of fluency in writing that was almost impossible to attain without a secondary education. The biographical sketches of one journalist after another in the early nineteenth-century *Biographie universelle* begin with the remark that the subject "was a good student." These men—the few women in the field, of course, had not had access to the *collèges* of the Old Regime—had thus gone through the conventional course of general studies in the eighteenth-century schools. They shared an easy familiarity with the great classics of Latin and French literature, which gave them a common frame of reference with their educated readers but which set them apart from the vast majority of their countrymen. Jacques-René Hébert's fictional Père Duchêne quoted Montaigne; Camille Desmoulins's *Révolutions de France et de Brabant* was virtually a course in Roman history. If, like Hébert, they had shared the hovels of the prerevolutionary poor, they had done so as unexpected visitors from another planet. The journalists, regardless of their political persuasion, were an intellectual elite group, more heavily drawn from the educated professions and the milieu of *gens de lettres* than was the political elite that governed the country after 1789, but equally far removed in mentality and life-style from the mass of the population.

The journalists of the 1790s came to the profession for a variety of reasons. For many, and certainly for most of those who became most celebrated, it was a way of furthering an ideological commitment. This was as true for the prominent revolutionaries Camille Desmoulins and Marat, who claimed he sought nothing more than "the glory of sacrificing myself for the country,"[9] as it was for a dedicated royalist like the abbé Royou. Moderation, too, had its true apostles, such as Antoine-Marie Cerisier, whose *Gazette universelle* preached the values of a constitutional government dominated by the educated and propertied classes that its editor had spent more than a decade elaborating before 1789,[10] and Charles Lacretelle, another nineteenth-century liberal ahead of his time who spent over a year in prison during the Directory. The annals of the decade's journalism record very few genuine turncoats who changed their tune for opportunistic reasons (although almost every journalist had occasion to revise his views on some issues during the rapid flow of events after 1789).

From the outset of the Revolution, leaders of the movement urged its supporters by exhortation, and in the case of Mirabeau by example, to consider patriotic writing as a form of service to the country and the good cause. In his pamphlet series published in Brittany during the prerevolutionary crisis of 1788, C. F. Volney had become only the first of many to proclaim himself the *Sentinelle du Peuple*, the people's watchman.[11] In a celebrated passage, Camille Desmoulins asserted that "today, journalists exercise a public function; they denounce, decree, judge, absolve, or condemn."[12] Typical of those who embraced journalism as part of a larger sense of ideological mission was Nicolas Bonneville, the guiding spirit of the *Cercle social*, a group of idealists who combined enthusiasm for the Revolution with a quasi-mystical religious passion. He and his friends founded several journals, most notably the *Bouche de fer*, as part of a wider campaign to promote their ideas, which included public lectures to a mass audience, the formation of a club, activism in Paris municipal politics, and the publication of books and pamphlets.[13] Bonneville retained his devotion to his original ideals throughout the Revolution and, despite the disasters of the Terror which claimed many of his original colleagues as victims, was still trying to promote them in a paper called the *Bien Informé* late in the Directory period. The right-wing journalists were in a different position: they had no public mandate to make themselves spokesmen for the cause they defended. The hapless Louis XVI dared not openly summon journalists to his aid, and indeed the shrill rhetoric of the self-appointed defenders of his cause often undercut the plans of the king and his circle. But this absence of public encouragement in no way dampened the enthusiasm of the writers who took up the counterrevolutionary cause, proclaiming their mission to remind readers "of what everyone in France . . . owes to his religion, his country, and his king."[14]

The personal commitment to ideals that characterized many of the period's journalists and eventually led a good number to the guillotine was often a very sudden one. Pierre-Barnabé Farmian De Rozoi, the royalist editor of the inflammatory *Gazette de Paris* who was executed in 1792, had a long and checkered prerevolutionary career that suggested anything but firmness of character, but once he had committed himself to the cause of counterrevolution, he displayed the loyalty of a true believer.[15] Similarly, Camille Desmoulins, a young man who had never managed to commit himself to anything prior to 1789, identified himself instantly and totally with the cause of liberty during the crisis leading to the storming of the Bastille. In other cases, journalists' work during the Revolution was the expression of long-standing views that pre-dated 1789. The abbé Royou had been a vigilant opponent of the *philosophes* long before 1789: he was the successor to their notorious enemy Elie Fréron as editor of the former's journal, the *Année littéraire*. He saw the campaign against the Revolution as a continuation of an old battle: "Fréron alone foresaw and warned against the misfortunes we are now suffer-ing."[16] Marat and Brissot had both written lengthy denunciations of the evils of the Old Regime long before it fell. But the connection between prerevolutionary and postrevolutionary view-points was a complex one, and in many cases too little is known about leading journalists' political views before 1789 to judge how their later positions were related to them.

Personal conviction was one of the forces that propelled individ-uals to become journalists in 1789; it worked perhaps most strongly on the most prominent and successful, and it would be unduly cynical to overstress the fact that these writers, once they had made their mark, stood to lose the reputation they had acquired if they started flagrantly contradicting views they had expressed earlier. Jean-François Laharpe, the acolyte of Voltaire and editor of the literary section of the *Mercure de France* until 1793, was one of a handful of prominent journalists to make a genuine recantation of his earlier views: the experience of the Terror caused him to become a devout Catholic, who expressed his new-found horror of the Revolution in the right-wing press of the Directory period. The repentant sinner was of course welcomed by the other counterrevolutionaries, but to most of his colleagues he was "the renegade Laharpe" for the rest of his career. Unlike the more tolerant English public of the period, which put up with its journalists' unexpected conversions from ministerialism to opposi-tion and back as part of the newspaper game, the society of revolutionary France would not forgive a journalist who revised his views.

Nevertheless, devotion to principles was not the only motive driving the journalists of the period. For some, the lure was less the chance to promote particular ideas than the opportunity to occupy a grandstand seat at the century's most exciting spectacle. Charles Lacretelle, whose memoirs are the most engaging account of a journalist's career in the 1790s that we have, gladly traded the unglamorous job of grinding out articles for Panckoucke's enor-mous *Encyclopédie méthodique* for a seat in the galleries at the

National Assembly. For a newcomer from the provinces, too young to aspire to a deputy's place, arriving at the hall at midnight to reserve a seat for the following day and exercising his imagination to flesh out the speeches that he had barely been able to hear was great fun. In addition, thanks to his profession, "I had ten to twelve seats to distribute to elegant people, and especially to the ladies."[17]

All this and a regular paycheck, too. For journalism during the Revolution could pay very well, and the desire to make a living reinforced the urge to make a statement or to serve a cause as the principal motive for pursuit of the profession. Elysée Loustallot, himself one of the best-paid revolutionary writers, rejoiced in the high salaries that the profession offered: he claimed that the patriotic cause would always be sure of spokesmen as long as journalism promised "wealth and glory."[18] Careers like that of Jacques-René Hébert, the Père Duchêne, who discovered his vocation through the accident of a meeting with an acquaintance willing to pay him to try his hand at writing and went on to become one of the most effective prorevolutionary journalists, vindicated Loustallot's proposition.[19] Lacretelle earned more than 3,000 livres a year for his anonymous reportorial work in the early years of the Revolution, and the stars of the journalistic firmament made far larger sums: 10,000 livres a year for Camille Desmoulins, upwards of 12,000 livres for Jacques Mallet du Pan as editor of the political section of the *Mercure de France*, a reported 25,000 livres a year for the young Elysée Loustallot on the *Révolutions de Paris*.[20] These fabulous salaries went to writers who were not even co-owners of their papers: those who were could aspire to even greater revenues. This was a far different world from the one in which Rousseau had sold the rights to the great best-seller of the 1760s, his *Emile*, for 6,000 livres. Even though many of the successful journalists managed to let most of their salaries slip through their fingers—Marat, Hébert, and Desmoulins all died poor—they had earned more with their pens in less time than any other writers before them. The journalists of the French Revolution, the largest group of professionals writing for pay that France had yet seen, blazed the way for the writers in other genres who would succeed in tapping the growing mass market for literature in the nineteenth and twentieth centuries.

Those journalists who were in a position to do so drove hard bargains for their services. Isidore Langlois, barely out of his teens when he became a successful right-wing editorialist after thermidor, agreed to write for a daily known as the *Messager du Soir* in 1796 for a guaranteed minimum salary of 3,240 livres and a bonus of one percent of the enterprise's gross revenues for every subscription above 4,000 sold. But the contract also assured him of protection against the hazards of the trade. He was to receive half pay during "any imprisonment or forced absence caused by the journal"; if he had to emulate Marat and go into hiding he would at least have a regular income. A similar provision covered incapacitation due to illness, and another clause specified severance pay. The publisher was also obligated to provide his star employee with a heated and well-lit private office. For a journalist with less than a year's experience, it was a handsome arrangement.[21]

The frequent clashes between journalists and their employers are sufficient testimony to the seriousness with which many writers defended their pecuniary privileges. The publishers considered the periodicals as their property and expected to pocket the lion's share of the profits, as they always had throughout the eighteenth century, but the journalists saw the matter differently. Camille Desmoulins spoke for all his colleagues when he protested against his original publisher's effort to exercise his option to replace the editor of the *Révolutions de France et de Brabant* after its first six months in existence. "I call {it} my journal, although the publisher claims it is his," Desmoulins wrote. "I am truly father of my 26 previous issues, since I drew them out of my brain. . . . But this quarrel between the publishers and we unfortunate authors is an old one."[22] The abbé Royou, opposed to Desmoulins on almost every other issue, agreed with him on this one: "It is sad indeed . . . that writers are subjected to those who, by the nature of their functions, are not and cannot be anything but their agents."[23] Jean-Pierre Gallais, a successful author-editor of the Directory period, resurrected a famous passage from the prerevolutionary journalist Linguet to justify journalists' claims to proper remuneration for their work: "Why, then, should the writer for a periodical, a writer who devotes his nights and often sacrifices his comfort to instruct his fellow-citizens, why should he not, without ceasing to be honest and scrupulous, figure out the income from his paper, and count on a monetary reward? It is by not letting himself be stained by ignominious favors or partialities that he maintains his honesty, and not by refusing a salary he has legitimately earned."[24] Not many journalists were as open about this aspect of their profession as Gallais, but even fewer were indifferent to the rewards their efforts could earn them. It was not only the words the journalists produced that were for sale; some supplemented their earnings by taking bribes on the side. Accusations of such corruption were endemic throughout the decade, but the practice was probably not as widespread as contemporaries professed to believe, and certainly not as flagrant as it was in British journalism of the same period. Still, there is no doubt that ambitious politicians like the duc d'Orléans and interested parties like the British-funded royalists of the Directory period did enrich some writers.[25]

Although journalism during the revolutionary period could lead to riches, it could equally well lead to prison or worse. The Declaration of the Rights of Man and the Citizen might well have promised freedom of the press, but every successive revolutionary regime harassed leading newsmen. Marat, ordered arrested by the National Assembly, the Legislative Assembly, and the Convention, as well as by several lesser governmental bodies, was the most frequently prosecuted and spent much of his journalistic career hiding from the police. But his experiences were anything but unique. Royalist journalists had to dodge angry Patriot vigilantes in 1790 and were temporarily silenced after the king's unsuccessful flight in June 1791; the radicals were in jeopardy after the bloody repression of the republican demonstration of 17 July 1791. The right-wingers were targets again in the wake of the *journée* of 10 August 1792, during which François Suleau, one of their number, was lynched in the street.

Up until 10 August the worst fate journalists normally risked was imprisonment or forced flight to avoid it, but with the fall of the monarchy, the stakes went up. In addition to Suleau, the *journée* of 10 August 1792 claimed the life of De Rozoi, condemned by the temporary revolutionary tribunal set up in the aftermath of the insurrection. Jourgniac de Saint-Méard, another counterrevolutionary writer, was imprisoned and barely survived the September massacres; his firsthand account of his *Thirty-Eight Hours of Agony* became a best-seller. With the counterrevolutionaries largely silenced, it was the turn of the revolutionary journalists. The writers identified with the Gironde were imprisoned or forced to flee for their lives after that party's defeat on 2 June 1793, and most of the well-known ones—Brissot, Antoine-Louis Gorsas, Carra, Condorcet, and Brissot's collaborator Joseph-Marie Girey-Dupré—fell victim to the Terror, as did several counter-revolutionary writers who had escaped attention in 1792. In 1794 it was the turn of the radical journalists who had failed to fall in line with the policies of the Committee of Public Safety: Hébert, Jacques Roux, and Desmoulins. The Great Terror also claimed the head of the Old Regime's most successful journalist, Linguet. Most of the journalists guillotined in Paris during the Terror were prominent figures who were punished as much for their political deeds as for their words, but there were a number of less famous victims put to death solely for their writing, such as the *Gazette universelle*'s founder Pascal Boyer and A. A. F. Coutouly, the crypto-royalist editor of an obscure sheet known as the *Trois Décades*, while numerous others spent months in jail or in hiding with the threat of execution hanging over them. Altogether, at least one-sixth of the journalists known to have been active in Paris in 1790–91 were executed during the Terror. Provincial journalists suffered along with their Parisian colleagues, particularly if they had helped to put out papers during the Federalist revolts in 1793: in Bordeaux at least ten newspapermen were executed for their part in the resistance to the Montagnard government.[26]

Thermidor brought a lessening of the risks involved in journalism—Gracchus Babeuf and his colleague Augustin Darthé, acquitted on charges of conspiring to overthrow the government in 1797 but executed for promoting "anarchism" in Babeuf's *Tribun du peuple*, were the only ones to suffer capital punishment for their published writings—but no end to the war against oppositional newsmen. More than a dozen of the counterrevolutionary editorialists were imprisoned or forced underground after the failed *journée* of 13 vendémiaire IV (5 October 1795); several radical writers were swept up in the repression of the Babeuf conspiracy; and the republican coup of 18 fructidor V (4 September 1797) resulted in warrants for the arrest of over thirty writers and editors, some of whom consequently endured lengthy prison stays. Extralegal assaults continued, too; the Director Paul Barras arranged a well-publicized beating for one editor he particularly disliked. Throughout the eighteenth century, French writers had suffered *embastillement* and exile when their works displeased the authorities, but repression had never been so extensive nor so deadly as it was during the revolutionary decade. Not until the years of the German occupation during World War II would French journalism again become as hazardous an occupation as it was in the 1790s.

Although journalism during the Revolution offered both unprecedented rewards and unprecedented hazards, it left its practitioners ample time for other activities. A number of journalists also wrote pamphlets, plays, and verse along with their editorials. Joseph Fiévée managed the *Chronique de Paris*'s printing shop as well as contributing to its columns. Even more important, many journalists simultaneously pursued political careers. Mirabeau and Bertrand Barère in the National Assembly, Brissot and Condorcet in the Legislative Assembly; those two and Marat, Gorsas, Carra, and several others in the Convention; and Jean-Baptiste Louvet,

Pierre-Samuel Dupont de Nemours, and François Poultier in the Directory's Councils combined service as a deputy with journalism. At various times Robespierre and Hébert worked as journalists while holding posts in the Paris municipal government. Journalists were active in the assemblies of Paris's districts and their successors, the sections, as well: Bonneville, Brissot, and Marat were involved in such local politicking in 1789, and in 1795 the vendémiaire insurrection against the Convention was largely directed by a group of counterrevolutionary journalists who had seized control of their sections after thermidor. Journalists were also active in the political clubs, from the Jacobins, well-staffed with newsmen at every stage in their evolution, to the counterrevolutionary Club de Clichy during the Directory. In the provinces, there were hardly any full-time newsmen and the combination of journalism, political activism, and a paying occupation was the norm, as in the case of the Perpignan Jacobin activist Jaubert, editor of the lively *Echo des Pyrénées* and director of the town's *collège*, and the Avignonnais editor Sabin Tournal, who was lieutenant colonel of the local citizens' militia during the violence that preceded the region's annexation to France.[27]

Journalistic success was not an automatic route to political power, of course: the journalist-deputies were an exception among their ink-stained colleagues, and of those who reached high posts by virtue of their writings, few were genuinely successful as politicians. But for those who combined the necessary talents, simultaneous activity as journalists and politicians offered a way to stand out from their rivals in both professions. "How does it happen that this petty individual does so much harm to the public welfare?" one of Brissot's Jacobin enemies demanded in late 1792. "It's because he has a newspaper . . . it's because Brissot and his friends have all the trumpets of renown at their disposal."[28]

Brissot achieved a leading position both as a newsman and as a politician, but the record of others who combined both activities was mixed. Mirabeau's journal started out as powerful as his oratory, but it quickly declined when he turned it over to a team of ghostwriters. Condorcet, a talented writer, was a poor speaker, but he did accomplish a good deal of important legislative work; Marat's biographers agree that he proved a surprisingly effective debater in the face of an overwhelmingly hostile assembly. But in many cases, successful journalists who won elective office proved relatively ineffectual in their new positions. Gorsas, Desmoulins, and Poultier were a few of the many editorialists who never managed to exert as much influence in the legislature as they were able to do through the columns of their papers, whereas Robespierre, no great success as a journalist, was quite effective as a parliamentarian. The talents needed for success as an orator or a committeeman were not necessarily the same as those required in journalism. Furthermore, the voters, willing to pick a large number of prominent journalists for the Legislative Assembly in 1791, turned against candidates who had made their reputation with their pens in the later years of the Revolution. In 1797 the electors, while returning primarily right-wing candidates, ignored the vigorous campaigns of the prominent counterrevolutionary journalists and preferred obscure local notables.[29]

Whether or not they had political talent, the journalists of the revolutionary period needed certain specific abilities to fill the columns of their papers. The "news work" that the journalists of the revolutionary era performed varied with the nature of their functions on their particular newspapers. The editorialists followed political events closely, either by attending the debates in person or by reading press accounts, and usually wrote about issues already under discussion or matters that they wanted the deputies to tackle. Like the national press columnists of today, they cultivated contacts with leading politicians, if they did not, like Mirabeau and Brissot, simply combine the two roles. Editorialists might be essentially paid publicists for a single politician, taking instructions from him, like Mirabeau's "ghosts" Etienne Dumont and Jacques Du Roveray, or they might meet on equal terms with like-minded politicians and collaborate in setting a political agenda. They also talked to their press colleagues:

during the postthermidorian period, the leading right-wing editorialists organized themselves into a regular group to plan press campaigns.[30] The journalists of the 1790s already had their favorite rendezvous for these informal exchanges with politicians and colleagues: they haunted the cafés and restaurants in central Paris, such as the Procope and the Caveau.

The revolutionary journalists earned their influence and their celebrity by working harder and more steadily than any of their predecessors. The prerevolutionary world of letters had been a mix of gifted amateurs, holders of sinecures, and "poor devils" earning an irregular income from hack writing;[31] all worked on erratic schedules. Revolutionary journalism was a much more professionalized milieu, and it demanded a new skill from its practitioners: the ability to produce on a fixed schedule. The revolutionary newsmen were among the first writers to have to accommodate themselves to the rigors of meeting daily deadlines. Most of these writers were expected to furnish at least a few paragraphs on a daily basis, seven days a week. They had to be able to write quickly. Madame Roland recalled that one reason for her friend Brissot's success was that he "worked very easily, and he composed a treatise the way someone else would copy a song."[32] Hostile critics seized on the fact that newspapermen had to produce on demand to downgrade the profession. "The necessity of writing every day," Benjamin Constant proclaimed, "is the tomb of talent."[33] Even journalists themselves admitted that "it is hardly possible . . . to write every day, at a fixed time, on the same subject, with the same force and the same elegance."[34] The demands of the profession did favor some mediocre wordsmiths whose main talent was their ability to meet deadlines: there is no other explanation for the durability of an editorialist like Antoine-François Lemaire, who worked successively for the *Lettres bougrement patriotiques du véritable Père Duchêne*, the *Trompette du Père Duchêne*, the *Courrier de l'Égalité*, the *Journal du Bonhomme Richard*, the *Orateur des assemblées primaires*, and the Directory-era revival of the *Patriote françois*.

The successful journalists learned, of course, to minimize the creative strain on themselves by various time- and thought-saving stratagems. Reliance on repetitive formulas was indispensable: after a while, Hébert's *Père Duchêne* could be counted on to provide one "grande colère," one "grande joie," and one piece of "bon avis" per number. By the winter of 1794 the public grumbled that "he has done nothing but repeat himself for the last six months."[35] Plagiarism was another handy crutch: editorialists borrowed ideas and sometimes whole articles from each other or from other sources. Camille Desmoulins took most of one issue of his *Vieux Cordelier* directly from a tract by the English commonwealthman Thomas Gordon, and Jean-Pierre Gallais, one of the liveliest Directory-era newsmen, copied a number of his most striking articles directly from the pages of Linguet's prerevolutionary *Annales politiques*, which did not keep him from publishing a vehement denunciation of those who duplicated his own articles, whom he labeled "manufacturers of news reports to measure, who don't bother to keep up the slightest pretense of honesty, as long as they can trick the public into trusting them and giving them money."[36] One way or another, the journalists of the 1790s were seldom found at a loss for words.

Those journalists whose job was primarily assembling information rather than commenting on it had their own routines. Few engaged in the active uncovering of news that was not presented to them in a public forum: Marat, who sometimes followed up on the detailed denunciations of specific individuals such as the "dishonest intriguer" who one reader had told him was illegally selling reserved seats in the public galleries of the National Assembly,[37] was one of the few precursors of investigative reporting in the revolutionary era. The most important reportorial job for most papers was the coverage of legislative debates. This required little legwork: the reporter, if he was not himself a deputy—even as distinguished a thinker as Condorcet did not consider it beneath himself to furnish a daily summary of legislative discussions—sat in the tribunes or public galleries and jotted down what the speakers had said as best he could. Initially, the reporters had to scramble for seats along with the general public; later they had reserved places, and the stenographers for the *Logographe*, which purported to furnish a complete literal transcription of the proceedings, had a private booth or *loge*. The acoustics in all the meeting halls used during the Revolution were miserable, however, and no one could hope to capture every word said in the often chaotic debates. Gorsas's *Courrier de Versailles à Paris, et de Paris à Versailles*, one of the earliest of the revolutionary papers, warned its readers at the outset that its parliamentary coverage would never be faultless: "It is very difficult not to make mistakes sometimes in an Assembly composed of 1200 people."[38] Etienne Dumont, who wrote up the debates for Mirabeau's *Courrier de Provence*, never pretended to make a literal record of the debates: "A few words written in pencil, sufficed to call to our recollection the arguments of a speech and the order of a debate. We never intended to give all the idle prating in the tribune." According to Dumont, some speakers were grateful for the pruning and editing the reporters did on their speeches. Most deputies spoke from written texts, and the enterprising reporter could avoid reliance on notes by asking for the manuscript.[39]

The legislative assemblies of the revolutionary period were not only a major news story in themselves, but they also served as a source of extraparliamentary news that the journalists thus obtained without having to make any investigative efforts on their own. Particularly after the start of the revolutionary war in 1792, the Legislative Assembly and its successors functioned as a daily press conference from which reporters could gather most of what they needed to know about the situation of the armies. During the Directory period, the executive branch of the government took a greater role in distributing news, even publishing its own official daily newspaper, the *Rédacteur*. Editors regarded it as the government's obligation to provide them with the information they needed: the editor of the *Echo des Pyrénées* in Perpignan threatened to abandon his enterprise when the local army commander and the departmental authorities failed to answer his requests for copy.[40] The success of the press during the revolutionary wars in providing more news about the fighting and printing it sooner than in the prerevolutionary period was entirely due to the government's efforts to obtain more and better information from the commanders, rather than to any independent journalistic initiative.[41]

For their other extra-Parisian news, the press of the capital relied heavily on readers' letters and out-of-town newspapers. Prior to the invention of the electric telegraph in the 1840s, newspapers from different locations were each others' press service, and editors who went to work on their colleagues' products with a pair of scissors in order to fill their own columns were simply following standard practice. In the case of foreign news, this meant that the Paris papers were heavily dependent on journals published in countries hostile to the Revolution; as a result, there was often a jarring discordance between the official reports furnished with the summary of the legislature and the news from other sources, a discrepancy that the journalists made no effort to resolve for their readers. Except in the case of civil conflict involving the armies, the revolutionary governments did not systematically collect and disseminate news from the provinces. The papers were consequently heavily dependent on the provincial press and on unverified reports from readers. Editors used these frequently, but they knew better than to place complete faith in them: the *Journal de Perlet*, bombarded with letters about candidates in the 1797 legislative elections, demanded that such missives be signed (but how was the journalist, sitting in Paris, to verify the signatures?) and that they give "precise facts proper to show that [the candidates] are really unworthy of their fellow-citizens' confidence."[42]

The end product of these journalistic endeavors invariably bore the stamp of the personalities who had written and assembled its contents. The sprightly and frequently obscene satire and verse in the *Actes des Apôtres* were the very image of the cynical aristocrats and men of letters who composed that disdainful rejection of the

Revolution, just as the cautious, pedantic, but encyclopedic *Moniteur* reflected the nature of its creator, Panckoucke. In the unstable and competitive environment of the revolutionary press system, there was no one model of journalism so successful that most practitioners felt compelled to follow it. The multiplicity of printers and publishers on the lookout for talented writers and the absence of dominating "press barons," together with the fact that most papers employed only one editorialist rather than a team, made the 1790s a period in which journalists had a maximum of freedom to try new methods. True products of the revolutionary era, with its encouragement of individual initiative, the French journalists of the revolutionary decade achieved a public status that few subsequent practitioners of their profession have been able to match.

The Press Industry

The dozens of competing newspapers in revolutionary Paris were the expression of their authors' individuality, but they were also the product of a printing industry that had had to transform itself in a matter of months to meet the French nation's greatly increased demand for news. Prior to 1789 printing and publishing had been tightly controlled by the government and by the printers' guild. The number of printing shops was limited to thirty-six in the capital and 266 in the French provinces. These licensed printers had every incentive to cooperate with the authorities in preventing the emergence of new competitors and little reason to question a system that guaranteed them a good living with a minimum of entrepreneurial effort. Printing licenses were hard for outsiders to obtain, and the vast majority of the compositors and pressmen who worked for these privileged employers knew they had no chance of ever becoming master printers in their own right.

The Revolution shattered the old legal and guild restrictions, and forced printers and publishers to adopt new strategies to make profits. Newspaper publishing was one of the main resources to

"The Freedom of the Press" (1798): This well-known revolutionary engraving telescopes the processes of printing and distributing newspapers into a single image that effectively conveys the competitiveness and urgency of the market for newspapers. Source: Bibliothèque nationale, Paris.

ruined the old publishing trade," a journalist wrote in 1790. "A new type of trade has replaced it . . . kept going only by these frivolous sheets that, like flowers, bloom in the morning and disappear by evening, to be replaced by new ones the next day."[43] Although the old publishers' guild was not formally abolished until 1791, it had lost all ability to enforce its regulations against unlicensed competitors.[44] Anyone who wanted to could now open a printing shop or become a publisher, and dozens did. Furthermore, it was mostly these newcomers—former printing-shop workers, printers from the French provinces, and even printers from abroad—who took up the challenge of producing the newspapers that were suddenly so much in demand. On the basis of this and the other new opportunities the Revolution provided, the Paris printing industry grew to an unheard-of size. By 1798 there were 221 printing shops in the capital.[45] Over ninety of these were putting out at least one periodical. The result of their efforts was to make political news and opinion into a mass-produced commodity whose price, although by no means negligible, was low enough for even some of France's lower classes to afford. And because following the press was a means of taking part in revolutionary politics, these commercial entrepreneurs in effect made it possible for anyone who could afford the price of a newspaper to join the active citizenry.

Entry into the news market was fairly easy. M. S. Boulard, one of these new entrepreneurs, sought to cash in on the printing boom by publishing a manual for newcomers to the trade, even if they had no knowledge whatever of printing procedures. He assured his readers that a decent printing shop could be furnished for little more than 8,000 livres, a fairly modest sum for a middle-class investor, but he was convinced that a newspaper enterprise could be launched for even less. According to his calculations, a single press, a single font of type, and the other minimal requirements of the trade should cost only 2,146 livres; allowing 1,200 livres for advances on wages and rent, he concluded that all it took to become a newspaper publisher was an investment of 3,346 livres, an amount not out of reach even for many master artisans.[46] Thanks to the fact that subscriptions were paid in advance, "the journalist has his enterprise assured, he takes no risk, he makes no advances, all his expenses are covered, he has already pocketed all his income before he spends a sou on his subscribers," another writer commented.[47] If a newspaper found readers quickly, the new-fledged publisher had an assured source of regular income; if it flopped, he had at worst a few reams of unsold copies to dispose of, and no matter how few subscribers he had been able to collect, in the furious competition of the revolutionary press market, he could always find a competitor who would pay something to add them to the ranks of his own readers. In 1797 the measly 300 subscribers of the *Déjeuner* struck the owners of the equally shaky *Aurore* as worth a third of the stock in the combined enterprise plus enough money to cover the debts of the failing party of the first part, which amounted to only 300 livres in any case.[48]

Boulard's calculations help explain why so many of the newly minted Parisian printers and publishers turned to putting out newspapers, and why it was so difficult for successive revolutionary regimes to discourage this trade. The ease with which newcomers could plunge into the business horrified men like Charles-Joseph Panckoucke, who had been a major figure in the prerevolutionary publishing world. He compared the situation in Paris in 1790 unfavorably with the press industry in London, dominated by large, heavily capitalized newspapers employing numerous journalists. Such papers had to "be circumspect in order to avoid being disturbed, and running the risk of losing their capital and the money invested in them," a condition Panckoucke applauded.[49] The structure of the press market in revolutionary France worked in a very different way, favoring small enterprises that required little capital and had little to lose from political unrest. This situation also affected journalists: instead of being gathered together into elaborate journalistic *équipes*, the talented writers of the revolutionary period were dispersed among the galaxy of competing papers, each of which could afford to support only one or two truly able contributors.

To be sure, many more newspapers failed and quickly disappeared than succeeded, but there were enough dazzling fortunes made in the business to keep attracting new entrants. Jean-Charles Poncelin de la Roche-Tilhac had been an anonymous hack writer before the Revolution. By 1797 he was the publisher of two successful newspapers and owner of one shop worth 40,000 livres and a third-interest in another, worth 10,000 livres, as part of a total fortune that he estimated at 164,000 livres.[50] The publisher Lenormant had been a journeyman printer before 1789; he set up in business for himself, specialized in counterrevolutionary titles and eventually became the printer and part-owner of the immensely successful *Journal des Débats* of the Napoleonic era.[51] And behind every other successful newspaper of the revolutionary era there was a hard-working entrepreneur. Indeed, these largely anonymous men and women—for a number of newspaper enterprises, including those of Marat and the abbé Royou, had female managers—were the unsung heroes of the press during the revolutionary era: without their enterprise and organizational ability, the flow of political information on which the Revolution depended would have been choked off.

The offices and printing shops of the new press spawned by the Revolution bunched together in the center of the capital, within blocks of the sites where the drama of the Revolution was played out. The largest concentration of enterprises was on the Left Bank, in the narrow streets west of the Sorbonne to which prerevolutionary regulations had confined the capital's authorized printers. Here radical, moderate, and royalist journals lodged in uneasy proximity. The neighborhood was a hotbed of political activism. The heart of the newspaper district was the section du Théatre-français, the political subdivision of Paris that was home to the radical Cordeliers club, stronghold of Danton and Marat, but these same streets were also home to the politically cautious Charles-Joseph Panckoucke and the royalist editor and publisher of the *Ami du Roi*, the abbé Royou. On the right bank of the Seine, newspaper bureaus clustered around the Louvre and the Tuileries, and a few spread east toward the Hôtel-de-Ville, Paris's town hall. From these locations, the papers had easy access to the revolutionary legislatures and the doings of the city government. Almost without exception, the Parisian newspapers of the revolutionary decade were written and printed virtually on the scene of the events they recorded. Seldom has the connection between events and their journalistic representation been so close.

The newspaper publishers who flourished in this politically charged environment needed skill, dedication, tremendous energy, and luck. They had to cope with new technical challenges, restless workers, an uncertain legal and institutional environment, and the threat of political violence. The most committed and imaginative ones were concerned with every aspect of their publications. Joseph Duplain, an aggressive book publisher under the Old Regime, was among the most innovative newspaper entrepreneurs of the revolutionary era. To promote his *Courrier extraordinaire, ou le Premier arrivé,* he set up a system of private stagecoaches to deliver his paper ahead of competitors who relied on the regular mails. He also suggested that readers form a network of clubs that would discuss the actions of the National Assembly and exchange their opinions through his paper, and in 1790 he became the first journalist to report regularly on the sessions of the Jacobin club in Paris. When France became involved in war in 1792, he offered substantial sums to soldiers who could "write legibly" and would send bulletins to his paper. Unlike most revolutionary newspaper publishers, he eagerly, if not very successfully, sought commercial advertising for his paper.[52] Duplain's fate illustrates the special problems of newspaper publishing during the revolutionary era, however: he ran afoul of the revolutionary government and was guillotined in 1794.[53]

Denis-Romain Caillot, who put out a number of papers in the course of the Revolution, was another publisher who worried about all aspects of his enterprise. In his pursuit of profits, he worked all sides of the political fence: in 1791 he was simultaneously printing the prorevolutionary *Lettres bougrement patriotiques du véritable Père Duchesne* and doing job-printing for the abbé Royou, editor of the *Ami du Roi.*[54] In early 1797 Caillot left Paris to try to set up a system of special-delivery coaches like the one Duplain had established in 1790. As he went from town to town making arrangements for this express delivery system, he also took a reading of public opinion and bombarded the editor in Paris with conflicting instructions on how to tailor the paper's content. He kept up with rival papers and chastised his own editor when a competitor scooped him on a major story. Caillot recruited correspondents to expand his paper's newsgathering network and suggested that his editor steal a march on the other Paris papers by bribing a worker in the government's printing shop to obtain advance copies of new laws, even stipulating what should be paid for such service. Even though the *Courrier de l'Égalité* had more than four years of successful publication behind it by the time of Caillot's trip, keeping it going and trying to improve it remained a full-time job.[55] As if publishing a newspaper was not sufficiently demanding, many entrepreneurs also engaged in other activities. Joseph Fiévée, who printed the successful prorevolutionary daily *Chronique de Paris* in 1790–93, also published books, pamphlets, plays, and a magazine to keep his seven presses occupied, and when the *Chronique* needed additional copy, he sometimes penned it himself.[56] Charles-Frédéric Perlet, publisher of the paper that bore his name, put out books and also cashed in on the tremendous increase in printing caused by the multiplication of new government agencies during the Revolution: in 1793 he was the official printer for the *Cour de cassation,* France's highest court of appeal.[57]

The busy entrepreneurs of the French press during the Revolution had little time to experiment with new ways of producing their products. They relied on the familiar wooden hand-printing press, still basically the same machine that Gutenberg had invented more than three hundred years earlier: the chaotic conditions of the press market discouraged investments in new technology of the sort that led to the invention of the more efficient Stanhope iron hand-press in England just after 1800. French printers did not even adopt the faster but more complicated and expensive wooden Anisson-Duperron press invented in their own country in the 1780s. To increase production, they simply added more presses: by 1794 Charles-Joseph Panckoucke, publisher of the *Moniteur* and the *Mercure de France,* was presiding over an establishment with twenty-seven presses, employing ninety-one workers.[58] Panckoucke's establishment was a large one for the period, overshadowed only by the gigantic government printing shops, such as the *Imprimerie des administrations nationales,* which had forty presses and several hundred employees in 1794–95, and the even larger *Imprimerie nationale.*[59]

Even the smaller shops that published most of the newspapers during the revolutionary decade needed numerous workers and had to adopt new methods of organizing their printing work. To put out the four separate impressions of the modest *Journal de Perlet* that can be identified by the tiny press numbers in their lower margins would have required a minimum of eight compositors, eight pressmen, and a foreman. In fact, considering that the paper appeared seven days a week and that additional workers were needed to do tasks such as cleaning and redistributing type that normal printing-shop workers did on days when there was no other work to handle, the *Perlet*'s workforce would have had to be even larger, including various less-skilled workers such as the *plieuses* who folded the printed sheets and put preprinted address labels on copies for the mail.

All these workers had to be hurried along on a time schedule very different from that characteristic of work in eighteenth-century book-publishing or job-printing shops. Whereas book printers worked on an erratic schedule suited to the irregular nature of their production, newspaper printers had to achieve regular, dependable output at high speed. To meet the public's demand for the freshest possible information, they had to print at night, which made the work more difficult and forced them to pay higher wages: Boulard indicated that the pressmen, who normally earned six to eight livres for a day's work, expected a premium of three livres for night work, and two livres for work on Sundays and holidays.[60] Exactly how work was organized in the crowded Paris printing shops where the fifteen to thirty compositors and printers it took to put out a successful daily paper scrambled about by candlelight to jam hastily set type into printing frames, ink them, and manhandle the balky presses to produce the printed sheets we do not know. But although the owners and workers who rushed about producing the papers of the Revolution used old artisanal methods, they were working under unrelenting time pressure alien to the preindustrial world, but only too familiar in the factories that became common in the nineteenth century.

Despite these rigorous working conditions, newspaper publishers had little difficulty luring workers away from more traditional printing enterprises. In 1790 Panckoucke, one of the few Old Regime publishers who was also successful in the revolutionary press market, complained that all workers cared about was the extra money they could earn from night work. "They have been seduced by the money they can make; but you can be sure that they will soon recognize that this work ruins their health," he warned. But defenders of the new printing shops replied that Panckoucke and his colleagues among the prerevolutionary publishers still believed that "while making immense fortunes out of the sweat and long hours of their workers, they had the right to treat them with contempt, and subject them to humiliating controls." If the workers flocked to new shops that offered higher wages, it was because these jobs offered "the hope of putting something aside for their old age."[61]

Higher wages did not ensure harmony in the workshops: compositors and printers organized in 1790 to protest the employment of poorly trained newcomers who accepted lower wages.[62] During the terrible inflation of 1795, newspaper printing workers met to design a common strategy for bargaining with their employers. Their plan had already been applied at some papers: the *Courrier républicain* of 10 December 1795 informed readers that "our compositors decided to raise the price of a form to 450 livres from its previous level of 200. This excessive and unforeseen demand having created some problems between them and us, they immediately quit work." A few months later the same paper had to print an apology to its workers after blaming them for the numerous typographical errors in a previous issue.[63] But the fact that newspapers of every political persuasion continued to appear except during the Terror, and the apparent absence of denunciations of publishers and journalists stemming from workers during that period, indicate that workers did not attempt to influence the content of the papers they put out. Newspaper printing workers were loyal to their trade and came to have a strong stake in the survival of the newspaper industry. After the Directory's decree of 18 fructidor V (4 September 1797), which put over thirty counter-revolutionary papers out of business, the police discovered that some of the suddenly unemployed workers from the banned papers' shops had joined together to establish their own paper "to give themselves a means of making a living."[64]

Although there were always willing compositors and pressmen to manufacture newspapers, the quality of the work they did was often poor. The irascible Marat took time off from his denunciations of political conspiracies to lament that "workers without education and civic spirit pitilessly mess up my paper, to save themselves an hour of work."[65] More familiar with the difficulties of hurried printing, Joseph Duplain told his readers that the errors in his *Courrier extraordinaire* were unavoidable: "The speed with which I have to write, the lack of time for the workers to make corrections . . . the unavoidable necessity of never reading more than one proof, all that is an invincible obstacle to my goal of putting out work more worthy of you."[66]

Organizing the work process and managing the printing shop were only part of the task of the revolutionary press entrepreneur. He also had to see to the distribution of his paper and collect the money due from its subscribers. Publishers sent out thousands of prospectuses to launch new titles and often provided free trial subscriptions to attract readers. In Paris most papers employed a corps of hawkers who peddled single numbers of each issue in the streets and cafés. Their loyalty and good will were essential for the success of any paper; journalist-entrepreneurs like Marat and Hébert went out of their way to cultivate dependable vendors.[67] When the Paris city government tried to limit the number of street hawkers early in the Revolution, Marat came to their defense, proclaiming that such regulation was "the cleverest of attacks against the freedom of the press, which becomes meaningless if authors' productions cannot be publicized."[68]

Provincial subscribers received their copies through the mail or via distributors in the larger towns. Maintaining subscription registers and keeping track of distributors' payments involved considerable clerical work. Duplain's *Courrier extraordinaire* dealt with distributors in fifty-seven provincial cities in 1797, and the *Journal de la Montagne,* published for little more than a year, accumulated one set of registers listing 5,575 individual subscribers and a second keeping track of the paper's income and expenses.[69] In 1791 the *Gazette de Paris* employed an office manager and three to five clerks to cope with this sort of record-keeping.[70] The slowness of mail delivery to the provinces was a constant irritation to newspaper publishers, as Duplain's and Caillot's efforts to set up their own delivery systems indicate. Copies often went astray in the mail, and some papers, like the *Nouvelles politiques* of the Directory era, maintained a regular register of subscribers' complaints.[71] Provincial distributors had to be courted; the more energetic of these put out lists of the journals they handled, and they sometimes reminded the Paris publishers of their indispensability. "Without my zeal for you, [he] would have subscribed to another paper," one agent noted in forwarding a customer's money.[72]

The newspaper entrepreneurs of the revolutionary decade, harried enough by the difficulties of overseeing the production and distribution of their publications, faced the additional challenge of operating in a viciously competitive marketplace without any legal protection and in a situation where political crises could destroy their enterprises at any time. The demand for political journals was great enough to sustain a large number of titles, but there were always more newspapers trying to carve out niches for themselves than the market could really support. Cutthroat competition was the rule, overriding even political solidarity with like-minded sheets. Under the Directory, when the counterrevolutionary *Précurseur* tried to get copies to its subscribers in southern France faster than its rivals by setting up a satellite printing operation in the Midi, the owners of the equally right-wing *Quotidienne* appealed to the same republican authorities they assailed every day in their columns to punish their rivals for violating the post office's monopoly on delivery.[73]

With the disappearance of the monarchy's system of royal privileges for periodicals, there were no laws defining the property of a newspaper. With such enticing profits at stake, bare-knuckled combat was the rule rather than the exception. Every time a journalist or a publisher came up with a formula that attracted an audience, rival editions, either counterfeits copied verbatim from the original or imitations that used the same techniques, and frequently the same title, were sure to follow. The weekly *Révolutions de Paris,* one of the instant best-sellers started immediately after the fall of the Bastille, warned readers against unauthorized imitations as early as its eighth issue. In the space of a few months, readers were faced with a rival version of the paper, also titled *Révolutions de Paris,* as well as imitations called the *Révolutions nationales* and the *Révolutions de Versailles et de Paris.*[74] The same fate befell the outspokenly counterrevolutionary *Ami du Roi*: it began as a single enterprise in June 1790, but by the following September there were three rival daily papers claiming the same title, all following more or less the same political line while exchanging scathing insults with one another.[75] The confusion among the half-a-dozen rival publications based on the character of the hot-tempered *Père Duchêne* has bedevilled bibliographers down to the present day, and even the inimitable Marat faced rivals who appropriated his title of *Ami du Peuple.* They "fight among themselves for my title, my epigraph, my name, my other features," Marat lamented, later remarking of one imitator that "in a country where justice prevails, he would be condemned . . . to have his hand cut off."[76] Even assassination did not protect Marat from those who sought to cash in on his journalistic success:

after Marat's death, the *enragé* spokesmen Jacques Roux and Leclerc de Lyon undertook posthumous imitations.

Cases such as the multiple editions of the *Révolutions de Paris* and
the *Ami du Roi* demonstrated that the most dangerous rivals a
successful newspaper owner faced were his own collaborators. The
two competing *Révolutions de Paris* were the result of a clash
between the author and the publisher of the original work: in this
case, Louis Prudhomme, the publisher, triumphed over Alex-
andre Tournon, the author. The dispute over the title of the *Ami
du Roi* saw the original publisher, Crapart, face off with two of the
editorial contributors, the abbé Royou and Galart de Montjoie.
Combatants in these family feuds knew no restraints. Private
contracts among the collaborators in a paper, such as the agreement between the publisher and the printer of the *Miroir* obliging
the latter not to undermine the former's right of property in the
paper "directly or indirectly during and after the period of the
present agreement either by forming or cooperating on another
paper under the same name or by any other act of invasion of the
journal and its income,"[77] were intended to forestall such civil
wars, but their value depended entirely on the good faith of the
parties: by the time a court judgment could have been obtained in
such a case, it was most likely that either the newspaper-reading
public would already have rendered a verdict in favor of one or the
other of the disputants, or the paper might well have been suppressed for political reasons.

One reason these conflicts were so common was the number of
political accidents that could befall a successful paper. The civil
war among the three co-owners of the *Courrier universel de Husson,* a
highly successful postthermidorian revival of Duplain's *Courrier
extraordinaire,* illustrates this. By the fall of 1795 this paper was
being run by three partners, all veterans of the counterrevolutionary movement. After the unsuccessful right-wing putsch against
the thermidorian Convention on 13 vendémiaire IV (5 October
1795), one of the three was imprisoned. His two associates,

evidently unwilling to see their profitable enterprise dissolve because of their comrade's misfortune, promptly started a paper without him under a different name, the *Rôdeur.* A few months later the police caught up with one of the two remaining co-owners, who was jailed in his turn. While this second man languished in prison, the first arrestee managed to launch his own paper, the *Véridique,* which in place of the usual prospectus carried the sad tale of how the editor's partners had attempted to defraud him, despite a signed agreement made at the time of the putsch that guaranteed him his rights while he was in hiding or in jail.[78] He evidently had some friends among the old employees of the *Courrier universel,* because the *Rôdeur* charged that "with unprecedented bad faith and infidelity, one of our employees has corrupted the women who fold the paper for mailing. Our list of addresses has been stolen . . . our readers should be on guard against this maneuver, which will certainly revolt honorable people."[79] But in the meantime, the one member of the original trio who had managed to stay out of jail altogether had apparently decided to proceed with business on his own, inasmuch as a paper titled *Courrier universel de Cit. Beyerlé* had appeared on the market; the said Beyerlé, despite his counterrevolutionary convictions, had also appealed to the republican government's ministries of police and justice for help in defending his rights against his quondam associates.[80] And so the public was left to choose among these bickering titles, until after many other adventures two of these enterprises faded away and the third was merged with yet another paper that had split away from the trunk of the Duplain enterprise in 1795 and the new combination became the basis for the *Journal des Débats,* the leading newspaper of the Napoleonic period.

The political misadventures that led to the three-way split of the *Courrier universel* were part and parcel of the risks that hung over all press enterprises throughout the Revolution. Regardless of the Declaration of the Rights of Man's guarantee of press freedom, newspapers were never secure from various forms of harassment that could affect printers and publishers as well as authors. In November 1790 a group of supporters of the Revolution visited the offices of the leading right-wing papers. The abbé Royou reported to his readers that the delegation had asked to see his presses and had warned him "to change tone and principles or we will not be responsible for the consequences."[81] The increasingly agitated tone of Parisian politics in 1792 and 1793 heightened the risks for newspaper enterprises. On 10 August 1792 the *sans-culottes* who toppled the monarchy also settled accounts with the right-wing press, sacking and burning several printing shops. In March 1793 radical activists smashed the presses of papers that supported the Girondins: the printer of the *Chronique de Paris* summoned the local police commissioners, who reported that "we found seven presses so battered and broken that the damages suffered . . . appeared irreparable. The printing type is so damaged and mixed up and in such disorder that it will have to be sent to the foundry and everything in this printing shop, tools, woodwork and other necessities of printing bear the traces of a veritable pillaging."[82] Newspaper printers in the provinces risked similar legal and extralegal harassment. A. J. Simard, the printer of the militantly Jacobin *Vedette, ou Journal du département du Doubs* in Besançon, was arrested in June 1792, and he claimed that he had come close to being massacred by a hostile crowd two months later.[83]

The triumph of the Montagnards in June 1793 brought an end to this sort of unauthorized violence, but it substituted more efficient police repression. Although the Terror fell more heavily on journalists than on printers and publishers, some of the latter, such as Joseph Duplain, came to grief. The authorities of the year II regarded the efforts Duplain made to promote the special express-mail version of his paper as signs of a desire to circulate antigovernment propaganda.[84] Several provincial publishers, especially those whose papers supported the federalist uprisings, also lost their lives during the Terror.[85] The Directory, exasperated by the ease with which publishers replaced one banned title with another of the same political coloration, included them and printers along with counterrevolutionary journalists in the decree of 19 fructidor V, and Charles-Frédéric Perlet, publisher but never the author of the newspaper that bore his name, was one of the few right-wing newspapermen to actually suffer deportation to Guiana in the wake of that coup.[86] Whenever police raided a newspaper office, they left seals on the printing presses that prevented the shopowner from working, even if it was the editor rather than the printer who was being sought. Throughout the revolutionary decade, newspaper publishers and printers thus faced very real risks to their persons and property.

The newspaper industry nonetheless never lacked for eager entrepreneurs and willing workers. Despite the political risks, the lure of jobs and profit was simply too great. Even after the Terror and the violent inflation that affected newspapers as it did every other branch of business in France in 1794–95, a journalist-publisher of the period was certain that "newspapers remain, in spite of their losses, the most lucrative branch of French literature."[87] The break-even point for a newspaper was low, perhaps as few as 400 to 450 copies per issue,[88] and the rate of profit mounted rapidly after that. Documents from two royalist papers whose records were seized in 1792 indicate that the *Gazette de Paris* earned a clear profit of over 25,000 livres on sales of 2,300 copies a day and that Royou's *Ami du Roi* may have brought in as much as 88,000 livres in its best year.[89] These high profits resulted from the fact that the revolutionary papers, which competed in every other area, did not challenge each other over prices. Most set their subscription rates close to the thirty-six livres a year that had been standard for the high-quality foreign gazettes before 1789; those that were significantly cheaper, such as the weekly *Feuille villageoise,* delivered many fewer total pages. It is curious at first glance that the newspaper publishers of revolutionary Paris, vigorous risk-taking capitalists in most respects, did not see the logic of sacrificing some of their profit margin to increase their total sales, but there was some reason for their behavior. Because an increase in sales beyond a certain point meant paying compositors and pressmen to make another printing of the paper, the marginal cost of production did not necessarily drop as sales expanded. Joseph Duplain pointed this out to would-be subscribers in 1792, explaining that he would not be able to accept new requests for copies until he had enough firm orders "to go on to a new composition."[90] Furthermore, sticking to the high standard subscription price meant that a paper would cover its costs even if it sold only a few hundred copies and that profits would be highly satisfactory if it sold a few thousand. The high-price policy was a safe one for the publisher; it compensated for the extraordinary risks of the revolutionary market. As a result newspaper publishers could ride out the economic fluctuations of the revolutionary decade without much risk. Even the hyperinflation of 1794–96, which reduced the value of advance subscription payments, seems to have bankrupted only a few marginal papers: most were able to raise their subscription prices fast enough to avoid disaster, and if necessary, they resorted to the legally dubious but pragmatically unavoidable course of simply shortening the length of pre-paid subscriptions.

The variety of newspapers that graced the shelves and reading tables of an establishment like Madame Vaufleury's *cabinet de lecture* thus reflected a substantial transformation in the French publishing industry. While the Revolution disrupted the production of books, it spurred the sudden growth of a sizable new branch of business, whose participants exhibited all the drive and imagination often said to have been lacking in the French economy. Together with the manufacturers who turned out tricolor ribbons, pottery decorated with revolutionary symbols, board games, playing cards, and other items whose purchase represented a form of political commitment, these publishers helped to make France more of a "consumer society." By inspiring the sale of these mostly modestly priced goods, the Revolution increased the range of manufactured products intended for a mass market in France; the production of periodicals and these other items related to the Revolution constituted one of the few growth areas in an economy badly disrupted by 1789 and its aftermath.[91] The growth of the press industry also provided employment for printing-shop workers, street hawkers, and distributors throughout the country. More importantly, by making acquaintance with the latest political news and opinions affordable—if not for everyone, at least for a far larger sector of the population than had ever before had access to them—the press industry contributed to the broadening of political participation that was one of the essential features of the Revolution.

Readers

The readers who came to peruse the products of the newspaper industry displayed in Madame Vaufleury's Cabinet Littéraire Nationale in Paris's Palais-Royal were a privileged elite: for the six sous that they paid to enter the establishment—a sum that would have added up to the cost of three annual newspaper subscriptions—they had a choice of over thirty products of France's burgeoning newspaper publishing industry to read and, no doubt, well-informed company with which to discuss them. But in the streets outside the Palais-Royal and in the towns and villages of the French provinces, there was a newspaper audience that was no less interested in the press even though it had less access to it. This audience included at least some of the poor and uneducated urban and rural masses of revolutionary France; it included the soldiers on revolutionary France's frontiers; it included women; it even included some of those who could not read. This diverse public, limited though it was by illiteracy and poverty, nevertheless constituted a larger proportion of the total population than had ever been included in political life in any other European country. And through the various kinds of demand they provided, these readers, like the journalists and the publishers, were a vital force in shaping the press of the revolutionary period.

Literacy and the ability to afford a newspaper defined the size of the potential audience for newspapers during the Revolution; the

Geschichte der gegenwärtigen Zeit.

CCXXXIV.

Straßburg, Freytag, den 24sten Brachmonathes, 1791.

Im zweyten Jahre der Freyheit.

Criminal-Straf-Gesetzbuch; An unsere Mitbürger; Inländische Nachrichten; Auswärtige Nachrichten. — Mittel gegen die Wuth. — Nachrichten.

Criminal-Straf-Gesetzbuch.

Sechste Abtheilung des Tit. I.
Verbrechen gegen das öffentliche Eigenthum.

1) Ein jeder, wer es auch seyn mag, der überwiesen worden, daß er National-Münze oder Geld, die im Umlaufe sind, nachgemacht oder verfälscht hat, oder dazu beygetragen, daß solches falsches Geld in das französische Reich eingeführt worden, soll mit dem Tode gestraft werden.

2) Die nämliche Strafe ruht auch auf dem, welcher National-Papiere nachgemacht hat, die den Werth, wie Geld, haben.

3) Wer überwiesen worden, daß er das Staats-Insiegel nachgemacht hat, soll fünfzehn Jahre zur Kettenstrafe verurtheilt werden.

4) Wer den National-Stempel nachgemacht, soll mit einer zwölfjährigen Kettenstrafe belegt werden.

5) Wer den Stempel auf Gold, Silber und auf andere Waaren des Staates nachgemacht, soll eine zehnjährige Kettenstraf ausstehen.

Titel II.
Von den Verbrechen und Vergehen gegen Privat-Personen.

Erste Abtheilung.
Verbrechen und gewaltthätige Angriffe gegen Privat-Personen.

1) Wer wider seinen Willen, ohne Unklugheit und Nachlässigkeit, jemanden getödet hat, ist keiner Strafe schuldig.

2) Wer zwar wider seinen Willen, aber aus Nachlässigkeit oder Unklugheit, jemanden getödet hat, soll zwar nicht als ein Verbrecher behandelt werden; dennoch aber haben die Richter nach Maaßgabe der Umstände eine Warnungs-Strafe zu bestimmen, wie auch eine etwanige Wiederersetzung eines verursachten Schadens.

3) Wer gesetzmäßig jemanden tödet, ist kein Verbrecher.

4) Die Tödung ist gesetzmäßig, wenn sie von dem Gesetz, oder durch eine rechtmäßige Gewalt befohlen ist.

5) Die Tödung ist rechtmäßig, wenn sie unumgänglich nöthig war, zur natürlichen Vertheidigung seiner selbst, oder eines andern. S.

An unsere Mitbürger.

Wir schreiten morgen zu einer äußerst wichtigen Wahl. Wir sollen diejenigen Männer unter uns ernennen, welchen wir die Vollmacht geben, die nächsten Repräsentanten der Nation, wie auch auf zwey Jahre lang die großen Volks-Beamten zu ernen-

234

Spreading the revolutionary message: This issue of the German-language *Geschichte der gegenwärtigen Zeit,* published in Strasbourg, shows one of the ways in which the press tried to reach parts of the population that could not read French. Papers like this also served to spread revolutionary ideas in Germany. Source: Harvard College Library.

newspaper industry's productive capacity limited the size of the press's actual audience. On the eve of the Revolution, adult literacy, which had been increasing throughout the eighteenth century, was still far from universal in France. It varied dramatically from region to region: the figures of percentages of adults who could sign their own name in 1786 from the celebrated Maggiolo survey show a solid block in northern France where more than two-thirds of all men could read, contrasted to a less-educated region including the provinces of the center and the south, where adult male literacy was often less than fifty percent. Female literacy was lower than male literacy in every region and only exceeded fifty percent in a small number of departments.[92] Regional studies have nuanced this picture, showing that rural literacy rates lagged behind urban ones and that there were often sharp differences between neighboring cities and from neighborhood to neighborhood within them. Literacy also varied greatly with occupation and social standing.[93] The capital stood out because of the high percentage of its artisan population who could read and because female literacy there had almost reached the male level by the end of the century: unlike the provincial population, Parisians could almost all be reached via the printed word.[94] In any event, illiteracy was not a complete bar to contact with newspapers. The German visitor Johann Heinrich Campe described how a group of uneducated workers in Paris would find "one of their comrades, who possesses the rare advantage of being able to read" and have him read the newspaper aloud.[95] The curé, the village mayor, or some other literate person might read the press aloud in public; in the provinces where French was not the spoken language, the village priest might even have to translate it for his listeners. Of France's linguistic minorities, only the German-speaking population of Alsace had access to an extensive newspaper press in its own language, thanks to the initiative of publishers in Strasbourg.

Illiteracy was not the only potential obstacle to newspaper reading during the Revolution. Regular subscriptions to Parisian daily newspapers remained quite expensive throughout the revolutionary decade, ranging from thirty to thirty-six livres at the outset and climbing to forty-two livres by 1798, after the imposition of a stamp tax. At a time when a day laborer's wage was normally around three livres, an individual subscription was clearly a luxury that most of the population could not afford. There were a number of ways besides taking out an individual subscription by which a determined reader could gain access to a newspaper. Poorer readers sometimes banded together to share the cost of a subscription; they might buy one of the cheaper papers designed especially for a lower-class audience, such as the weekly *Feuille villageoise,* which cost only seven livres and four sous per year in 1789, or a single issue of a pamphlet-journal like the *Père Duchêne,* which normally went for a mere two sous. The provincial papers were also cheaper, although they provided fewer pages per week and carried much less news. One could read the papers in a *cabinet de lecture,* although these too charged fees, or one could find them in a café or cabaret for the price of a glass of wine. Even those who were completely penniless were not entirely cut off from access to the press: some newspapers were given out for free, like the version of the *Père Duchêne* whose editor condemned his rivals for publishing out of desire for gain, and some newspapers were published as wallposters so that they could be read without charge.[96]

Neither illiteracy nor poverty thus constituted a complete bar to access to the press during the Revolution: newspaper articles could become part of an oral culture that, as French historians Roger Chartier and Daniel Roche have pointed out, nonetheless differed from traditional popular culture precisely because it was based on the reading aloud of printed materials.[97] But it would be naive to overstate the degree to which the poor and uneducated were actually able to share in the regular communication of political news through the press. Most of the newspapers published during the Revolution were clearly not written primarily to be read aloud, and those who had to depend on listening for their news had no way of telling whether they were getting the full message conveyed in the paper. In 1789 the Occitan-speaking peasants of Quercy suspected their curés, who summarized the news bulletins about the Estates-General during their services, of leaving out important details, but how were they to find out for sure?[98] A police agent pointed out in 1793 that readers dependent on the free wallposter-papers subsidized by the government would lose access to the news when cold weather drove them indoors.[99] Poor readers were undoubtedly less likely to read several different papers and to develop a well-informed critical perspective on the press. The lower classes in France, the overwhelming majority, were like the bystanders on the edge of a large crowd: they could tell that something was happening and occasionally catch a few phrases from the center where the action was, but they were much less informed than were the privileged minority that could actually see and hear the action for themselves. And because they bought fewer newspapers, the poorer members of the audience had less influence on the press market than the wealthy did: they had to accept papers designed for them by zealots like Marat or the editors of the *Feuille villageoise,* whether or not these publications truly reflected popular interests.

Illiteracy and poverty limited the size of the potential newspaper audience in revolutionary France; technology limited the number of newspapers that could actually be put into circulation. Printers continued to use wooden hand-presses, one of which could turn out no more than about 3,000 copies of a normal revolutionary paper per day, and the papermaking industry continued to use artisanal methods that did not allow a rapid increase in the supply of newsprint.[100] No satisfactory figures exist for the total number of copies of newspapers published at any given date during the Revolution, but a number of approaches suggest an order of magnitude of about 300,000 copies a day as an upper limit. This would have been the equivalent of 100 simultaneously appearing titles with an average press run of 3,000 copies each, a substantial circulation for any given paper and certainly higher than almost any of the provincial papers ever attained. Paris consumed a disproportionate share of the total number of papers printed. Postal records show that 80,000 papers a day were mailed from the capital during 1793;[101] the capital alone probably absorbed at least that number in addition. Several period sources give an estimate of 150,000 copies published per day for the Parisian press during the Directory period, when the price of newspapers had gone up and the excitement contained in them had diminished; while this figure cannot be documented, it was repeated often enough at the time to indicate that contemporaries found it plausible.[102] Even this reduced figure was a very impressive performance in comparison with other countries in the same period or with subsequent periods in France. The total daily circulation of the London press in 1780 is said to have been 45,422 copies.[103] The total daily press run of all Paris papers was only 33,000 copies in 1802, 110,358 in 1836, and 180,291 in 1846.[104] Modest as total newspaper production during the revolutionary period seems to have been by comparison with the levels it reached after 1850, the 1790s were certainly an exceptional decade in the history of the French press.

The figures for the press runs of individual papers during the revolutionary period are only slightly better documented than the figures for global numbers are. Perhaps the only indisputable figure we have is provided by a tiny scrap of paper that the Directory's police seized from the printing shop of the *Indispensable* in 1799, which reads *"tirer à 2800"* ("print 2,800"): it was the publisher's instruction to the printer.[105] Most of the figures from the period were printed in the papers themselves and are subject to caution, because publishers normally wanted to inflate the success of their title. Aside from the exceptional figures of 60,000–80,000 copies for single numbers of Hébert's heavily subsidized and frequently reprinted *Père Duchêne* from 1793–94, only one of these period estimates exceeds 20,000; most journalists seem to have thought that they were making a sufficiently impressive claim if they asserted that their circulation was between 10,000 and 12,000 copies per issue, a level that can be confirmed from documentary evidence for several papers.[106]

The papers that sold the largest number of copies were often those that deliberately avoided political controversy: the pusillanimous *Journal de Perlet* once claimed a circulation of 21,000, and the colorless *Journal du Soir* also topped 10,000.[107] The papers that contemporaries regarded as the most significant often had much lower press runs. Marat's printing shop had only two presses in January 1790, indicating that his press run could not have exceeded 5,000–6,000; in fact, most estimates from the period credit him with sales of only about 3,000.[108] The abbé Royou's *Ami du Roi* had a peak circulation of 5,300 copies in early 1791.[109] The only comparative survey of newspaper circulation from the period shows that six leading dailies from the late Directory period had press runs between 2,500 and 5,200 copies.[110] Clearly a newspaper could have substantial public impact with a press run as low as 2,000–3,000 copies. More obscure papers survived at a much lower level of circulation; sales of 400–450 copies per day were probably sufficient to cover the cost of producing a paper.[111] Provincial papers hardly expected to reach the levels of the successful Paris titles: Perpignan's *Echo des Pyrénées* had only 400 subscribers in May 1793.[112]

The number of copies a paper printed was not a measure of its total readership. Individual copies were undoubtedly read by several people: if a newspaper was read aloud at a Jacobin club or some other public gathering, a single copy could conceivably have served an audience of several hundred. In 1801 Pierre-Louis Roederer, the editor of the *Journal de Paris* during the Directory period, estimated that ten people saw each copy of every newspaper that circulated in Paris, and four read each copy sent to the provinces.[113] If we ignore the fact that some readers read more than one paper and take Roederer's proposed multiplier of ten readers per copy as a rough estimate—his figure for the provinces seems suspiciously low—and apply it to our equally rough estimate of 300,000 newspapers per day at the height of the Revolution, we would have a maximum newspaper audience of 3 million out of a French population that is estimated to have been around 28 million in 1789. Newspaper readership was evidently the privilege of a minority even of the adult male population of about 7 million (children were not likely to begin to read papers until the age of 10 or 11);[114] the others either lacked the means to acquire or to read the press or like the subscriber who forgot to send in his renewal because he was "a man of very advanced age" and "has just married for the third time, to a young woman," had other things on their minds.[115] The newspaper press of the revolutionary decade never succeeded in becoming a true mass medium capable of reaching the entire adult population.

It is a privileged minority of these newspaper readers who we meet in the subscription registers to a few newspapers that have survived in the French archives. These documents come overwhelmingly from papers that were raided by the revolutionary police at some time during the 1790s: we are thus much better informed about the subscribers to ultra- and counterrevolutionary papers than we are about the readership of more moderate journals. Our documents have other shortcomings as well. They say very little about newspaper readership in Paris, where papers were most often sold by number in the street or delivered by carriers employed by the publishers, and above all they do not tell us how many readers beyond the nominal purchaser were likely to read a given copy of a paper.

The subscription registers of the abbé Royou's *Ami du Roi* and De Rozoi's *Gazette de Paris,* seized by the police in mid-1791 and late 1792 respectively, show that these vehemently counterrevolutionary publications had a substantial following among members of the prerevolutionary privileged classes. Twenty percent of the 7,000 names in the *Ami du Roi*'s registers can be identified as nobles, and an equal percentage were from the clergy. Of the readers whose letters to the *Gazette de Paris* are preserved, 52 percent were nobles—two-thirds of them army officers—and 15 percent clergy. Not all the royalist papers' readers were diehard opponents of the new order, however: a full 10 percent of the *Ami du Roi*'s subscribers held judicial posts in the new courts established after 1789.[116] It is hard to compare the readership of these royalist papers with those of the papers whose registers date from later in the Revolution, because in the later lists former nobles and clergy can rarely be identified as such. The analysis of six such lists, three from prorevolutionary papers and three from counter-revolutionary titles, shows a consistent pattern (see table 4). In all cases, subscribers from the middle classes clearly predominated; among the readers who listed themselves as *cultivateurs* or *propriétaires,* it is doubtful that we have many genuine peasants, whereas we certainly find a number of former nobles now reduced to the status of ordinary citizens. Even the *Feuille villageoise,* ostensibly aimed at the rural population, in fact reached more city dwellers than true peasants. Of the published letters to its editors, no less than 57 percent were from priests or ministers.[117] Merchants and shopkeepers were especially well represented among the subscribers of the *Journal de la Montagne,* but that paper also had a higher percentage of subscribers from the educated professions among its provincial readers than any of the Directory-era titles did. There were some artisans among the readers of all the papers except the short-lived *Tribune publique,* a right-wing paper from 1797, but they were a minority even among purchasers of Gracchus Babeuf's radical *Tribun du Peuple.* It is clear that provincial subscribers were drawn from the stratum of *notables,* the educated, prosperous, and influential members of their small communities. The overwhelming majority of subscriptions went to private individuals, rather than to cafés, *cabinets de lecture,* or other institutions that fostered collective reading.

The subscription registers and other documents also give us some information about the geographic dispersion of newspaper reading, but not enough to map the distribution of political opinion in revolutionary France. Because there were always competing titles with similar political views, the distribution of readership of any one title depended on its luck in capturing

Table 4. Occupations of Provincial Newspaper Subscribers, 1793–97

Occupation	JM[1]	"X"[2]	GF[3]	TP[4]	TdP[5]	AP[6]
Agriculture	10%	12%	22%	13%	6%	2%
Commerce	36%	24%	19%	14%	28%	34%
Government	12%	22%	21%	34%	22%	33%
Professions	30%	22%	28%	21%	16%	8%
Artisans	7%	8%	6%	—	9%	15%
Collective	6%	8%	2%	10%	10%	6%
Other	9%	4%	2%	8%	9%	2%

1. *Journal de la Montagne;* figures from Hugh Gough, "Les Jacobins et la presse: le 'Journal de la Montagne' (juin 1793–brumaire an III)," in *Girondins et Montagnards,* ed. Albert Soboul (Paris: Société des Etudes robespierristes, 1980), 269–96, based on subscription registers in AN, T 1495 A and B.
2. Unidentified right-wing paper, 1797; documents in AN, F 7 3447.
3. *Gazette française;* documents in AN, F 7 6239 A and B.
4. *Tribune publique;* documents in AN, F 7 3446.
5. *Tribun du peuple;* figures from Albert Soboul, "Personnel sectionnaire et personnel babouviste," in *Babeuf et les problèmes du babouvisme* (Paris: Editions sociales, 1963), 109–19.
6. *Ami du Peuple* [Lebois]; figures from Max Fajn, "The Circulation of the French Press during the French Revolution," in *English Historical Review* 87 (1972): 100–105.

particular regional markets for itself, often as a result of its editor's or publisher's personal contacts. Thus the *Gazette française,* one of many similar counterrevolutionary papers in the Directory years, had an extraordinary concentration of subscribers in Bordeaux, where a local royalist agent recommended it,[118] but relatively few readers in the Rhône valley, where other counterrevolutionary papers apparently outsold it. Newspapers did penetrate to every corner of France: the 864 known individual subscribers of the *Gazette française* were dispersed among 400 different towns. Police surveys undertaken after the fructidor coup, which had eliminated over thirty papers, still found that thirty-four different newspapers had subscribers in the department of the Haute-Vienne, seventeen circulated in the Aube, eighteen titles had readers in the small market town of Tulle in the Limousin, and even in isolated Corsica there were four French titles and one Italian paper available in 1798.[119]

Readers' motivations for perusing newspapers naturally varied considerably, as did their reasons for selecting a particular title. A desire to keep up with the news was undoubtedly the most prevalent motive, particularly in a period when so many sensational and unexpected events occurred. From the point of view of readers who simply wanted rapid reports of ongoing events, the political slant of their papers was secondary: the Marquis de Ferrières, a moderate noble deputy to the National Assembly, sent his wife back home the *Moniteur* because "although democratic, it is accurate."[120] Readers motivated primarily by a desire for information were often put off by the bias of the partisan press: a distributor in Bayonne warned one of the counterrevolutionary editors of the Directory period that he was losing readers because "your partiality comes through in every paragraph."[121] Some readers, particularly the subscribers to the provincial press, turned to the newspapers for practical information that often had nothing to do with politics. Many of the provincial *affiches* or advertising journals carried on after 1789 as if nothing unusual was occurring in France, and even papers like the *Journal du département de la Vienne,* which offered considerable political news, also gave long listings of *biens nationaux* for sale and recorded the price of wholesale goods in the market towns of their region.

Whatever their reason for selecting a given paper, readers of the revolutionary period regarded their purchase as a commercial transaction and demanded a quality product for their money. The publishers' notices or *avis* that appeared from time to time in most papers indicate that readers complained regularly about typographical errors, bad paper, and worn type that was hard to read; they demanded more extensive coverage of provincial and foreign affairs, blamed the publishers for papers that were delayed in the mail, and tried to protect themselves from inflation by paying in advance for long-term subscriptions. [122] Readers, even those from the lower classes, also maintained a critical attitude toward their papers. Members of the Paris Jacobins, an educated elite group, worried about the effect of royalist press propaganda on "the class of readers which has the least education and is least likely to raise questions," but on the whole, readers from all classes seem to have taken their papers with a grain of salt. During the Terror a police agent reported overhearing remarks to the effect that "the journalists are charlatans; everything they say is lies. . . . They always try to fool us." [123]

Nevertheless, political orientation was the main attraction that most of the national newspapers offered. The woman subscriber who risked nine livres on a subscription to the right-wing *Gazette universelle* of 1795 in the hope that it would "respect religion, and defend the priests who, loyal to their consciences and to their God, have had the courage to renounce a country that they cherished, and to prefer exile and poverty to a criminal oath," and the reader who renewed his subscription to the equally counter-revolutionary *Précurseur* two years later because "its hatred for the criminals who have troubled us for so long, the sagacious and energetic observations with which it abounds, have made reading it infinitely agreeable," obviously wanted reading matter that would agree with their personal views. [124]

The numerous Jacobin clubs around the country that took out subscriptions to newspapers were also selective; guided by the Paris mother club's lists of papers "suitable to sustain patriotism, to spread public spirit, to extend enlightenment, to encourage alertness," they leaned heavily toward titles that supported the Revolution without endorsing radical extremism, and they rejected both the numerous royalist papers and Marat's *Ami du Peuple*. [125] The Paris Jacobins divided on the question of whether they should publicly read and discuss hostile papers, but even those who favored this did so because it would "teach the public to recognize poisonous writings" rather than out of a conviction that there was anything positive to learn from considering opposing points of view.[126] It was readers of this sort who the moderate politician Baudin des Ardennes had in mind when he told the Directorial Councils that "everyone subscribes for the public papers in which he finds the principles he was already attached to":[127] these readers turned to the press above all to strengthen their preexisting political convictions. Readers whose letters were published in the papers were almost invariably in sympathy with their chosen title's policies; this process of self-selection ensured that the provincial news in each Paris paper, usually provided by volunteer correspondents, invariably matched its ideological slant. And because there was no unanimity of political opinions in revolutionary France, readers' tendencies to look for papers that echoed their own views helped guarantee the political diversity of the press.

There were, of course, some readers who approached the reading of the press in a more critical frame of mind. The Marquis de Ferrières's letters portray an exceptionally sophisticated reader who turned to different papers for different purposes. Although he occasionally lost his patience with Panckoucke's paper—"the *Moniteur* lies," he exclaimed in one letter—he generally regarded it as a reliable source of information: "this paper reports everything; the bulletin of the assembly depicts fairly accurately what is done there, and what is said."[128] He read and recommended other papers, such as Mallet du Pan's *Mercure de France,* because they agreed with his constitutional-monarchist views. But this did not mean that he avoided papers that disagreed with his own prejudices. He read radical publications like Desmoulins's journal: "he is a madman, totally crazy, he seems to be delirious; nevertheless, if it will amuse you, you shall have it," he promised his wife. Amusement was not his only motive for reading the revolutionary papers. Commenting on the *Chronique de Paris,* he remarked, "one must read everything, be acquainted with everything, otherwise one is nothing but a stubborn fool." Those who stuck exclusively to the journals of their own party, like some of the aristocrats he knew, lost all sense of public opinion.[129] The marquis was obviously sensitive to the differences between papers and determined to avoid becoming the dupe of any one journalist, even one who shared his convictions. Ferrières was of course an exceptional reader—a resident of Paris, a man of letters, a legislative deputy, and a subscriber to a *cabinet de lecture*[130]—but even in the small towns of the provinces there were newspaper consumers who could articulate the view that "it is good to know the polemics of all the parties."[131] For such readers, the perusal of a newspaper was only part of a process in which they exercised their individual judgment, perhaps after discussion with other readers, in order to come to a reasoned opinion about the events described in the paper and the publication itself.

The Marquis de Ferrières's letters show that he read his newspapers in both private and public situations: sometimes alone and sometimes at a *cabinet de lecture*. Because it took place in public, the practice of collective newspaper reading is mentioned more often in our sources from the period than is the unobtrusive perusal of newspapers in private homes, which may in fact have been the manner in which most bourgeois subscribers read their copies. Newspaper publishers motivated more by profits than by political zeal had an interest in encouraging private subscriptions and discouraging reading in public establishments, "where two or three copies suffice for a great number of the curious."[132] The better-off readers who had individual subscriptions were undoubtedly the ones most likely to bind their copies and make them part of their permanent libraries, thereby preserving them for the benefit of historians.[133] But as Ferrières's example shows, it would be misleading to contrast wealthier readers consuming their papers at home with poorer ones reading them in public places. The wealthy were in fact the people best able to afford the entry fees required for entry to reading rooms with large newspaper collections, as well as the stiff membership fees charged by the Jacobin clubs in the early years of the Revolution. Despite their obvious importance, we know little about the *cabinets de lecture* of the revolutionary period. In 1810, when the Napoleonic authorities imposed a registration requirement, there were 456 of these institutions in France, and there is some evidence that their number had increased during the revolutionary period; they were much more common in the northern third of the country than in the center and the south. [134] Large establishments like Madame Vaufleury's offered an impressive array of newspaper titles, but their entrance fees were correspondingly high: six sous per visit for access to Madame Vaufleury's, with six foreign and thirty-four domestic papers; four sous for the less pretentious *Chambre patriotique et littéraire* on Paris's Left Bank, which offered twenty-four periodicals. [135]

Poorer readers were less likely to enjoy the luxury of reading their newspapers privately at home. In his exhaustive study of the Parisian *sans-culottes,* Albert Soboul found that few of these revolutionary militants—and they were by no means the poorest members of the city's population—actually read even the papers aimed specifically at them on a regular basis. Hardly any kept collections of papers, other than a few scattered numbers of Marat or Hébert. [136] But the institutions for collective reading that were available to these readers were also less elaborate than those to which bourgeois readers could repair. The numerous cafés and cabarets that kept newspapers as one attraction for their *sans-culotte* clientele certainly had less extensive selections of papers than the *cabinets de lecture* did.

In *cabinets de lecture* and cafés, the public picked and chose from a variety of available newspapers and read them individually; in other institutions, selected newspapers were read aloud for an audience. Sometimes these gatherings were informal: in Caen the politically active tobaccanist Jean Michel Barbot read Gorsas's *Courrier des départements* aloud outside his shop every day. [137] But they could also be regularly organized. Municipal governments frequently subscribed to Paris papers and read them aloud at public gatherings. [138] The reading of the Paris papers was the central feature of many provincial Jacobin clubs' meetings, which were often timed to follow the arrival of the mail. These clubs were more numerous than the *cabinets de lecture,* although they also tended to be shorter-lived. At least 1544 communes are known to have had a club at some point between October 1791 to June 1793; larger cities often had several. The army also encouraged collective reading: in 1793–94, the War Ministry purchased up to 31,000 papers a day for this purpose. [139] In contrast to the readers in cafés and clubs, these audiences had their papers selected for them, and received their contents aurally rather than by reading them. Those who "read" their newspapers in such public gatherings were less able to form any independent judgment on the value of their content and more likely to react according to their judgment of the person reading it: if they trusted him, his credibility would be transferred to the printed sheet he read from. Because the decision to read a paper aloud at club meetings or similar gatherings implied an endorsement, the choice of papers to be broadcast often became the object of intense debates.

Although the main reason subscribers obtained newspapers was to read them, the French public employed these small printed sheets for other purposes as well. One might obtain a particular newspaper as a way of making a statement about oneself: during the Terror, one memoirist recalled, those who feared being arrested as suspects made a point of purchasing and displaying copies of Hébert's *Père Duchêne*: "The image of the orator smoking his pipe and molding his furnace parts served as an icon of safety on the dressers of the prettiest women, in the studies of the learned, in the salons of the rich and in business offices." [140] Just as one might ostentatiously associate oneself with a particular paper, one might also make a spectacle of distancing oneself from one. Political activists frequently burned offending newspapers as a way of making a political statement. One of Marat's readers sent him an outraged account of such an incident at the famous café Procope involving the *Ami du Peuple*: "a barrister's clerk, long suspected of anti-patriotism, cried out that your paper deserved to be burned . . . he made a motion to that effect; at that moment, a crowd of lowlifes, on the alert in another room, came to his support, and their leader . . . ran to the middle of the street to set fire to your work." In this case, "several patriots ran after him, put out the fire that was ready to devour it, and collected the fragments," disrupting the ritual,[141] but on many other occasions, groups succeeded in making an *auto-da-fé* of a condemned paper. These burnings were highly symbolic: under the Old Regime, printed works condemned by the courts had been burned by the public executioner. By performing this ritual execution themselves, the political activists of the Revolution asserted their claim to exercise sovereign authority. These symbolic punishments were also meant to intimidate the offending journalists, who were warned that their newspapers were targeted only because their authors were not at hand; the public decision to "treat their productions as they deserve" was frequently linked to an explicit demand that the authors "be punished as disturbers of the public peace."[142]

The impact of the texts that the hardworking newsmen of the revolutionary decade scratched out with their quill pens and that the energetic printers and publishers of the day transmuted into print was thus determined by the many ways in which their audience used and interpreted them. Readers reacted differently to the press depending on which papers they read, and on whether they read papers of opposing points of view or only publications whose viewpoints reinforced each other. Their reactions were also likely to be influenced by whether they read their papers privately in their own homes, publicly in a café or *cabinet de lecture* where reading was likely to be accompanied by discussion, or whether they listened to the news when it was read aloud in a public place. However they reacted to them, the members of the newspaper audience during the Revolution were nevertheless all part of a new collectivity, created and structured by their reading matter. This newspaper-reading public cut across class lines to an extent unmatched by any other genre of printed material, and it was affected simultaneously, or nearly so, by the same news. Newspapers organized their readers into a cohesive collectivity, capable of reacting to the same events at the same time. Even though the newspapers never succeeded in reaching the entire adult population during the revolutionary period, it was the press as much as any other revolutionary institution that transformed the French population into a political nation.

3. THE JOURNALISTIC TEXTS OF THE REVOLUTION

THE BOND THAT BROUGHT THE JOURNALISTS, PUB-lishers, and readers of the revolutionary decade together was the newspaper itself, a flimsy piece of paper covered with printed words. Those words were what made the press a revolutionary force, for words were at the center of the struggle for power in a France whose traditional structures of authority had collapsed. As French historian François Furet has written, the politics of the Revolution was "a competition of discourses for the appropriation of legitimacy."[1] And the pages of the nation's newspapers were the place where that competition was carried on. The newspapers captured the fugitive words uttered in parliamentary debates and club meetings, carried some of them beyond the walls within which they were spoken and gave them permanency, and, by omission, condemned the rest to oblivion. But they did more than merely select some of the spoken words around them for transmission to their readers: they put those words in new contexts and added their own words of commentary, interpretation, and refutation to what they transcribed. Furthermore, the newspapers had the task of creating verbal descriptions of revolutionary events and of representing the social and political groups whose actions were now supposed to make up national politics. The result was a complex depiction of political reality that was far more than a simple copy of what the journalists of the Revolution saw and heard.

The Presentation of Newspaper Texts

Regardless of their journalistic intentions and their political orientation, all the newspapers of the Revolution operated under the same constraints in presenting their words to their readers. Some of these limitations were technological: the hand-operated wooden printing press could only accommodate relatively small sheets of paper, and there was no easy way to integrate words and images into a unified whole, as the newspapers of today can. Some of the constraints on the press were cultural: the papers of the Revolution used the French language as it had developed over the centuries, and they could not depart too far from what French readers expected in a printed text without risking a total lack of comprehension. Within these constraints, however, there were many possible ways of presenting a journalistic text. The newspapers of the Revolution adopted some of these and shunned others; the result of their choices was the distinctive physiognomy of the revolutionary press.

Just as the most radical revolutionaries had difficulty freeing themselves from some aspects of the Old Regime, the newspapers had a hard time liberating themselves from the long-standing conventions of book design. The English press of the eighteenth century had begun to take on some of the characteristics of the modern newspaper: the London dailies used large folio-sized sheets of paper, bigger than all but a few special kinds of books, and they divided their text into three or four columns. Their pages formed a mosaic made up of short articles of varying length, divided from each other by printer's rules or by individual titles. Like modern newspapers, these English papers carried both advertisements and news, and their ads often included small woodcut illustrations—a sailing ship for shipping announcements, for instance. The Dutch newspapers also broke with book-printing conventions: they had the habit of running advertisements sideways in the margins between their news columns. All these innovations reflected the combination of political and commercial motives in the uninhibitedly commercial societies of England and the Netherlands. They also reflected a growing awareness that a newspaper was something different from a book. The newspaper's essence was diversity, and readers could not be expected to devour it systematically from beginning to end. In a newspaper, as in a public marketplace, each individual item needed to draw attention to itself, through the use of a drawing, a headline, or its placement on the page, so that readers could easily identify the items that interested them.[2]

The French newspaper of the Old Regime was much less the image of a confused and variegated marketplace than its English and Dutch cousins. French printers and the foreign printers whose gazettes aimed at the French market continued to present the newspaper as something much akin to the book: even the provincial advertising journals, the *affiches*, arranged their material in orderly sequences and eschewed the woodcuts and large lettering that enabled English newspaper ads to call attention to themselves. A distaste for clutter and a neoclassical emphasis on order still governed French-language newspaper printing as well as book design. Periodical publishers used the small formats common in the book trade and an arrangement of text that made it difficult to pick out individual items of interest within the paper. The most sophisticated papers, like the *Gazette de Leyde*, had evolved a complex set of typographical conventions, such as the use of italics for proper names, that made it easier to read their densely packed columns of type, but they rejected headlines and other English-style devices to break up the page.

The newspapers of the early years of the Revolution continued the typographical traditions of the prerevolutionary French press. The experienced publisher Charles-Joseph Panckoucke's attempt to popularize the three-column folio format of the London daily press in his *Moniteur* inspired few imitators, and even the *Moniteur*, which had few advertisements and no headlines designed to pique the reader's curiosity, had a distinctly neoclassical purity

and monotony of style that distinguished it from the messy
vitality of the English papers.

The vast majority of the printers who began producing newspapers in 1789 adopted the octavo format, producing eight-page
newspapers in which the printed lines ran all the way across the
small page, as in books and pamphlets. The octavo was familiar,
easy to set and to print, and required no special equipment, as the
large folio format did. Street hawkers preferred these little booklets, which were easy to carry around, and protested when a
publisher announced that he was thinking of shifting to the larger
quarto format.[3] The octavo's popularity reflected the expectation
that readers would want to keep the copies of their paper and
eventually have them bound: publishers were sure that the small-
sized paper was "the most convenient both for the reader and for
libraries,"[4] and printers provided signature markings at the bottom of their sheets, just as they did in books, to help the binders
get the pages in the right order. Newspapers of all political and
journalistic tendencies adopted the octavo format: it was used by
the counterrevolutionary *Actes des Apôtres* and the *Petit Gautier*, and
by the radical *Ami du Peuple* and the *Révolutions de France et de
Brabant*, by such nonpolemical journals of information as the
Journal des Débats and the *Journal de Perlet*, by the didactic *Feuille
villageoise*, and by the majority of the papers published in the
provinces. Nearly two-thirds of the titles included in one contemporary list of papers published in the fall of 1790 used the octavo
format.[5]

The papers published in octavo format normally gave their
readers an eight-page daily issue, folded into a small brochure.
The bi- and triweeklies and weekly pamphlet-journals—a genre
that included some of the Revolution's most celebrated titles, such
as the *Père Duchêne*, the *Révolutions de Paris*, and Camille Desmoulins's *Révolutions de France et de Brabant*—were sometimes larger,
running to as many as sixty-four pages per issue. Octavo-format
papers did adopt some forms of journalistic organization, includ-

ing a regular sequence of materials, rubric titles to separate various forms of content, and a summary of their contents on the front page, often designed to be cried aloud by street hawkers. Publishers learned that readers quickly became accustomed to a particular pattern of features and needed to be reassured whenever it was changed. When the *Journal de Perlet* experimented with putting its account of the Convention's daily debates at the end of each issue rather than at the beginning, the printer promised that "this will not mean that will be less complete, or less extensive. This change [is] purely typographical, and . . . will not result in any change in editorial policy."[6] But the octavo format deprived the papers that used it of a fundamental resource of modern newspaper design: the ability to use the placement of the item on the page to indicate its significance relative to other items in the paper.

The growing popularity of the quarto format over the course of the revolutionary decade marked the gradual evolution of French newspapers away from the model of the book, but this was a slow process, and the first French papers to abandon the conviction that their copy had to be presented in one continuous sequence, starting at the upper left of page one and ending at the bottom right of the last page, did not appear until the Napoleonic era. The quarto format, with the pages laid out in two vertical columns, had been used by a number of papers during the Old Regime, including the provincial edition of the *Gazette de France*, the first Paris daily, the *Journal de Paris*, and the extraterritorial gazettes. During the Revolution, quarto-format newspapers typically published a four-page issue each day. The larger format had the advantage of allowing the printer to cram in more type per sheet of paper: typically, a quarto paper carried about thirty percent more words per week than an octavo rival using the same type size.[7] A publisher who tried (unsuccessfully) to change over from the octavo layout in 1792 explained to readers that a quarto paper would allow him "to insert more articles in the numbers of the paper, and to make it more interesting and piquant by making the content more varied."[8] Quarto papers often had a fairly standard allocation of space, with foreign news occupying one page, a summary of the legislative debates another, and regular articles on Paris and provincial news and the editorial column the remaining two; this arrangement made it much easier for readers to find the news they were interested in than in an octavo paper. Rubric headings and titles, usually set in italic type of the same size as the paper's body type, served to set off articles.

Like the octavo format, the quarto was not the monopoly of any one political tendency. Brissot chose it for his *Patriote françois*, but it was also the format of the *Ami du Roi* and several other royalist papers. If the octavo could be adapted to every style of journalism, however, the quarto was less flexible. From the start of the Revolution, the quarto design was a symbol of newspapers that were sober and serious in their language, and in which there was some genuine news content as well as polemic. None of the famous journalistic tribunes of the Revolution—Marat, Desmoulins, Hébert, Babeuf—employed the quarto format, nor was it ever used by the satirical royalist papers like the *Petit Gautier* or the *Rocambole*. The quarto bespoke an institutionalized and less personal journalism. From the outset of the Revolution, although quarto papers were rarer than octavos, a higher percentage of them tended to survive journalistic infancy and live a relatively long life: only 21 percent of the journals founded in 1789 that used the octavo format lasted as long as a year, but 64 percent of the much less numerous quarto newspapers survived that long.[9] By the Directory period, the quarto design had clearly established itself as the standard form of the Parisian newspaper, although the provinces continued to favor the smaller format. Of twenty-nine Paris papers suppressed in the coup d'état of 18 fructidor V (4 September 1797) that can be identified, twenty-one were quartos, and of the eight octavos, five were titles that had been founded prior to 1793, whose publishers might have changed format had readers not complained that "the collection would not be uniform in appearance."[10] The papers suppressed in fructidor were largely counterrevolutionary, but the republican press showed the same tendency: of nineteen papers subsidized by the Directory government after fructidor, fourteen were quartos and only two were octavos. This triumph of the quarto format meant that the serious newspaper had emerged as a distinct form of text, clearly separated from the book, the pamphlet, and the magazine—these periodicals, less oriented toward current news, continued to use the octavo format during this period—and also from the *petits journaux*, the satirical, polemical, and subversive periodicals that reemerged after the end of the Napoleonic period. Even so, the French quarto-format newspapers of the revolutionary decade remained considerably more restrained in layout and typography than those in the English-speaking countries: they made little effort to sell either themselves or the articles they contained through forceful visual presentation.

Typographical conservatism was not the only reason why the newspapers of the French Revolution lacked visual impact. The printing technology of the period prevented them from combining words and images in the manner of the modern newspaper. Engraving, the method used to reproduce the numerous prints and caricatures published during the revolutionary era, required a printing process the reverse of that used for books and newspapers: ink was poured into the grooves cut by the artist, and the paper forced down into them, whereas in book printing, the inked printing surfaces of the type stuck up from the form. As a result, it was impossible to print engraved images and text set from movable type on the same page in one operation. The illustrations that were sent to subscribers to a number of revolutionary-era journals, including the *Révolutions de France et de Brabant*, the *Révolutions de Paris*, the *Actes des Apôtres*, and the *Accusateur public*, were thus printed separately from the papers and were united with the text they illustrated only when the subscribers had their copies bound.[11] Only the various editions of the *Père Duchêne*, a genre meant to look like the chapbooks and almanacs traditionally produced for a lower-class audience, used woodcut illustrations, which could be combined with printed text because the inked lines of the design projected upward, like printing type. A woodcut portrait of the imaginary Père Duchêne, smoking a pipe and brandishing an ax, was an identifying feature of several rival versions of that paper in the years from 1791 to 1794, but this illustration was not a cartoon or caricature in the normal sense: the same picture was used in all issues. In 1799, however, R. F. Lebois, the last revolutionary journalist to employ the *Père Duchêne* persona, adopted a momentous innovation: he found a woodcut artist speedy enough to make a new cartoon featuring the paper's suppositious author for each of its triweekly issues. Lebois's *Père Duchêne* seems to have been the first newspaper to produce new images as fast as it produced new words and to combine both into a single, unified whole: this obscure publication is one example of the innovative spirit that characterized the press of the revolutionary decade.

Although limited in their typographic formats and restricted in their use of illustrations, the revolutionary newspapers were completely unfettered in their search for distinguishing titles. With so many enterprises competing for the public's attention, journalists and publishers were hard put to find a tag that would both identify their product as a newspaper and distinguish it from its rivals. The conventional eighteenth-century labels for news publications— *gazette, courrier, chronique, annales, journal, mercure*—were combined with almost every possible modifier, but only alert and sophisticated readers could readily distinguish among the *Gazette Nationale de France*, the *Gazette universelle*, the *Gazette de Paris*, and the *Gazette française* or sort out the *Courrier des départements*, the *Courrier de Provence*, the *Courrier républicain*, and the *Courrier français*. Journalists desperate to find a niche amid all this confusion often chose *titres de fantaisie*: the Revolution saw newspapers entitled *Journal du diable, Tout ce qui me passe par la tête, Le Plumpudding, Le Thé*, and many more, but with a handful of exceptions such exotic plumage failed to get its bearer airborne. At the opposite extreme, there were publishers who often deliberately sought to confuse purchasers by making their paper's title identical with that of another publication. When a split produced rival editions of a paper, each naturally tried to keep the original title, as in the case of the three *Amis du Roi* or the multiple *Pères Duchêne*. Some newspapers had titles, such as the *Ami du Roi*, the *Journal de la Montagne,* or the *Tribun du peuple*, that indicated their bearer's political orientation, but most gave little clue to their paper's policy. By the Directory period, some of these ideological titles had become downright misleading, as the one-time prorevolutionary *Courrier républicain* turned counterrevolutionary without changing its name and the *Courrier de l'Égalité* denounced the principle celebrated on its masthead.

The newspaper title was supposed to be the main distinguishing feature of each publication, but it often failed to perform its function because of the intense competition in the press market and the rapid course of revolutionary events. Typographical appearance was also not of much help in telling papers apart. Aside from the choice of format and perhaps a decorative title block, there was not a great deal to separate rival papers. Apart from the German-language papers in Strasbourg, all used small Roman-style type, and none employed such distinguishing features as large headlines. But it was indispensable for newspapers to include some signs that would truly identify them. The surest clue to a journal's identity was the printer's imprint or address. Like a fingerprint, this modest feature, often tucked away at the bottom of the last page or hidden in small type under the title, was a genuine distinguishing mark. It proved that the publication in question was an ongoing enterprise that could actually be located. It was not the law that made the address a feature of almost every newspaper. For the publisher, the inclusion of an address, normally accompanied by an announcement of the subscription price, was a business necessity: how else could would-be subscribers know where to send their money? And it was the one feature of the paper that a rival could not duplicate without losing the fruits of his efforts. Hence one of the many competing versions of the *Père Duchêne* actually incorporated its address in its title: *Je suis le véritable Père Duchêne, Moi, Foutre, Mon Imprimerie qui est celle de Henri IV, étoit ci-devant rue du Vieux Colombier.*

The publisher's address was one key feature of any newspaper that intended to put out more than a few issues; others were the dating and serial numbering of its issues. These features were often missing from the very first issues of the new publications founded in 1789, but they quickly appeared in those that were transformed into ongoing enterprises.[12] They not only served as definitive evidence of a paper's identity, but also as proof that it *was* a newspaper and not some other genre of publication. The numbering of issues was an indication of continuity, an assurance that a reader would be able to count on a regular dialogue with the publication; dating enabled the reader to situate each issue in the context of ongoing events and implied that each issue was valuable because it was fresh and up-to-date.

The newspapers of the French Revolution thus put their words into molds shaped by existing technology, long-standing cultural traditions, and the new necessities of the newspaper market. These conventions dictated that papers use familiar typographical formats and stick to their chosen formats once they were established; they limited the range of titles that could be employed with a chance of success; and they compelled publishers to give their papers at least one indubitable form of identification, its address. Only at the very end of the revolutionary decade did one journalist achieve the combination of up-to-date words and constantly changing images that has become one of the hallmarks of the modern press. Revolutionary in its content, the French press of the 1790s remained conservative in its form, still anchored in a typographical Old Regime even as it contributed to the destruction of old political structures.

The Press and Parliamentary Politics

The small, conservatively laid out French periodicals of the 1790s were texts with a mission. Newspapers in other times and places have provided many things besides political news and comment: the London dailies of the 1780s gave half their space over to commercial advertising and a considerable share of the rest to entertainment, cultural items, and even sports reports. But the French press of the revolutionary decade was much more single-minded. Politics was virtually the only concern of the majority of the new papers. Brissot had proclaimed the newspaper press the modern version of the public forum of the classical city-states: he and his fellow journalists would ensure that the papers exhibited the sober seriousness befitting political debate modeled after the proceedings in Athens and republican Rome. There were, of course, many ways to write about politics seriously. The bitingly satirical royalist *Actes des Apôtres* of the early years of the Revolution, Camille Desmoulins's often light-hearted *Révolutions de France et de Brabant* with its personal tone, and the earthy *Père Duchêne* in its various incarnations were all political papers with serious messages. But no journalist of the revolutionary period ever echoed the Dutch editorialist of the Patriot period in the 1780s who had told his readers that "our greatest misfortune . . . is that we are too serious."[13]

Stressing the importance of politics during the Revolution meant giving pride of place to the successive national assemblies whose debates were the center of political life: the National Assembly of 1789–91, the Legislative Assembly of 1791–92, the National Convention and the legislative councils of the Directory. In all of these bodies, the nation's elected representatives publicly debated the gravest issues facing the country and made decisions that had drastic and immediate effects. For the press the assemblies provided an inexhaustible supply of copy—in that respect, newsmen during the Revolution were much better off than their London colleagues, because the British Parliament spent half the year in recess—and most newspapers were built around these legislative reports. The summary of the day's debates was the latest-breaking news most papers carried, and the entire process of manufacturing the paper was scheduled to allow the inclusion of the most up-to-date reports from the Assembly.

What the papers provided, however, was much more than a neutral transcript of the debates. Even those newspapers that claimed to do no more than to give the actual words of the speakers in fact reshaped what had happened in the assemblies in various ways. Each journalist decided which speeches he would give *in extenso* and which he would dismiss with a few words of summary. Furthermore, most journalists did more than merely report; they also commented on the proceedings they were transcribing. Signed or unsigned articles in the paper created a dialogue between the paper and the politicians: each journal applauded some and denigrated others. The conventions of parliamentary debate invariably restricted the range of what could be said in speeches; the conventions of journalism were different and left room for insults, insinuations of base motives, polemical exegeses of speeches, and a variety of other comments that made parliamentary journalism far more than the printed equivalent of what the politicians had said and done.

This form of political journalism, based on the publishing of legislative debates with commentary and interpretation, was already familiar to British readers; newspapermen had won the right to publish the proceedings of Parliament in 1771, thanks to the efforts of the radical John Wilkes.[14] In revolutionary France, however, it was an innovation. Before 1789 there had been no national legislature and so no debates to serve as the backbone of a newspaper, the core text around which elaborate commentary could be woven. The extraterritorial gazettes had sometimes treated the Parlement of Paris as a debating assembly and had occasionally larded their reports with a certain degree of comment: during the crisis resulting from the Brienne ministry's last-ditch effort to ward off bankruptcy by abolishing the parlements in

1788, for instance, the *Courier du Bas-Rhin* had accompanied its publication of the Parlement of Paris's eloquent protests with sarcastic footnotes demolishing the pretentions of the "judgocracy."[15] But the prerevolutionary gazettes' specialty was international news coverage, and the tacit agreement by which they won the right to circulate in Europe normally required them to eschew commentary of their own. "A journalist who makes comments is a vulgar person," wrote one respected prerevolutionary authority.[16] The events of 1789 offered the opportunity for the creation of a press much more heavily oriented toward French domestic politics and much more open to the expression of journalistic opinion.

The first papers founded in the early weeks of the Revolution, such as the future Jacobin Barère's *Point du Jour*, were devoted almost exclusively to coverage of the Estates-General's public sessions. Papers like Barère's met a widespread practical need: they satisfied those who wanted "an accurate, brief, clear and up-to-date relation of what is happening at the Estates-General," as the Italian observer Filippo Mazzei wrote in recommending the paper to a foreign correspondent.[17] Mazzei expressed no skepticism about the possibility of such a neutral, nonpartisan summary of the National Assembly's proceedings, and this dream of a perfectly neutral newspaper remained powerful throughout the Revolution. Within a few months, however, it became clear that it was unexpectedly difficult to produce a report on the National Assembly that would be universally accepted as accurate and unbiased.

Lehodey de Saultchevreuil's *Journal des Etats-Généraux* and its continuation, the *Journal logographique*, were among the most important of the journals that set out to meet this goal. Lehodey's intention was to report "literally, with the most complete fidelity, everything said in our Representatives' Assembly. . . . Nothing, absolutely nothing, will be omitted." Carrying out this promise required the invention of a primitive method of stenography. This effort was directed toward an idealistic purpose: Lehodey meant to ensure that, in reading it, "the inhabitants of regions furthest from this capital . . . will virtually be present at the sessions of this august Senate, as if they were attending in person." The *Journal logographique* was to be a completely neutral medium, exercising no influence whatsoever over its readers' reactions to the Assembly's proceedings. Its editor condemned both rival papers that "interpret in their own sense or that of the party they want to favor what is said there" and lazy readers "who, incapable of thinking and reflecting, want someone else to spare them the trouble."[18] The journalistic result of the logographic process was not exactly what the legislators may have had in mind, however: the Assembly appeared as a scene of long-winded confusion and chaos, with speakers—identified by name or sometimes not at all but never by any party label or any other clue as to their position on major issues—competing with the faithfully recorded murmurs and applause of the galleries for space in the newspaper's columns. By swinging to the opposite extreme from the laconic official press of the Old Regime, which gave no background information at all on the governmental decision-making process, the *Journal logographique* underlined the transformation that the Revolution had wrought in French politics, but at the cost of making that process nearly as unintelligible as it had been before 1789.

The *Journal logographique* bore more of a resemblance to the English *Hansard's* or to the American *Congressional Record* than to what we conventionally think of as a newspaper. Its appeal was more limited than that of Charles-Joseph Panckoucke's creation, the *Moniteur*. The *Moniteur*, like the *Journal logographique*, promised that the legislative debates would be "the essential object of our paper," and it set out to provide an almost full transcript of them by adopting the large folio format of the London daily papers and by giving itself an extra day to publish the deputies' remarks, compared to the smaller papers. Unlike the Lehodey enterprise, however, the *Moniteur* sought to be a comprehensive newspaper rather than simply a record of debates. Its prospectus made specific reference to the model of the English press and promised foreign and domestic extraparliamentary news, coverage of literature, science, and the arts, plus an advertising section.[19] In practice, neither the cultural articles promised nor the advertisements managed to create a niche for themselves in the paper, but it did combine parliamentary and extraparliamentary news successfully enough to establish itself as revolutionary France's "newspaper of record."

Panckoucke had initially promised something more: he had proposed to make his paper "a political arena where the most vigorous athletes from both parties can measure themselves against each other at all times. . . . The public will be the spectator and judge."[20] The debates of the Assembly would be paralleled by a public discussion of the legislators' actions, as in the London press, and the paper itself would be a public forum in which conflicting viewpoints could be expressed. But in practice Panckoucke quickly retreated from the notion that partisan polemics could be combined with news coverage. With France going through "the beginnings of a just-born liberty," he decided that it was necessary "to be respectful of the delicate constitution of the public spirit" and to publish "only irreproachable principles and unquestioned conclusions."[21] This was a wise business decision: the *Moniteur* learned to adopt the "irreproachable principles and unquestioned conclusions" of each successive revolutionary regime, so that in June 1793 its editor could ingratiate himself with Robespierre by calling his attention to the fact "that the *Moniteur* has always given the speeches of the Mountain at greater length than the others."[22] But Panckoucke's decision was also a panicky refusal to admit that public disagreement was an inherent and legitimate part of the new politics created in 1789. Whereas the British papers provided in their capacious columns a structure within which conflicting views could be aired, the French papers either identified only one set of views as legitimate or else, like the *Moniteur*, refused to admit the necessity of choosing any viewpoint at all. Both policies amounted to a condemnation of the politics of public disputation featured in the columns devoted to legislative reporting.

Papers like Lehodey's and the *Moniteur*, based primarily on extensive transcripts of public speeches, made a definite niche for themselves as repositories of record, but they never became the dominant journals of the Revolution. Other journalists were quick to point out the shortcomings of these journals of record. "Summaries which are, uncontestably, easier to read than a slavish transcript of what happened, would also be more instructive," the author of a journal aimed at supporters of the Jacobin movement suggested.[23] The publishers of a *Collection of Decrees of the National Assembly* pointed out that newspaper accounts were necessarily as chaotic and hard to follow as the debates themselves: "today they talk about the constitution, tomorrow, about administration or laws, and, most often, all these subjects become confused together. . . . Often one doesn't know if a decree was accepted or sanctioned."[24] Most readers preferred journals that edited and summarized the Assembly debates and gave their outcome as soon as it was clear, but there were many ways to accomplish that task. One could simply copy the formula of the prerevolutionary *Gazette de France* and give only the final results of the Assembly debates, as the *Journal des Décrets de l'Assemblée nationale, pour les Habitans des Campagnes* started out to do, although the editor soon had to admit that "it would be more attractive and useful if one provided a summary of the principal arguments raised in the preceding discussions."[25] But what he provided bore little resemblance to parliamentary reporting as conventionally practiced: speakers' names were omitted, and the arguments for and against each measure were reduced to a few sentences in each case, reorganized into simple lists of pros and cons. This formula yielded a portrait of the Assembly as a rationalized law-making machine devoid of passions—and completely different from the depiction of the same body in the *Journal logographique* or the *Moniteur*.

Between these two extremes of objective parliamentary reporting there were many other journalistic formulas. Most differed from those employed by the newspapers just described because they involved both more active and visible intervention on the part of the journalist and the juxtaposition of news about the

Assembly with other reports. In the *Feuille villageoise*, a highly successful weekly aimed at a rural audience, the emphasis was on explaining the significance of the issues raised in the debates, rather than on transcribing them. Unlike the *Journal logographique*, this paper assumed that if the average Frenchman could listen to his representatives debating, he would be utterly bewildered, and its political articles were conceived in the same didactic spirit as its propaganda for agricultural improvement. The weekly summary of the Assembly's sessions made up only a small part of the paper, considerably less than the space devoted to articles aimed at clarifying the issues. The *Feuille villageoise* habitually analyzed arguments rather than summarizing debates and rarely identified the deputies who had spoken, although it contributed to a sense of the Assembly as the battleground of opposing forces of good and evil by referring to "aristocrates" and "patriotes," while struggling to preserve the image of the latter as a unified group. Although hesitant to emphasize such party labels, it was not reticent in identifying the central issues at stake. Typical of the paper's presentation of controversies was an article on royal authority from 1791, beginning, "If the least educated villager took it into his head for a minute to reflect on the word 'king,' the first idea he would come up with, is that a king is a man like himself, simply entrusted with a very important function."[26] When the paper did break with its normal practice of giving only very short summaries of parliamentary sessions in order to provide fuller coverage of Louis XVI's appearance before the Convention during his trial, it still did not leave readers on their own, but told them that this report would show them "the solemn dignity of the representatives of a great people, the humiliation of the former king, his denials, his subterfuges."[27]

The success of the *Feuille villageoise*—it had perhaps 15,000 subscribers in 1791[28]—proves that this condescending attitude did not offend potential subscribers, but journalists interpreting the revolutionary assemblies' debates for a more sophisticated audience had to take a different tack, particularly if they intended to be part of the political fracas as well as to report on it. Brissot and Condorcet, both well-known writers on politics during the prerevolutionary period who were nevertheless passed over for election to the Estates-General before being chosen for the Legislative Assembly in 1791 and the Convention the following year, were among the masters at this form of parliamentary and partisan journalism.

Brissot's *Patriote françois* was justifiably considered one of the best prerevolutionary newspapers. Unlike the authors of the *Feuille villageoise*, he addressed his comments on the Assembly's work not only to the public but also to the deputies themselves, chiding and directing them in line with his "patriot" outlook. Brissot understood himself as having a teaching role: "The point is to spread the enlightenment which prepares a nation to receive a free constitution, by instructing the people about the National Assembly's operations," he stated in his first issue. But the paper was not merely an adjunct of the Assembly nor merely a reflection of the public mood. "It will devote itself above all both to defending the rights of the people . . . and to keeping it from allowing itself to be led into continual fermentation, which would perpetuate disorder and postpone the constitution."[29] The paper's Assembly reports, only one part of its larger news coverage, were designed to guide the deputies in their work and to forestall external obstruction to it by either an unenlightened populace or by the forces of aristocratic reaction.

Brissot immediately demonstrated his willingness to teach both the Assembly and the people in his earliest numbers. "One does not *create* the rights on which any free constitution is based, one can only state them," he thundered in a preface to his report on an early debate about the constitution in 1789, denouncing hesitant deputies who feared giving the people too many freedoms.[30] The *Patriote françois*'s treatment of the famous confrontation over the royal veto later in 1789 gives a good example of its method of presentation. Rather than leaving matters in the hands of the speakers, the *Patriote françois* began by framing the question itself: "The celebrated matter of the *veto* is beginning to become clear." The terms being employed in the debate, such as "suspensive veto," were "rather abstract," but "that is the case with many new words." The paper was pleased to see that the members of the Assembly had now succeeded in grasping the concept. "Our readers will also succeed in understanding it well, by following the different explanations of the greater or lesser power accorded to the king," Brissot continued, and then proceeded to give a masterful summary of the points made by the principal opponents of an absolute veto for the king.[31]

Condorcet, who wrote the legislative coverage in the successful *Chronique de Paris* in 1791–92, proceeded in a similar fashion. He, too, sought to disengage the heart of the matter from the verbiage in which his fellow deputies tended to conceal it. Should there be legislation against the Catholic priests who refused to take an oath to the Civil Constitution of the Clergy? "Everyone agrees that religious worship . . . should be free, and that no cult should be excepted. . . . But when a group turns a religious system into a pretext for a conspiracy against public order . . . can this group not be the object of special laws?" he asked.[32] He was more than willing to criticize the misuse of parliamentary procedure and thereby to imply that the diligent readers of comprehensive transcriptions were wasting their time; of one debate, he wrote, "the art of holding up the deliberations by irrelevant proposals, by calling the previous question, by all the petty means that the interpretation of the rules provides, was carried to the point where it exhausted the most stoic patience."[33]

Partisan journals like those of Brissot, Condorcet, and their emulators among the other political factions served not only to dissect the content of the debates, but also to identify and categorize the participants in them. It was the newspapers, for example, that identified and labeled the party groupings in the National Assembly of 1789; their tendency to impose a bipolar division into "good" and "bad" factions gave a simple dramatic structure to the proceedings that was not necessarily evident to the deputies themselves.[34] The party labels adopted by the press reflected a deeply rooted hostility to the very notion of party: the *Journal de Perlet*'s division of the Convention at the time of Louis XVI's trial into a "pure and respectable majority," meaning the Girondins and the *Plaine*, or center, and a "disorganizing faction," referring to the Montagnards, was typical.[35] However negatively weighted, party designations were an indispensable element in making sense of legislative politics, and the partisan press was the principal means by which the public learned to recognize the different factions.

The emphatic tone adopted by the partisan journalists, and their assurance to readers that their deputies also needed the press's enlightenment on constitutional matters, illustrated their conviction that the press was not simply a passive medium by which the deputies could reach their constituents. It was an indispensable third element in a representative government, on a level with the people, the source of sovereignty, and the legislature, the people's chosen representatives. Where the literal record of the Assembly's debates produced confusion, the journalist's summary and his comments brought clarity. He drew for the deputies themselves the proper conclusion from their own proceedings and simultaneously urged the people to recognize the expression of its own will in the decisions of the legislators, so long as they conformed to the principles of patriotism as the journalist defined them.

This type of parliamentary journalism recast political life into comprehensible patterns, and its practitioners modeled for their readers an active, critical attitude toward their representatives. In the absence of political parties in the modern sense—organizations bringing together legislators and voters in pursuit of common goals—this form of parliamentary press served as a vital link between politicians and the public. Its activities might infuriate the politicians—who, after all, had given the journalists a mandate to interpret and contest their motives, or to dismiss them as irrelevant windbags?—but it quickly became apparent that this style of journalism was inseparable from modern parliamentary politics. Journalism of this type flourished in the periods of the

Revolution when parliamentary politics prevailed, particularly from 1789 to 1792 and from 1795 to 1797; its suppression during the Terror and under Napoleon was a sure sign that the life had gone out of the country's public parliamentary institutions. Indeed, this style of serious political journalism has become a permanent feature of all representative governments based on the power of a public opinion that is not simply the manipulated creation of those in power: it is Brissot, Condorcet, and their numerous emulators rather than the *Moniteur* or the *Logographe* who are the ancestors and blood relatives of today's *Le Monde*, the British *Guardian*, and the *New York Times*, papers that assume it is their mission to pick out what is essential in legislative debates and to measure whether the politicians are adhering to constitutional principles.[36]

Whatever their private feelings about this style of journalism, the deputies of the French revolutionary assemblies had much stronger reactions to the extremist press of left and right, which mentioned their debates only to deny the political legitimacy of the entire legislative enterprise. The most celebrated radical paper of the Revolution, Jean-Paul Marat's *Ami du Peuple*, epitomized this style. From the moment his paper began to appear in September 1789, Marat's commentary on the Assembly was clearly more important than the sketchy and exceedingly biased summary he gave of its proceedings. A typical number of Marat's *Ami du Peuple* began with a highly compressed account of the latest Assembly debates. Then, as if he could restrain himself no longer, Marat would break in with his expostulations against the deputies, denouncing those he disliked in the strongest possible terms. He lambasted the views of one supporter of the royal veto as "more than suspect; they are the ideas of aristocracy covered with the veil of love for order and the public good," and he expressed astonishment that any deputy could defend a bicameral legislature or the veto, while reminding readers somberly that the enemies of the people would never have made any concessions "without the bloody scenes that followed the storming of the Bastille."[37] Condemnations of the Assembly were mixed with overt attempts to mobilize the force of the people against "the criminal faction" in the Assembly, and when he looked back on the first revolutionary parliament from the perspective of the spring of 1792, it was only to conclude that "cruel experience has taught the whole nation that its deputies to the Estates-General sold out its imprescriptible rights and its most vital interests to the monarch, and only seven or eight came out pure."[38]

Often, however, Marat simply omitted any coverage of the Assembly, refusing to accept its claim to be the center of the political universe. During much of the winter of 1791, he pursued his private campaign against Lafayette, the commander of the National Guard, and largely left the deputies to their own devices. Until the second revolution of 1792 and the election of the National Convention, Marat refused to accept the legitimacy of Assembly politics. The deputies responded by repeated refusals to accept the legitimacy of Marat's form of journalism: the *Ami du Peuple* was the occasion for repeated calls for repressive legislation, culminating in its author's trial before the Revolutionary Tribunal in April 1793. And the editors of the papers that paid serious attention to parliamentary politics also recognized that Marat had gone beyond the boundaries, even if they defended his freedom to publish. Brissot defended Marat's patriotism but disavowed his "tantrums"; the *Chronique de Paris* asked whether he was a secret agent of the counterrevolution.[39]

The royalist press, which flourished as extensively as the pro-revolutionary papers in the first years of the Revolution, shared Marat's indignant rejection of the National Assembly and all its works but not, of course, for the same reasons. The *Ami du Roi* depicted the Assembly in terms not very different from Marat's, as a criminal conspiracy against the people, "a colossus already grown to an immeasurable height" and oppressing both people and king.[40] The *Ami du Roi* was a serious journal, just as much oriented toward the actions of the legislature as the *Patriote françois* was. Its tone and its format were the same as those of the serious patriotic press, although its evaluation of the Revolution was at the opposite extreme. The paper can hardly be said to have represented a loyal opposition to the dominant prorevolutionary party, inasmuch as Royou and his associates rejected the constitutional framework the National Assembly was piecing together, claiming that the "learned architects who were at work on the reconstruction of the state" had destroyed all existing institutions "when these wonderful ideas by which they were to be replaced had not yet been conceived."[41] The National Assembly, far from being a forum for the rational discussion of political issues, had become a cockpit for men who were "slaves themselves to violent passions that clash and struggle. . . . Our destinies are decided in a boxing ring rather than in an Areopagus."[42] But Royou practiced what might be called parliamentary oppositional journalism: whereas Marat frequently went off on tangents of his own, Royou dogged the steps of the hated deputies, blasting their decrees day by day, lamenting their disrespect to the king, but nevertheless doing them the honor of making their actions the main theme of his own reflections.

The many satirical counterrevolutionary journals of the early revolutionary years took a much less respectful attitude toward the deputies' doings. The *Actes des Apôtres*, the most notorious of them, showered the "buffoons of the grand national theater"[43] with abuse in every issue, mixing obscene verses, often blasphemous parodies of the Catholic liturgy, with straightforward calls for the hanging of the Assembly's entire membership. The *Journal général de la Cour et de la Ville*, better known as the *Petit Gautier*, expressed its disdain for the Assembly by giving it no more than a six-line paragraph in most issues, discrediting the subject by trivializing it. In a typical number, it apostrophized the deputies: "Courage, gentlemen . . . fill your pockets well, all means are good. . . . Plunder, steal, do whatever you want, but do it quickly. . . . The people who suffers misery while you are overwhelmed, not with assignats but with gold coins, might well demand an accounting from you." The *Sottises de la semaine* announced that "it is so rare for the National Assembly to make a good decree that one could cite them all in an epigram."[44] As far as these satirical papers were concerned, the legislators' work was so absurd that it deserved no serious discussion. Like Marat's paper on the far left, these counterrevolutionary journals denied any legitimacy to the parliamentary Revolution.

In the same way that its summaries and commentaries recast the workings of the revolutionary assemblies in shapes that the legislators had never anticipated, the newspapers transformed all the other institutions of public discourse they represented, such as the political clubs and even the press itself. The organizers of clubs, particularly the nationwide network affiliated with the Jacobins, were acutely aware of the importance of the press for spreading the ideas articulated in their assemblies. Provincial Jacobin groups took the initiative in establishing papers under their own control even before the Paris society did so.[45] In Paris the central club patronized several initiatives by members, such as Choderlos de Laclos's *Journal des Amis de la Constitution*, founded in late 1790. Nevertheless, the Jacobins hesitated for years before deciding to create an official journalistic record of their own debates, fearful that such a journal would become the tool of an individual or a faction within the club. The vicissitudes of the paper they finally created, the *Journal de la Montagne*, showed that this caution was well motivated. The paper, founded in June 1793, became a widely read and highly influential spokesman for the Jacobin movement and the revolutionary government of the year II.[46] Its content was explicitly intended to demonstrate the unity and wisdom of the legislature and the club, both now purged of their perfidious Girondin members, while the paper's reports from the frontiers and the provinces recorded the Republic's victorious progress.

In fact, however, the literal transcription of speeches at the Jacobins could be highly unsettling. What were readers to make of things in 1793 when a member "raised some suspicions about Danton's *civisme*" or when a deputy came to the club and urged it to demand yet another purge of the Convention?[47] The paper itself became the occasion for public dissension within the organization. Members protested that not all speeches were published in it: two days of angry debate in March 1794, duly recorded in the paper for its readers' edification, concluded with Robespierre proclaiming that it was inopportune to abolish the *Journal de la Montagne*, but that it had nevertheless been edited "less in the interest of truth, than for private personal interests."[48] Perhaps the greatest demonstration that even a newspaper of record could not be a politically neutral medium came two weeks later, when the paper's Convention report began with the deputy Legendre's stunning announcement, "I have just learned that four of our colleagues were arrested last night; Danton is among them."[49] In the Convention, Legendre's protest came close to derailing the Committee of Public Safety's coup against the Dantonists; one can only imagine the impact its publication had on public opinion.

The independent newspapers that recorded or commented on the Jacobins and other clubs were, naturally, even less restrained than official organs like the *Journal de la Montagne*. During the struggle with the Girondins, the dominant Montagnard faction in the Jacobin club repeatedly protested the way the club's sessions were written up in the general press. The club banned hostile reporters, and the members voted to choose censors who would examine printed reports for "every sort of Brissotist, Rolandist, Girondist or Buzotist proposition."[50] Things had not changed in 1799 when the right-wing *Feuille du Jour* decided to give readers news about the neo-Jacobin Club de Manège's public sessions. "We have omitted several sessions where they did nothing but give out inarticulate cries. . . . We will choose only what is most important, that is, most horrible," the paper promised.[51] Left-wing clubs were not the only victims: during the Directory period some of the right-wing press campaigned against the Club de Clichy, a gathering place for counterrevolutionary deputies, on the grounds that clubs were by their very nature evil institutions. "The provinces will no doubt not like to learn that their representatives, instead of preparing themselves by meditation and silence for the work of the assembly, pass their time yelling, arguing, and perhaps intriguing in a club," one of the papers subsidized by British and royalist agents proclaimed.[52] Like the deputies of the revolutionary assemblies, the militants of the revolutionary era's clubs found that the press fundamentally changed the nature of their activities, both by amplifying them and by subjecting them to criticism.

Like the assemblies and the clubs, the press itself was affected by its own power of amplification and distortion. Journalists commented freely on their colleagues, sometimes with praise but more often with criticism. This process in which each journalist pinned labels on his rivals served to reveal the partisan underpinnings of the press, even though many a partisan journalist tried to convince his own readers that he was truly impartial. In his prospectus the editor of the *Gazette universelle* asserted that "we are, and we only want to be, historians"; but other journalists had different names for him: "this dog of a gazetteer" and "master scoundrel"; clearly, its opponents had succeeded in redefining the nature of the paper's text.[53] The royalist *Quotidienne*'s review of the republican press in 1797 was typical of the way partisan journalists warned readers not to take the content of other papers at face value: it contrasted the outspoken *Ami des Lois*, "the buffoon of the Revolution," with the more insidious *Clef du Cabinet*, "where they lie with gravity, with dignity, where they cleverly disguise what the others flaunt," arguing that both really represented the same discredited revolutionary policies.[54] Journalists argued that this unmasking of their competitors was an essential part of their function. Faced with complaints that assaults on the royalist newspapers occupied too much space in his *Lettres bougrement patriotiques du véritable Père Duchêne*, A.-F. Lemaire replied, "If people were as convinced as I am of the harm that 20,000 aristocratic newspapers continually sent to the old provinces do, they would applaud my zeal."[55] For the most part, each journalist intended his partisan attacks for his own audience; they constituted a form of preaching to the converted. Nevertheless, most journalists felt compelled to respond to hostile criticism, often indulging in prolonged slanging matches with their opponents. The net effect was to make the entire press appear as a cacophony of contradictory voices, each calling the other's honesty into question, and to discredit the entire medium.

No journal demonstrated the importance of these cross-references in other papers as powerfully as Jean-Paul Marat's *Ami du Peuple*. Marat himself asserted that "the multiplicity of so-called patriot writers" describing events differently "muddles all the reader's ideas" and promised to be the first to quit if one authoritative journal were set up. Other journals' comments on his paper proved his point. Even those journalists who were prepared to acknowledge that "his lash has often been useful and necessary to ward off the enemies of the Revolution, or the hidden traitors," normally felt obliged to distance themselves from what Brissot called "the tantrums, the doubtful or calumnious assertions" in Marat's work.[56] But unadulterated denunciation was more common. A pamphlet in the pseudo-popular *poissard* style from early 1790 reminded readers that Marat, who had once held an appointment as physician to the king's brother's bodyguards, was not one of the common people he claimed to speak for: "I don't trust a former doctor of the Comte d'Artois, even if he calls himself our friend." This author used language meant to resemble that of the common people to disassociate them from Marat's bloodthirsty prescriptions: "Look here, I'se not up for deviltry, I'se not wanting to hurt a dog."[57] After Marat's assassination, a provincial Jacobin journalist who might have been expected to honor him concluded that "Marat knew that he served as a pretext for declamations by the aristocrats; that his name alone damaged the cause he defended; that much of France blamed the violence of his opinions: his duty was to give way, to condemn himself to an obscurity useful to his country."[58] As he surveyed the reaction to his articles, Marat had good reason to boast "My pen has caused some sensation."[59] But in fact it was other journalists' words that defined the significance of his own text and elevated it to its unique position.

Brissot's and Mirabeau's prerevolutionary vision of the newspaper press as the invention that would restore to modern democracy the immediacy and the participatory quality of politics in ancient Greece and Rome thus failed to anticipate the actual effects of dependence on journalists and their words. The prerevolutionary monarchy had put itself on display in Versailles's Hall of Mirrors but had contrived to control the reflection it gave off; the actors in the new public political culture of the Revolution had the feeling of being depicted by the distorting mirrors of a carnival funhouse. The French revolutionaries were among the first to confront the paradox inherent in freedom of the press under a representative system of government: the people may choose their representatives, but they do not necessarily let those representatives define themselves. At the same time, the press encouraged a critical attitude toward the clubs that claimed to guide the legislators and even toward its own operations.

The evolution of the press after 1789 shattered the optimistic belief that unlimited public debate would lead to a reasoned consensus on how France should govern itself. The relatively nonpolemical *Journal de Perlet*'s comment on the debates in the National Convention summarizes the judgment that the press rendered on the public politics of the Revolution as a whole:

> Those who attend the Convention's sessions often have occasion to make scandalized remarks on this battle between orators who want to talk, one on this topic and the other on that, who insult each other, break into each other's speeches and turn the assembly of the people's representatives into an arena of conflict. . . . One would be inclined to think better of laws passed by the Convention, if they had been discussed with gravity, considered calmly, and if they did not seem to be more the fruit of disputes and tricks, than that of wisdom and reason.[60]

It was a disturbing picture of the nation's leaders, and of its new political process.

The Press and Extraparliamentary Politics

Important as the war of words in the assemblies, in the clubs, and in the press itself was, it was not the whole Revolution. The revolutionary decade was also punctuated by great public crises, from the storming of the Bastille in 1789 to Napoleon's coup d'état of 18 brumaire ten years later. As inciter, chronicler, and interpreter of these events, the press was at the center of these *journées* and crises. This was true even though the French press of the 1790s was not geared to sudden events as much as the daily press of the late nineteenth and twentieth centuries was to be.[61] It was the regular flow of parliamentary words that permitted the rise of a large-scale news industry in revolutionary Paris; the newspapers of the 1790s, creations of that large-scale event, the Revolution itself, nevertheless lacked the technology to capitalize financially on sensational occurrences. Limited by the slowness of the wooden hand-press, they could not rush out extra editions, and because most papers were dependent on subscription sales, they could not make windfall profits from sudden news developments, even though interest in the news obviously increased during crises. Paris newspapers also had to face the fact that journalistic involvement in one of these high-stakes dramas being played out in the streets around their offices meant risking the existence of their enterprises and, after 1792, the very lives of the newsmen and publishers.

The Old Regime press had already provided coverage of sudden and spectacular events, or what the age referred to as "revolutions," in the plural.[62] But the French Revolution made the connection between these crises and the media much closer and more immediate than ever before. The most fully informed prerevolutionary gazettes had normally been published far from the scene of the occurrences they described, and their reports conveyed a sense of their difficulty in discovering what had occurred. As the French press scholar Pierre Rétat has written, they "revealed this process . . . by their hesitations, their successive approaches over time, with the event being treated first as a rumor" and only gradually taking on the outlines of something definite and certain.[63] The events that these papers were reporting invariably appeared as "something that had already occurred, usually abruptly and without the conscious choice of human actors," as Keith Baker has put it in analyzing the prerevolutionary understanding of the phenomenon of revolution.[64] Jean Luzac, editor of the *Gazette de Leyde*, was acting in accordance with this tradition on 21 July 1789 when he told his readers that he would withhold the reports that he had received of events in Paris a week earlier because he did not want to relay rumors "of blood spilled by the troops in the middle of the capital and all the horrors that presage a civil war" without positive assurance of their truth.[65]

Long before the *Gazette de Leyde*'s cautious account of the storming of the Bastille had reached Paris, however, the French journalists on the spot had invented a completely different way of treating such news. In the 15 July number of his *Courrier de Versailles à Paris*, Antoine-Louis Gorsas, the paper's editor, gave a quick summary of the occurrences that had resulted in the capture of the royal fortress the day before, written from the perspective of the participants themselves: "What to do? There was only one choice: oppose force with force in order to shore up our endangered freedom. . . . One took up arms." As Rétat has written, the revolutionary journalist, in contrast to his cautious prerevolutionary predecessor, "gives the impression of living from day to day" by describing events as though he was directly in the middle of them, and "this immediacy . . . allows him to be the conscious explicator of the event, its interpreter."[66]

The capture of the Bastille, the great founding event of the French Revolution, demonstrated more clearly than any subsequent crisis the way in which the media transformed the ephemeral moments of the Revolution into symbolic stories whose impact could then be transmitted through time and space. The storming of the Bastille was a public event, witnessed by a large crowd, but it would not have been beyond the capacities of the prerevolutionary media to consign it to virtual oblivion. This had been, after all, the fate of the first insurrectionary *journée* of the revolutionary period, the uprising in Grenoble on 7 June 1788. Passed over in silence in the French domestic press, it was chronicled in some detail in the foreign-based gazettes, but as Jean Sgard's recent study has shown, these journalists "hastened to bring the story to an end." Their concern was to "integrate the unheard-of event into a legalistic account" that emphasized the return to normality: within a few weeks, it was as if the rioters' successful challenge to royal authority had never occurred.[67] The officially authorized press in France treated the storming of the Bastille as it had treated the Grenoble affair: not a word about it appeared in the *Gazette de France* or the *Journal de Paris*, and in the *Journal général de France* the event surfaced only via published documents such as the emergency decree establishing a citizen militia, the National Guard. The foreign-based papers published delayed reports, as they had about the Grenoble riot, and they tended to emphasize the disorder and violence in Paris rather than the political significance of what had occurred. The *Gazette de Leyde* spoke of "a vile populace" which, "in giving itself over to the most frightful pillage and lawlessness, spread fear and terror everywhere," and praised the Parisian bourgeoisie, not for standing up to the king, but for arming themselves to contain the people.[68] The *Courrier d'Avignon* was more positive about the uprising and more emphatic in indicating that a major upheaval in French life had occurred. "One only has to know the French character to know how quickly all these things were carried out, and how eagerly everyone demonstrated what is now called patriotism," the paper's report of the events of 14 July concluded.[69] These reports, often quite detailed about what had taken place, included no speculation about its meaning: the traditional press did nothing to transform an admittedly sensational *fait divers* into a myth symbolizing the people's power.

To establish itself as a revolutionary event, the Bastille had to create its own media. The new periodicals that had been launched since the convocation of the Estates-General had only a modest role in spreading the details of what had occurred there: focused on the parliamentary proceedings in Versailles, they were poorly prepared to cover developments in Paris. Even the *Courrier de Versailles à Paris*, the most informative of them on the events leading up to the revolt, did not get around to recording the events in Paris until the last three pages of its issue dated 15 July 1789, where it accorded one paragraph to the actual storming of the Bastille, mentioning the name of the fortress only once. Mirabeau's *Lettres à ses commettans* and Jean-Charles Poncelin's *Courrier français* stressed the importance of the creation of a bourgeois militia, the *Garde nationale*, more than the people's success in destroying a symbol of royal authority.

To find both the details of what transpired on 14 July 1789 and the earliest versions of the revolutionary myth that eventually made that date France's national holiday, readers had to turn to pamphlets rushed out in the wake of the events, such as the dramatist Jacques Beffroy de Reigny's *Exact Summary of the Taking of the Bastille, written before the eyes of the principal actors who took part in this expedition, and read the same day at the Hôtel de Ville*. Of the twenty-odd accounts of the storming of the Bastille published immediately after the event that they studied, the German scholars Hans-Jürgen Lüsebrink and Rolf Reichardt found only two that subsequently grew into newspapers, and only one of these, the *Révolutions de Paris*, lasted more than a few issues.[70] But the news-hungry public was served by a flood of pamphlets, illustrated broadsheets, and other improvised media that conveyed the unmistakable message that the people had seized power.

The domestic newspaper press did its part, not by dwelling on the events of 14 July 1789 themselves, but by serving as living demonstrations of their significance. Gorsas's *Courier* of 15 July 1789 might have been short on factual details about the capture of the Bastille, but it was quick to interpret its importance: "Yesterday will be forever remembered in the records of our history: it opens the way for the greatest and perhaps the most fortunate revolutions." In the first issue of his paper after 14 July 1789, Mirabeau, after curtly remarking that he had had no time to chronicle events, went to work defining their significance: they amounted to nothing less than "the restoration of our rights," the people's resort to violence, although regrettable, had been necessary, and the National Assembly would now be able to proceed to the making of a constitution.[71] By describing the National Assembly as the locus of power and by disregarding the censorship, the press made it clear that the storming of the Bastille had in fact transformed the political situation.

The press that came into existence as a result of the fall of the Bastille replaced the improvised media of July 1789 and institutionalized the new relationship between the press and revolutionary events. This new press was much closer to the events it described than the papers before 1789 had been. The Paris news industry, of secondary importance in the European journalistic world before the Revolution, had suddenly become the world's largest center of newspaper production, and its editorial offices and printing shops were located in the midst of the events its products depicted. The shift from weekly or biweekly papers to dailies meant that journalistic texts appeared within twenty-four hours of the events they described, soon enough to influence the outcome of the movements they reported on. The crumbling of censorship restrictions meant that the press could incite events as well as chronicle them after they had happened. Consequently, newspapers became an essential part of the revolutionary story they printed.

Collecting facts about the major events of the Revolution was the most traditional of the functions newspapers performed during the 1790s, but it was nonetheless of fundamental importance. The Revolution had its mythic dimension, but its power as a narrative came from the audience's conviction that it was a true story, the result of concrete actions at specific times by identifiable individuals and groups. Neither the Revolution as a whole nor the dramatic turning points within it told themselves, however. Even as the events were occurring, they had to be cast in the form of a coherent, chronologically organized historical account. The number of newspapers founded after 14 July 1789 that provided subscribers with a supplement giving an account of events from the start of the prerevolutionary crisis or at least from the assembling of the Estates-General up to the date of the newspaper's own first issue, such as the "Tableau of the Revolution in the Midi" that filled the first numbers of Carpentras's *Observateur du Midi*, launched in September 1792, is testimony to the strength of this drive to present the revolutionary story as a complete history.[72]

On the whole, the newspapers were reasonably faithful chroniclers of the spectacular events that dominated the Revolution. Even the most shocking and controversial occurrences of the decade, such as the massacres in the Paris prisons in September 1792 and the Federalist revolts against the Convention in the summer of 1793, were reported promptly and with a fair degree of accuracy. In this respect, the press of the Revolution broke decisively with the authorized newspapers of the Old Regime, which could be forced to suppress all mention of unsettling events, and they differed fundamentally from the controlled press of modern totalitarian regimes. Barère, the former journalist turned spokesman for the Committee of Public Safety in 1794, might fulminate against the papers' "gambling on driving public opinion up and down" by the printing of exaggeratedly pessimistic or optimistic news reports,[73] but even the dictatorial regime of the Terror never abandoned the idea that there was an objective truth about public events that the press had a right to publish.

The assembling of the facts about those events was not an easy task. Paris was too large and the elements of each revolutionary *journée* usually too complex for any one individual to be able to provide a reliable eyewitness account. The newspapers tended to provide structured narratives written from the viewpoint of an omniscient but anonymous reporter—first-person reportage like the account of 10 August 1792 by the *Hamburg Correspondent*'s informant, who mentioned that he had participated in the fighting at the Tuileries as a member of his section's National Guard battalion, was unusual[74]—but these apparently simple narratives concealed the work their authors must have gone through in assembling and reconciling as best they could eyewitness accounts of actions that had often taken place in widely scattered parts of the city. Frequently it is clear that the reporters were not eyewitnesses at all but had followed the events of a *journée* by noting down the reports delivered to the Assembly or the city government at the Hotel de Ville.

The structuring of a narrative about a controversial event already implied ideological choices, as the differing stories about the same incidents that appeared in pro- and counterrevolutionary newspapers often demonstrated. In 1799, the right-wing *Publiciste* and the neo-Jacobin *Journal des Hommes libres* both reported on a riot in the provincial city of Amiens. Both agreed that rioters had clashed with the mayor and his armed deputies and that several children had been killed in a fusillade. The *Publiciste*'s narrative said the incident began when the town's theatergoers demanded a presentation of the counterrevolutionary play "The Interior of the Revolutionary Committees"; the *Journal des Hommes libres*'s version maintained that the demonstration at the theater was only the second phase of a process whose real origin was resistance to the authorities' effort to round up young men subject to the draft. In the neo-Jacobin paper's report, the mayor's forces were insulted and stoned before they finally opened fire to defend themselves; no such provocations were reported in the *Publiciste*'s story. Both versions clearly depicted the same event, and indeed they were in basic agreement on the facts—an antirepublican riot, a confrontation with the authorities, the deaths of several innocent bystanders—but the inclusion or exclusion of significant elements gave the two rival narratives different significations.[75]

However they obtained their raw information, the revolutionary era's newsmen, like their modern-day successors, followed regular rules in casting it into intelligible form. Modern journalistic conventions require the journalist to highlight the most important and most striking aspects of his story and arrange subsequent details in order of diminishing importance. Revolutionary-era newsmen had not yet heard of this "inverted pyramid" procedure. Their stories tended to be strictly chronological, even when this meant burying the climax of the narrative deep within the paper. Offputting to the modern reader, this was a journalistic "strategic ritual" that served to persuade the eighteenth-century audience, unaccustomed to modern narrative structures involving flashbacks and other devices that break up the linear flow of time, that they were in fact learning of events exactly as they had unfolded.[76]

Only when the newspapers had completed their work of converting a congeries of isolated actions into a coherent narrative did a revolutionary event come into existence. In the course of constructing their narratives, however, the newsmen had already gone beyond describing what had occurred and begun labeling it. Louis XVI's effort to escape from Paris in June 1791 provided a striking example of this. A few radical journalists, such as Jean-Louis Carra, had forecast such an occurrence and, so to speak, classified it in advance, but there were no public indices that such a plot was afoot until the king was discovered missing from the Tuileries palace on the morning of 21 June 1791. Was the king's unexpected departure to be labeled an abduction, an escape, or a desertion? The *Moniteur* aided and abetted the mayor of Paris, Jean-Sylvain Bailly, and his legislative allies in their efforts to avoid holding the king responsible for his action: the paper led off its coverage on 22 June with Bailly's carefully worded announcement, "The king was carried off around 2 A.M. last night, and no one knows the route he took." To give additional credence to this version, the paper immediately shifted to its transcript of the National Assembly's session. The presiding officer was depicted accepting Bailly's statement without further question: "I have sad news to tell you. Monsieur Bailly has just informed me that the king and some of his family were carried off last night by enemies of the public welfare."[77] The paper's adherence to the chronology of the story as it had unfolded before the National Assembly allowed it to bury the uncomfortable fact that the king had left behind him a manifesto denouncing the Revolution and demolishing the fiction that his flight had been involuntary far down in its columns. Neither on this nor on the following days did the paper offer the slightest editorial reflection on the abduction theory or on the king's behavior. A reader depending on the Revolution's "newspaper of record" for a notion of what the king's flight meant would have had to assume that the whole affair had been an unfortunate accident that would not permanently alter France's constitutional set-up.

While the *Moniteur* thus acted to give credence to the Bailly version of an innocent king abducted by unnamed enemies, most of the French press conducted itself quite differently. The patriot press moved at once to define the king's departure as a deliberate flight. The Strasbourg *Geschichte der gegenwärtigen Zeit*, reacting to papers like the *Moniteur*, saw the situation clearly enough: "Some reports absolve Louis XVI, as if he had been given a sleeping potion and hauled away without his knowledge. This is no excuse." Carra's *Annales patriotiques* could hardly pass up the opportunity to point out its forecast of the event. For Carra, what had happened was clear: "Louis XVI, this morning, deserted the throne, the capital, the empire, and by this cowardly defection, promised to return, with foreign executioners, to reign over twenty-five million corpses." The more moderate papers were less explicit, but they did not participate in Bailly's effort to disguise the truth about the king's intentions: the *Journal de Perlet* clearly labeled his departure an "escape."[78]

The king's actions posed a different sort of problem for the outspokenly counterrevolutionary papers. The *Journal général de la Cour et de la Ville* held up distribution of its issue of 23 June 1791, in which the editor had imagined "the instant when these faithful subjects [the French emigrés], who had exiled themselves from this infidel land, threw themselves . . . into the arms of Louis XVI," for what the editor described as "very important reasons, which can easily be imagined."[79] Montjoie dropped the reference to the king from the title of his version of the *Ami du Roi*.[80] But within a few days, most of these papers not only admitted that the king had acted deliberately but openly defended his actions. "I salute you, king of the French. . . . The effort you have just made to break your chains, raises you in the esteem of all the French; it explains the mystery of your past conduct; it teaches them that you are worthy of being their king, and that the pure blood of the Bourbons flows in your veins," the *Journal général de la Cour et de la Ville* intoned less than a week after the event.[81] For different reasons, both the patriotic and the counterrevolutionary papers thus chose to describe Louis's flight for what it was and refused to aid the majority of the legislative deputies in leaving open the possibility of absolving the king from responsibility for his conduct.

The massacres in the prisons in Paris on 2, 3, and 4 September 1792, shortly after the *journée* of 10 August 1792, were another example of a surprise event that the press had not foreshadowed but that it was called on to label and categorize. Journalists were faced with the problem of reporting the killings without either discrediting the new regime set up after 10 August, unleashing further violence, or endangering their own lives by antagonizing the Paris crowd, which had massacred some of the prisoners almost within earshot of many newspaper offices. The most common journalistic strategy for presenting the violence was to start with the report that representatives of the revolutionary Commune, in power since 10 August 1792, provided to the Legislative Assembly on the evening of 2 September 1792. That report, as summarized in the press, was short and obscure and allowed the press "to draw a curtain over events which it would be too difficult at this moment to detail, and whose consequences cannot yet be calculated," as Condorcet put it in the *Chronique de Paris*. He added that it was "a sad and terrible situation, in which a naturally good and generous people is forced to commit such a vengeance."[82] If the *Chronique*'s anxiety to say as little as possible about the massacres was a natural consequence of its commitment to the revolutionary movement, the papers that had been opposed to 10 August 1792 were equally cautious in dealing with the subject. The *Journal de Perlet* hastened to assert that "if the people did take cruel vengeance on the days of the second and third [of September], one could fill a book with touching scenes of justice and humanity which it also took part in." The *Moniteur* insisted that there had been a real conspiracy on the part of the prisoners, and it absolved the Paris municipal authorities of any complicity in the killings. In Poitiers the moderate *Journal de la Vienne* limited itself to the publication of the Paris Commune's reports to the Legislative Assembly.[83] The counterrevolutionary press, suppressed on 10 August, was not around to attempt to exploit the massacres; when the first crypto-royalist papers began to show themselves a few weeks later, they had to be content with vague references to "the troubles and the afflicting scenes surrounding us."[84]

The intent of the press in September 1792, probably acting under instructions from the revolutionary authorities,[85] was to legitimate the prison massacres, minimize their significance, and propagate an image of Paris as calm and untroubled by agitation. The killings were not passed over in silence, as they would have been in the press of Nazi Germany or Stalinist Russia, but faced with a truly sensational event, the journalists sought above all to make sure that it did not stick in their readers' consciousness. In contrast to the flight to Varennes, where the papers provided radically different labels and suggested conflicting courses of action based on them, this instance of popular violence drove the press into a forced unanimity. Only two months later, when the revolutionaries' temporary unity following 10 August had dissolved and the responsibility for the killings had become a bone of contention between the Girondin and Montagnard factions of the Jacobins, could dissident papers like the crypto-royalist *Feuille du Matin* raise explosive questions such as "how many killers must be assembled, before a murder that they commit ceases to be a crime and becomes an act of the people's justice?"[86] And it was this relabeling of the events of September 1792, which became one episode of the Revolution that even the radical Montagnards of the year II preferred to pass over in silence, that proved durable.

For the victors in each of the great revolutionary confrontations, it was essential that this labeling process lead to the conclusion that the events that had occurred were a public manifestation of the will of the people. Without this confirmation of legitimacy from the press, the results of such *journées* as the October Days and the overthrow of the monarchy would necessarily remain in doubt. Hence the victors in every confrontation felt the need to reshape the press in order to guarantee favorable presentation of their achievement. In cases such as 10 August 1792 and 18 fructidor V, those papers that had backed the losing side were either suppressed altogether or intimidated into expressing only the desired views. Thus in the wake of 10 August the prorevolutionary *Chronique de Paris* could ignore the fact that perhaps half the press had warned against an insurrection and announce that "this time one can say, without exaggeration, that the people has risen up unanimously"; meanwhile, the *Journal de Perlet*, which had opposed the uprising, felt compelled to claim that there was now complete support for "the wise and energetic decrees that the Assembly has seen fit to pass for the good of the country."[87] Similarly, after fructidor, the right-wing papers were suppressed and the republican ones had a clear field to proclaim that the coup was not a violation of the constitution but a necessary measure of defense against subversion. The sudden disappearance of prominent newspaper titles identified with the defeated party in each of the Revolution's major turning points—the radical democratic papers after the suppression of the republican demonstration of 17 July 1791, the royalist papers in 10 August 1792, the Girondin press after the *journée* of 31 May–2 June 1793—was one of the most striking signs that a crisis had taken place, and the most reliable index of who had won.

Constructing narratives that tied disparate facts together into intelligible stories and labeling the significance of those stories were two fundamental features of the press's involvement with revolutionary events. But the most striking and innovative feature of that relationship, the one that differentiated the revolutionary papers from their Old Regime forerunners, was the papers' role in inciting and directing the actions that led to the famous revolutionary *journées*. For historians, the question of how important journalists were in guiding events has been the main criterion for evaluating the significance of the press during the Revolution: it has led to lengthy debates over, for example, the responsibility of Marat for the September massacres or the relationship between Hébert's *Père Duchêne* and the various manifestations of the *sans-culotte* movement in 1793. The mechanistic cause-and-effect definition of newspaper influence implied in these debates and the difficulty in weighing the impact of words against the impact of political and social movements and economic trends has resulted in a rather sterile debate over the role of the press, normally resolved by according primacy to underlying social forces and allowing the press only a secondary effect on timing and procedures. As Hugh Gough, the most recent historian of the revolutionary press, has put it, "it is . . . difficult to isolate the influence of the press from that of other forces at work in the revolution, such as hunger, habit, speeches, pamphlets, friendship or sheer accident. No single event in the revolution was caused exclusively by the newspaper press, but a great many of them were influenced by it in some way."[88]

Whatever historians may think, the journalists of the time did write as if the newspapers could set out scripts and guidelines to prepare the actors on the revolutionary stage for their parts. Sometimes these incitements to action were amazingly detailed and precise. On 8 July 1792, for example, the *Trompette du Père Duchêne* warned its readers that a crisis was approaching. "While the blonde one [Lafayette] makes up petitions, and while the Lameth brothers want to lead the army against Paris . . . the Prussians are advancing with great strides," its author, Antoine-François Lemaire, exclaimed. But he offered his readers a program: "We will act as one. We will come together. We will arm ourselves, and the time is coming when we will punish all the rascals who traffic in our blood and our treasure. In the meantime, patriots of all parts of the country, arm yourselves, THE TOCSIN OF LIBERTY WILL RING OUT! Spread this issue everywhere, reprint it, post it up."

For the next month, Lemaire kept up his campaign of incitement. Every day, he warned the people that they were not recognizing the dangers they faced, and urged them to "shake off your criminal lackadaisicalness." He pointed them toward their real enemy, Louis XVI: "It is he who fools us; it is he who ruins us and forces us to rise up; it is he who starves us; it is he who waits only for the right moment to see us slaughtered by his good friends the *honnêtes gens* of Coblentz, in order to be all-powerful and despotic." And he indicated the appropriate remedy: "we need, and urgently, a national convention." On 8 August 1792 Lemaire proclaimed, "the torrent is about to overflow, and I defy any human power to stop it." On the night of 9–10 August 1792 the Parisian *sans-culottes* did indeed take arms, sound the tocsin, surround the royal palace, and compel the Legislative Assembly to summon a national convention. The *Trompette du Père Duchêne* continued to stage-manage the journée even after the force of arms had settled the issue. Its issue of 12 August brought a breathless account of the day's events: Lemaire began, "I've just come from the Tuileries (on the tenth, at 4 PM in the evening); they are covered with bodies." He continued both by giving further instructions— "Departments, stay calm! In the name of the *patrie*, no bloodshed!" and by defining and labeling what had just occurred: "Liberty triumphs today."[89]

Lemaire's printed sheets provided a comprehensive script for the historical actors involved in the events of 10 August 1792.[90] He defined the *journée*'s goals, assigned the parts, and provided advance assurance of the uprising's success. Nevertheless, it was not his paper alone, or even the combination of his and the other Jacobin papers printing similar propaganda, that produced the insurrection of 10 August. The newspapers were not operating in a vacuum: indeed, they were not even the originators of this call to action. Journalists like the *Annales patriotiques'* editor Jean-Louis Carra, who subsequently boasted of his part in the elaborate planning that preceded the *journée*,[91] knew full well that the press campaign had been set in motion by a nucleus of determined activists, and that it had involved not only printed propaganda but also other preparations such as the gathering of troops—the *fédérés* who had been brought to the capital for the celebration of the anniversary of 14 July—and intensive politicking in the capital's forty-eight sections. And all of these conscious preparations had succeeded by exploiting long-established patterns of crowd behavior.[92]

Not only had the press not initiated the insurrectionary movement on its own, it had been anything but unanimous in promoting it. Many papers had done everything possible to forestall the event. In the week before the uprising, the *Moniteur* asserted that there was "no hope for the agitators of the people to lead it into the excesses that they desire and that they never cease to provoke"; the *Journal de Perlet* warned against raising the divisive issue of the king's status at a moment when the nation needed unity to fight off the foreign invaders.[93] Meanwhile, the royalist press openly urged the Prussians and Austrians to carry out the bloodcurdling threats contained in the Brunswick manifesto, or even condemned that document as too moderate.[94] And paradoxically, the radical journalist who had most persistently called for a popular insurrection against the monarchy and the Legislative Assembly during the preceding year was largely sidelined as 10 August approached: Jean-Paul Marat was busy evading the police and managed to put out only thirty numbers of his *Ami du Peuple* in the ninety days preceding the *journée*, and none between 22 July and 7 August.[95]

For that matter, even Antoine-François Lemaire did not get exactly the insurrection he had intended. Indeed, by 9 August 1792, just hours before it began, he had decided that the mere threat of an uprising would suffice to make the Legislative Assembly vote the removal of the king and he had tried to halt the insurrectionary process: "I invite my dear fellow-citizens to *foutre* a little water in their wine for a few days, and to be on their guard against those who want to get everything over with today." And his own account of the *journée* reflected distinctly mixed feelings on the part of a writer whose paper had seemingly incited the whole affair: "Liberty has triumphed today: it is horrible and beautiful all at the same time."[96] Reality never completely followed the wishes of the journalists: even when they seemed to be at their most effective, events stubbornly refused to conform precisely to printed instructions.

Striking as the parallels between Lemaire's calls to action and the events of 10 August are, they should not mislead us into assuming that a well-prepared press campaign automatically ensured results. The aftermath of the flight to Varennes showed that, while the press could label and define the king's action and no doubt heavily influence the public response to it, the journals were not the locus of sovereignty and, in the short run, they could not determine whether the monarch would be removed from office. On 15 July 1791 the majority in the National Assembly, swayed by the arguments of Antoine Barnave and other moderates, officially embraced the myth that the king had been abducted against his will and prepared to restore him to office. "The separation between the public will and the assembly was never so striking," the *Feuille villageoise* asserted, but like almost all the rest of the press, including even radical papers like Hébert's *Père Duchêne*, it accepted the deputies' decision.[97] The bloody repression of the republican demonstration on 17 July 1791 closed the issue, even for the radical papers that had openly favored the abolition of the monarchy until the Assembly's vote: Carra, who had called Louis a "traitor" ten days earlier, now set the example by blaming the trouble on 17 July on "paid agents of the aristocracy" and disassociating the demonstrators from the republican cause, whose press supporters were silenced for the time being.[98]

In the absence of a genuine insurrectionary movement and in view of the fact that the press itself was divided, with moderate titles like the *Gazette universelle* claiming that the Assembly's action had been "applauded by all good citizens,"[99] the newspapers that had branded the flight an act of treason and called for the logical reaction to it were powerless to translate their words into political realities. Nevertheless, the papers' acquiescence in the restoration of the king did not erase the impact of their reports on his flight: there can hardly be any doubt that the end result of the press's coverage was to increase public distrust of both the king and of the National Assembly. The memory of the weeks when the patriot newspapers had lambasted the king as "a cowardly deserter"[100] and the royalist journals had openly praised him for trying to drown the Revolution in blood was not erased when the National Assembly voted to restore Louis XVI to the throne. In August 1792 the Parisian crowd forced from power both the king and the assembly elected under the constitution drawn up by the National Assembly, accomplishing what the radical journalists of June 1791 had demanded.

The coup d'état of 18 fructidor V provided another demonstration of the limited power of the press in the face of determined governmental action. The legislative elections of April 1797 had been a clear defeat for the thermidorian republicans who had set up the Directorial constitution to keep themselves in power. From the moment the election returns had come in, the republican papers, a minority in the face of an ever-growing list of right-wing titles, had demanded strong action. "The royalists are chosen for public office, the patriots shamed and vilified, liberty in danger, the constitution on the point of being overturned," the former Girondin Louvet's *Sentinelle* warned, and the *Ami des Lois* urged the Directors to call on General Bonaparte for support, promising that "we will know how, if it becomes necessary, to make a campaign plan for the interior of France."[101] The five-man Directory, split into moderate and republican factions, wavered between following the program outlined in these republican papers and seeking a compromise with the more moderate right-wing deputies. The decision came at a meeting of the Directors on 30 messidor V, when Barras, the notoriously corrupt thermidorian who had been holding the balance between his moderate and republican colleagues, came down on the side of the latter.

No other supposedly confidential governmental decision of the revolutionary period was as thoroughly and accurately reported in the press as this one. A politically neutral paper, the *Républicain français*, gave the full details the next day, thanks to a leak from Lazare Carnot, one of Barras's moderate colleagues, and this article was extensively reprinted in the right-wing press. In the weeks that followed, the two dozen or more right-wing papers provided their readers with exquisitely detailed day-by-day coverage of the process by which Barras and the two other republican Directors prepared for a coup d'état to oust their two moderate colleagues and to purge the refractory legislative councils. The papers— acting in cooperation with the leading right-wing deputies in the legislative Councils—reported troop movements, they noted the public menaces of the plotters, they exhorted their legislative allies to stand firm, and they called on the voters who had chosen those deputies to prepare to resist. The ultra-royalist *Thé* proclaimed that "the Directory has raised the standard of rebellion" and demanded that Barras and his two accomplices be impeached and executed; Dupont de Nemours's moderate *Historien* warned against the dangers of the army's intervention on behalf of the government. [102] It was one of the most elaborate and broad-based press campaigns of the entire Revolution, even if its effect was marred when the more moderate right-wing papers began urging negotiations with a supposedly chastened Directory while the more overtly royalist titles continued to claim that "the worst evil would be to leave cruel and angry men in power . . . under suspicion of crime and therefore forced to defend themselves by despotic means."[103] The republican papers, for their part, barely bothered to disguise what was coming. The entire mechanism of the impending coup d'état was thus exposed to public view, but the course of events was entirely unaffected. When the three republican Directors, the *triumvirs*, called on General Augereau's troops to launch the long-awaited operation on 18 fructidor V (4 September 1797), it went off without a hitch: the side with the bigger battalions defeated the party with the bigger press corps.

The press's record as a force in shaping extraparliamentary events during the Revolution was thus a mixed one. Because the papers were never unanimous, events could at most correspond only to what a fraction of the journals had urged or forecast, and even an overwhelming advantage on the journalistic front could not offset a lack of popular support or the opposition's control of key instruments of power such as the bureaucracy or the army. The press could not propel the masses into action if they were not already inclined that way: Marat's furious campaign against the celebration of the festival of the Federation in July 1790 was a classic example of the futility of journalistic propaganda directed against the trend of popular opinion. From a narrowly instrumentalist point of view, the traditional conclusion that the press had only a secondary influence on the crises of the Revolution thus seems justified.

From a broader perspective, however, the press's influence in the production of revolutionary crises was greater than this traditional view suggests. When journalists did begin to publish scripts for a crisis, they may not have determined the actions that resulted, but they did produce an atmosphere of tension and expectation that made an explosion of some sort inevitable. Their texts were not merely barometers of the revolutionary weather, but powerful stimulants to the hopes and anxieties that were essential ingredients in all the revolutionary *journées*. Journalistic anticipations of violent confrontations created a reality that drove the revolutionary process forward: they were a powerful aspect of that "force of things" that Saint-Just saw governing the Revolution and overriding the conscious intentions of its actors.

Even if one accepts the consensus of most historians about the limited efficacy of press propaganda in determining the course of the Revolution, it is clear that the press was essential in constructing and transmitting the stories that constituted the "events" of the Revolution and in putting together that large, fast-paced drama that was the Revolution as a whole. Without its work of shaping and defining, the events of the revolutionary decade would not have been packaged as historically effective symbols. The way in which successive revolutionary regimes reshaped the press after each crisis is eloquent testimony to the importance of the press's role in labeling events. And the role of the press was essential in creating the situation in which a crisis could occur, even if not in dictating its outcome. The accelerated rhythm of newspaper publication after 1789 contributed powerfully to the sense of urgency, of crises crowding upon one another, that was a vital constituent of the revolutionary atmosphere. Just as the parliamentary life of the Revolution was inseparable from the medium that reported and commented upon it, the words of the press were an integral element of the dramatic climaxes that defined the Revolution.

Journalistic Language and Democratic Consciousness

Of the French Revolution's many contributions to modern political culture, none was more significant or more controversial than its summoning of the common people to play an active role in government. The doctrine of national sovereignty propagated by the abbé Sieyès and other revolutionary propagandists in 1789 made the people the ultimate basis of legitimate authority; the storming of the Bastille in July 1789 and the wave of peasant revolts known as the Great Fear that swept the countryside at the same time demonstrated that this power was not merely theoretical. But how were the people to be represented in the new political system? The experience of the Old Regime provided no precedents for mass involvement in the governing of the country. Above the local level of guilds and village or parish assemblies, the peasants, artisans, and workers who made up the overwhelming majority of the French population had never had a political voice.

The authorities had spoken to them on occasion through their curés, who read royal decrees and proclamations at services, but until the great national consultation of the Estates-General in 1789, the government of the Old Regime had never asked its ordinary subjects to express their opinion about politics, and it had certainly never proclaimed that their approval was necessary for its policies to be carried out.

Although they proclaimed themselves the representatives of the people in order to legitimate their revolutionary challenge to the king, the overwhelming majority of the deputies to the National Assembly of 1789 sincerely believed that the common people lacked the education and the experience necessary to participate directly in politics. The Assembly devised a voting system, incorporated in the Constitution of 1791, that imposed a property qualification for voting and a much stiffer requirement for eligibility to office. No institutions were proposed to make it possible for the government to know what the true will of the whole people was. The classical democracies of ancient Greece had been able to summon all their citizens to a single assembly, but all modern political theorists, including even Rousseau, the most outspoken advocate of the theory of popular sovereignty, had agreed that such a participatory system was impossible in a country as large as France.

With the overthrow of the monarchy and the Constitution of 1791 on 10 August 1792, the barriers to popular participation in politics were destroyed. The National Convention convened to draw up a new, republican constitution was elected by universal male suffrage; assemblies in the forty-eight sections of Paris and a network of revolutionary committees throughout the country gave the common people forums in which they could exercise their political rights. In practice, however, only a minority of the population was truly active in politics. In Paris, the most highly politicized part of the country, hardly more than ten percent of the adult male residents ever took part in their section assemblies; Albert Soboul, the historian of the *sans-culotte* movement, has concluded that its core amounted to a "tiny percentage" of activists out of an urban population of more than 600,000. [104] The great days of revolutionary action brought larger crowds into the streets, but even these occasions involved only a minority of the population: perhaps 20,000 to 30,000 active participants for the *journées* of 10 August 1792 and the protest of 1–4 prairial III in 1795. [105] The demands of everyday life and the unfamiliarity of their new role as citizens kept most of the population from taking an active part in politics.

For those activists who sincerely believed in the necessity of popular participation in politics, as well as for those more opportunistic figures who saw mass support as a way of gaining power for themselves, this absence of active and continuous participation from below posed a problem. How was the people's influence to be made effective if they would not or could not speak for themselves? The answer came from the radical journalists. Through their writings, they created a paper representation of the popular movement that had a coherent program, that was continuously active and ready to respond immediately to every challenge, and that served during crises as a means to mobilize the activists among the people.

Not all the journalists who claimed to write for the common people intended to convert their readers into an active political force. Many of them adopted a didactic approach that showed how little faith they had in their audience's political sophistication and how little comprehension they had of the lower classes' true concerns. The *Feuille villageoise*, for example, assumed that its audience needed explanations of terms as fundamental as *frontier*, and despite its avowed intention to cover rural issues, it gave minimal attention to the legislative enactments affecting peasants' lives and property. [106] But there were other writers, such as Marat and the several journalists who produced papers claiming to be the words of the mythical popular figure known as the Père Duchêne, who sought not merely to educate the people but also to spur them to action. These radical journalists made an effort to speak *to* the common people in ways they could understand, while at the same time creating a language that would demonstrate that they spoke *for* the ordinary people. In their writings they described and acted out ways in which the lower classes could exercise political power. As a result, they were pioneers in creating a democratic political culture—but also pioneers of the modern techniques for manipulating mass support for ends that were not always those of the people themselves.

Marat, the most controversial of the radical journalists, was also one of the first in the field. He launched his newspaper, best known under the title of *Ami du Peuple*, in September 1789. Friends and foes alike recognized that it was unique. At a moment when the prevailing political mood was still one of euphoria about the results of the Revolution, the *Ami du Peuple* warned of catastrophe; it urged suspicion of the heroes of the day who had led the movement against royal authority and privilege in the National Assembly. Marat's title, "The Friend of the People," indicated his intention to address the entire population, including the lower classes, but it also distanced him from his readers: he was their spokesman, their guide, willing to sacrifice himself, as he repeatedly proclaimed, to assure their salvation, but he was not simply one of them.

Marat's journalistic strategy was based on the assumption that the *peuple* did not know and could not articulate their own interests and that shock tactics were necessary to enlighten them. Each issue of his paper began with a brief *sommaire* or summary of contents on the first page, designed for the hawkers to cry aloud and phrased in the strongest terms in order to attract public attention. "Hair-raising conspiracy against the country and the friends of liberty—German regiments approach the capital—the National Assembly's alarming lack of concern—address to the people," ran a typical list of contents in 1790, the quietest year of the Revolution. [107] This sensationalism was not merely a tactic to sell papers; it was a deliberate device to get Marat's message across to the common people. "Everything is permitted to shake the people out of its deadly lethargy, recall to it the sense of its rights, inspire it with the courage to defend them; one cannot be a troublemaker, when one cries out only for the nation's interests," he wrote in justification of his methods.[108] When the patriot editor of the *Révolutions de Paris*, Elysée Loustallot, died in 1790, Marat issued a backhanded eulogy whose itemization of his colleague's shortcomings amounted to a portrait of what Marat saw himself as accomplishing. Loustallot, he remarked, never "knew the magical power of a horrendous scandal, he never struck terror in [the opposition's] breast . . . he never dragged them over the precipice. . . . Knowing nothing of the great forms of eloquence, of these burning arrows that start fires, carry all before them, overcome, he had none of the qualities of a statesman, capable of stopping a country ready to perish when it is on the edge of the abyss, and of inciting an ignorant, cowardly and corrupt people to break its tyrants' yoke."[109]

The democratic radicalism Marat sought to inculcate in his readers through his vivid language had taken shape long before 1789, and it took only a few months for him to sketch it out in the *Ami du Peuple*. From the outset, he proclaimed that government was a creation of the people and always dependent on its creators, who were "free to revoke it at any time."[110] But the exercise of power almost invariably fell into the hands of men who used it to mislead or enslave the rest of the population for their own benefit. "The people never sells itself, but it is almost always betrayed by its leaders."[111] Violent popular revolution offered a rare moment of opportunity to install a government under effective popular control, and the people had to be taught that its use of force was legitimate: "To want a nation that throws off the yoke to break its chains by legal methods, by gentle and peaceful means, is the height of insanity."[112] It was in the context of these appeals for the people to use their strength that Marat made his notorious estimate that "five to six hundred heads cut off at the time of the capture of the Bastille would have given us enduring peace, liberty and happiness," whereas by September 1790, "ten thousand heads cut off would hardly suffice to save the country,"[113] a quota that he raised on occasion as high as 500,000. Modern biographers have pointed out, convincingly, that these articles had little to do with the actual explosions of popular violence in 1789 and 1792, and that counterrevolutionary journals like the *Actes des Apôtres*, which regularly called for the hanging of most National Assembly deputies, were equally bloodthirsty. Like Marat's other characteristic recommendation, the appointment of a "tribune of the people" with temporary dictatorial powers, his regular call for executions distanced him even from the other patriot journalists and gave his opponents a handy stick with which to beat him. But both were concrete, easily understood proposals by which popular force could be converted into political power.

About the nature of the democratic state to be created by his longed-for insurrection and his dictatorial tribune Marat was quite vague. It seemed obvious to him that "a just, free and wise constitution can only be based on the equality of rights of all the citizens,"[114] and those rights had to include the power to participate actively in politics: "one is not a member of the state, when one cannot participate in the choice of the people's representatives, and one is an outsider to the country as soon as one is not allowed to take part in public affairs."[115] But beyond this, Marat never enumerated those rights he considered sacred. He frequently voiced his sympathy for the poor, "the only healthy part of the nation,"[116] but he was not a forerunner of socialism. He actually admired the self-made capitalists of eighteenth-century England and advised the National Assembly to make it easier for artisans to acquire their own businesses. "Give such a man a little bit of property, and let him some day reap the fruit of his labors."[117] On occasion, when he was utterly exasperated with the selfishness of the rich, he called on the poor to "divide up among yourselves the lands and the wealth of the criminals who have hidden their gold, to force you by means of hunger to submit to the yoke," but this appeal was made in the context of his usual argument that threats were needed to force the men in power to act in the people's interest. He urged the seizure of property because, he exclaimed, it was better to have the country "completely overturned from one end to the other" rather than to tolerate policies that were unjust to the poor; he did not suggest that property distribution would improve the economy.[118] Fundamentally, it was power and its exercise that interested Marat, not economic relations.

Marat made no attempt whatever to imitate the language of the common people; his vocabulary was severely classical and he resisted the neologisms and jargon coined by the Revolution. His normal tone was one of exasperated indignation as he surveyed a political scene of utter depravity and corruption. Vague in his depiction of the ideal polity he hoped to see created, he was excruciatingly detailed in his evocation of the evils of the world around him. He had an inexhaustible store of derogatory epithets: *scélérat, lâche, traître, infâme, atroce, affreux, funeste, criminel, fripon,*[119] and many more. Typically, he coupled every derogatory noun with at least one and often several intensifying adjectives. A decree against the recall of legislative deputies was "unfair, odious, revolting, oppressive, tyrannical."[120] Lawyers were untrustworthy because their profession taught them "to split hairs, to obscure things, to twist and denature them by means of subtleties and tricks."[121] As he strung together lists of evildoers and their execrable acts, his sentences grew to monstrous length, sometimes running for a full page as he worked his way through a denunciation of "the instruments of chicanery . . . the valets of the runaway princes . . . the skinflints, the royal pensionaries, the arrant aristocrats, the magistrates, the valets of the court, the public spies . . . the men ennobled for money, and sold out to the ministry, creatures of the prince, instruments of despotism, cowardly workers of iniquity" and other enemies of the Revolution.[122]

Marat's major stylistic model was the Bible.[123] Several times a week, Marat would conclude his issue with an "Address to the Citizenry" or some other message conceived in the spirit of the Old Testament prophets: "Blind and cowardly citizens, can you still doubt that Louis XVI, whom you stupidly proclaimed the *restorer of your liberty*, is the head of the conspirators against the country . . . ?" He enumerated the disasters that would fall upon his readers if they failed to heed his words: "Torn from your homes, you will fall under the swords of your executioners, after having seen your wives and your children disembowelled, your houses and your daughters will be the prey of a brutal soldiery, all those among you who took up arms for the country will have your throats slit, your faithful defenders will perish in the cruelest torments, and all those not put to death will be led away in chains."[124] And as his ultimate argument Marat reminded his audience that he would be "the first victim slaughtered if you weaken."[125]

Marat was not the only journalist of the revolutionary period to recognize that language and imagery drawn from religious sources would make his message easily comprehensible for a wide audience. His paper flourished alongside the counterrevolutionary *Actes des Apôtres*, whose title was biblical and whose pages were filled with parodies of the Catholic liturgy, and Hébert, before turning to the *Père Duchêne*, had begun his career as the author of a series of satires against the counterrevolutionary abbé Maury, in the form of fictitious *Sermons preached in the assembly of the Enragés*.[126] But whereas these rivals were children of the Voltairean Enlightenment, whose satirical use of religious formulas mocked their political enemies and the Christian religion simultaneously and conveyed the message that nothing in the revolutionary world was sacred, Marat borrowed from the Scriptures for serious purposes. Addressing the ordinary people of France in language they had previously heard on the most solemn occasions, he conveyed to his audience the sense that they were called upon to play a leading part in a great drama of redemption.

Like the Christian forerunners whose very words he sometimes appropriated, Marat succeeded if not in persuading at least in creating a scandal that could not be ignored. The numerous letters he selected for publication in the paper show that the *Ami du Peuple*

reached all sectors of the urban population,[127] although the sales
of his paper were less than those of many other titles. The degree
of attention he succeeded in drawing to himself and his paper even
as early as 1790, long before a recognizable popular movement
had taken shape in the streets, was eloquent testimony to the
power of journalistic words in creating political realities. But for
all his success in dramatizing the power of the people, Marat
remained apart from those to and for whom he spoke. His exalted
tone was certainly not the language of the people; his program of
insurrection and dictatorship was not a practical way for ordinary
citizens to participate in everyday politics. Marat put the issue of
the people's role in the center of revolutionary debate, but he left it
to other journalists to elaborate an image of the democratic citizen
that could truly serve as a model for such participation.

Marat's journal employed the resources of a religious rhetoric
that was the common property of the cultured and the uneducated
in eighteenth-century France, but there were other ways for journalists to talk to and speak for the ordinary people. For decades
before the Revolution, some writers and dramatists had produced
pamphlets and skits in a language that purported to represent the
speech of the common people. During the Revolution, journalists
put this tradition to political use. By far the best known and most
celebrated of these "popular" newspapers was the *Père Duchêne*
written by Jacques-René Hébert, who parlayed his journalistic
ability into a career in Parisian municipal politics and acquired by
1793 enough of a following to threaten the power of the Montagnard leaders of the Convention. Hébert's *Père Duchêne* was the
longest-lasting and the most influential publication of its kind,
but unlike Marat's *Ami du Peuple*, it was less the expression of its
author's individual personality than the successful adaptation of a
generic formula employed by a dozen or more writers. The *Pères
Duchêne* and their close relatives, the journals attributed to *Mère
Duchêne*, to the *Père Duchêne*'s comrade the old sailor Jean Bart, and
to other friends and relations, were a collective product not of the
Parisian *sans-culottes* themselves but of journalists who sought a

formula for addressing and representing the poorly educated common men and women of the revolutionary decade. They were not limited to Paris: original versions of the *Père Duchêne* were published in Rouen, Lyon, and the rural department of the Corrèze, and a "nephew of Père Duchêne" appeared in the columns of the Besançon *Vedette*. One of the most original aspects of the press of the Revolution, these pamphlet-journals faithfully reflected the dilemma of educated elites trying to promote the interests of or mobilize support among the people while recognizing that the majority of the French population could not articulate its own political goals directly.

The *Père Duchêne* formula for political journalism was invented at the very beginning of the revolutionary decade. The *Père Duchêne* enjoyed his greatest moments in the stormy years from late 1790 to early 1794, but he left the scene for good only with Napoleon's coup d'état. The first pamphlets reporting the words of this hard-drinking, hard-swearing stock character taken from the boulevard theaters of late eighteenth-century Paris appeared even before the opening of the Estates-General in 1789, at about the time that the popular playwright Louis-Archambault Dorvigny was enjoying a hit with his *The Père Duchesne, or the Bad Habit*. Dorvigny's "gruff, ill-mannered, warm-hearted stove setter" offended the more refined characters in the play with his liberal usage of the two common oaths *bougre* (bugger) and *foutre* (a vulgar term for sexual intercourse, which like similar expressions in modern English, conveyed a variety of other meanings as well), but he finally won them over with his kindness and honesty.[128]

The pamphleteers faithfully reproduced these characteristics when they made the Père Duchêne into a vehicle for political discourse. Antoine-François Lemaire, the journalist who exploited the formula most indefatigably during the Revolution—he produced nearly fifty percent more *Père Duchêne* pamphlets than Hébert did—was among the first to put on the persona, in a pamphlet entitled *Les Vitres cassées par le véritable Père Duchêne, député aux Etats-généraux*. Even at this date, many of the basic

Je suis le véritable père Duchesne, foutre.

LA CONFESSION

DU

PERE DUCHESNE

A L'ABBÉ MAURI,

ET CELLE DE L'ABBÉ MAURI
AU PERE DUCHESNE.

SA CONVERSION A LA CONSTITUTION, SON
ACCEPTATION D'UN VICARIAT DE
VILLAGE, SON DÉPART AVEC DES LETTRES
DE RECOMMENDATION DU PERE DU-
CHESNE.

L'ABBÉ MAURI, homme très charitable
pour le salut de son prochain, ayant appris que
le père Duchesne étoit dangéreusement malade,

Je suis le véritable Père Duchêne ci-devant
rue du vieux colombier n°. 20 actuellement
rue du Four St. Germain n°. 7.

LES CRIS

DU

PERE DUCHÈNE

Aux Parisiens, sur les dangers de la patrie et sur le grand coup de poupie qui
s'approche. Ses Instances de se mettre en
défense parts, et de vite faire cinquante
mille piques. Nouvelles du traitre Bouillé,
et grands masques découverts.

Sortez de votre stupeur, aveugles Parisiens, et rompez le rocher qui obstrue vos

R. F. LEBOIS.

LE PÈRE DUCHÉNE.

Ah !.... Ah !... Ah !.... Citoyens, le voilà !...
le voilà !... le père Duchesne ....— Il est
ressuscité... — Comme il est bougrement en
colère, contre tous ces coquins qui ont vendus
le peuple, qui l'ont musclé, et qui l'ont bail-
loné depuis deux ans. — Il faut le voir,
citoyens, comme il arrange Merlin-17-Sep-
tembre, Rewbell-Rapinat-Voleur-Forfait-
Grugeon, et ce scélérat, ce monstre de Sché-
rer, qui fait couler le sang de ces braves
bougres aux frontières. — Ah !.... comme il
est furieux contre ces jean-foutres de Di-
recteurs, qui ont escamoté ce pauvre Buo-
naparte à la République, parce qu'ils avoient
peur de lui.

Foutre !....me voilà enfin débaillonné, mille
num d'un tonnerre ; j'ai tant de choses à dire ; elles

Three versions of the *Père Duchêne*: An early number from
Hébert's edition (top left), an example of the abbé Jumel's edition
(lower left), and a copy of R. F.
Lebois's revival from 1799 (top
right). The Jumel edition includes a version of the "Memento
Mori" woodblock that was subsequently adopted by Hébert and
several other rivals and became
the Revolution's most widely circulated image of a *sans-culotte*.
The illustration in Lebois's version was changed for each issue,
apparently making it the first
newspaper ever published with
an editorial cartoon directly inte-
grated with the text. Source: The
Newberry Library, Chicago.

features of the Père Duchêne's personality were already evident, although in 1789 his favorite oath came out as "f—" rather than the fully spelled out *foutre* that was the most obvious characteristic of his speech later in the Revolution. Lemaire's proto-Duchêne already gave what would become the genre's standard justification for the use of vulgarity: he told readers to "put up with my declamation, this vigorous and resounding tone, and, under this rough covering, recognize the truth that inspires me." Lemaire's Duchêne, like all later incarnations, was on familiar terms with France's top leaders, up to and including the king. "If the King is there," he proclaimed, "I'll explain myself with even more assurance. I'll open my heart to him. . . . Anyhow he knows me well." This graphic depiction of a man of the people dealing with his sovereign on a basis of equality was more powerful than dozens of high-flown revolutionary speeches on the dignity of the citizen.

Lemaire's early version of the *Père Duchêne* genre included another feature that would become almost unavoidable in all subsequent embodiments: an indignant disavowal of a rival pamphlet using the same character. Nothing more clearly demonstrated the collective nature of the process by which the Duchêne image was built up than these ritualized protests against "false Duchênes," the "bunch of *bougres* who take it into their heads to use my name to write smut and lies,"[129] that every writer who employed the character lodged against his rivals. The *Père Duchêne* authors themselves understood the way in which this competition blurred and diffused the impact of their papers, particularly among their less-educated readers, so that it was to the genre as a whole and not to any particular version that the audience reacted. Because of the many competing editions, one writer lamented, the genre suffered from "a much too dangerous inconvenience: the Père Duchesne has a new issue, those who can't read say, and the number of those in this class may be a third of the population of the city. This causes murmurs and discord: everyone gives his opinion, preaches, those with evil intentions triumph, error and ignorance assure them of followers."[130] Like the competition in the press in general, the conflict among *Père Duchênes* of rival persuasions exposed the lack of a revolutionary consensus. Only when the Montagnards and the *sans-culotte* movement eliminated their rivals in the summer of 1793 was Hébert able to impose his edition, heavily subsidized by the government, as the sole *Père Duchêne*. Needless to say, his monopoly was broken with his death, and the doughty *marchand des fourneaux* was once again available for anyone to use during the postthermidorian period.

Although Lemaire's pamphlet shows that the character of Père Duchêne was already well delineated in the early months of 1789, the isolated pamphlets of this sort did not grow into regular series until 1790, and Jean Bart, not the Père Duchêne, was the leading character in the first of them, which appeared in February 1790 and soon inspired imitators.[131] In contrast to the daily and weekly papers that had begun to appear in mid-1789 and which sought to sell subscriptions for three months to a year at a time, the publishers of these pamphlet series issued individual numbers intended for separate sale at the price of two sous. The pamphlets commented on the affairs of the day, but they were normally undated and written in such a way that they did not risk being immediately rendered obsolete by the next day's events. If a particular issue did well, it could quickly be reprinted. Jean Bart had many of the same characteristics as the Père Duchêne, including the habit of "letting drop a *foutre* here and there . . . to make my style flow better,"[132] and the ritual denunciation of competitors.

In the Jean Bart series that began in April 1790 under the title of *Je m'en fouts*, the Père Duchêne appeared regularly in the subordinate role of an "old comrade" of the title character. Like the popular characters in some weekly American television comedies, he was eventually "spun off" into a pamphlet series of his own. Lemaire, who had used the character in 1789, began to employ him on a regular basis in his *Lettres bougrement patriotiques du véritable Père Duchêne* at the beginning of September 1790. In a matter of weeks it became clear that the Père Duchêne had an appeal that his comrade the old sea salt could not match. Several Paris publishers, on the look-out for a formula that would enable them to tap a new, more popular market and perhaps inspired by politicians increasingly anxious to influence the opinions of the lower classes, sought out journalists who could imitate Lemaire. Hébert, who may have written several earlier *Père Duchêne* pamphlets and who had already produced a similar series of brochures for one publisher, [133] was one of several who joined Lemaire in exploiting the character, and throughout 1791 readers had a choice of up to a half a dozen *Père Duchêne* pamphlet series.

This fierce competition for the *Père Duchêne* market forced publishers and editors to desperate expedients to differentiate their products without giving up their claim to the central character. The most important of these was the use of some sort of pictorial element on the front or back page, on the theory that this would distinguish their paper from imitations. Eventually the abbé Jumel, Hébert, and several other *Père Duchêne* journalists adopted a half-page woodcut showing the mustachioed, pipe-smoking Père Duchêne brandishing a hatchet, with his furnace, his musket, and his winebottle in one corner and a kneeling priest with the enigmatic motto "Memento Mori" ("Remember you must die") in the other. Reproduced three times a week on the front page of the paper, this was undoubtedly the period's most widely circulated visual image of the typical *sans-culotte*; its crude style and its depiction of a powerful masculine figure in contemporary dress contrasted sharply with the classically proportioned, female allegorical figures the deputies of the Convention usually chose as symbols of the Republic and its values. [134]

Because the woodcuts of the Père Duchêne in the rival versions of the paper were so much alike, they hardly served their ostensible purpose of enabling purchasers to spot the "true" *Père Duchêne*. But this pictorial element did serve to differentiate these pamphlets as a genre from the rest of the revolutionary press. Reminiscent of the crude illustrations in the popular booklets of the prerevolutionary *Bibliothèque bleue*, the woodcut images of the Père

Duchêne gave the pamphlets the appearance of literature for the common people, as did the worn type and the typographical errors that were even more common in these pamphlets than in the general run of the revolutionary press. Paris printers were perfectly capable of producing much more neatly printed pamphlets: indeed, Hébert's printer Tremblay also put out an entirely normal-looking *Journal du Soir*. The physical appearance of the *Père Duchêne* pamphlets—with the important exception of Lemaire's version—was a deliberate contrivance to make them look like "popular literature."

The deliberate "roughing up" of the *Père Duchêne* pamphlet series served two purposes that reflect the ambiguous status of this genre of political literature. In the first place, the various versions of the *Père Duchêne* were all intended to reach an audience that extended further down the social scale than the purchasers of the regular press, and the physical appearance of the *Père Duchêne* pamphlets made them look familiar to this class of purchasers. But these pamphlets were also crudely printed and made use of expressions meant to be taken as "popular" so that readers of all social classes would *interpret* them as expressions of the point of view of the ordinary people, the *sans-culottes*, regardless of their actual authorship. Like Marat's *Ami du Peuple*, the *Père Duchêne* papers were intended to substitute for and represent the voice of the people.

In reality, however, the journalistic *Pères Duchêne* of the 1790s remained what their boulevard-theater progenitors had been— artificial creations, sophisticated enough to comment ironically on their own artifices, as in one pamphlet in which Jean Bart praised himself and the Père Duchêne because they did not hide behind the veil of anonymity in their writings.[135] Intended to reach the people in their own language, these pamphlets were nevertheless not genuine products of popular culture; indeed, the element of parody in many of them linked them to the literature of the educated and gave them an audience that transcended class boundaries. Hébert, the most successful employer of the *Père*

Duchêne disguise, may have been able to choose effective themes because he had lived the life of a down-and-outer in prerevolutionary Paris, but he was the son of a well-to-do bourgeois father and a mother whose families had pretentions of nobility, and he had had ample educational experiences in his youth. [136] Lemaire too was, to judge by his writing, a well-educated professional writer; Jumel, another early *Père Duchêne*, had been a member of the prerevolutionary clergy.

As for the aristocratic or bourgeois purchaser who took up a *Père Duchêne* pamphlet to find out what the common folk thought, he too was in for a deception. For one thing, the various journals of this type did not express the same ideas. The *Père Duchêne* formula was as easily adapted to different political purposes as any other type of journalism; it was used at one time or another to express almost every political opinion. Although the majority of the *Pères Duchêne* were supportive of the Revolution, at least one version supported the king as the necessary mediator between "Messieurs the aristocrats and Messieurs the demagogues," and several of the *Mères Duchêne* were more moderate if not, indeed, frankly counter-revolutionary. [137] Hébert's early numbers were considerably less radical than much of the "educated" press; he supported Lafayette at a time when Marat had already proclaimed him the people's leading enemy and made himself out to be a bosom friend of Mirabeau at a time when much of the revolutionary left had turned against him. [138]

The *Père Duchêne* formula was thus not automatically associated with political radicalism, but it was associated with a certain kind of journalism in which political ideas were mixed with entertainment. Each *Père Duchêne* pamphlet was a self-contained publication, telling a little story in which the title character played the leading role, similar to the skits or *parades* that were a regular feature of the popular boulevard theaters. [139] The Père Duchêne might recount his visit to some important political figure: the king, the queen, Mirabeau, Lafayette, Marat. He might react to some recent event with one of his "grandes colères" or "grandes joies," formulas employed not only by Hébert but also by a number of his rivals. Or he might be in a mood to instruct his readers by delivering some "bon avis," a formula of which Hébert was particularly fond.

A typical *parade* from the abbé Jumel's series recounted the adventure of "the Père Duchêne in the King's chapel." The title character had taken it into his head to sneak into the mass at the palace. For a while he held his peace and merely observed "Toinette la blonde" (Marie Antoinette) and the two castrati singing in the choir, who inspired him to affirm his masculinity with the reflection that "Père Duchêne would rather have the voice of an ass and everything that goes with it rather than the throat of a nightingale and no longer be a man alongside his wife." But finally Père Duchêne could not contain his anger at the "calotin aristocrate" who was celebrating the mass. "I could not sit still any longer. . . . When the Père Duchêne takes a hand in something, he really does the job; I shoved the bugger back to the foot of the altar, and I said to him, 'Priest of Satan, tonsured dog, by the horns of Moses who delivered his nation from the aristocrats of Egypt, I order you on behalf of the patriots to say an *Oremus* for the nation.' "[140] The earthiness, the rough humor, and the story line in which the man of the people triumphed over or showed himself wiser and more patriotic than his social superiors were all constants of the genre. Where radical journalists like Brissot and Marat argued in abstract terms that the common people ought to rule, the *Père Duchêne* pamphlets recounted the triumphs (imaginary, to be sure) of democracy in action.

These amusing but serious vignettes were written in a language very different from that of the rest of the press, but one which was not really the language of the common people, either.[141] The best-known linguistic characteristic of the genre was the insertion into otherwise normal sentences of the two common oaths *foutre* and *bougre* at regular intervals. This deliberate use of vulgarity was meant to set the *Père Duchêne* genre apart from the majority of the press during the Revolution. Like Marat's calls for blood, these swearwords drew attention to the papers that printed them. "Delicate ears are shocked, they say, by the frankness of my expressions!" exclaimed one Père Duchêne. "Very well, those who condemn me don't have to read my sheets, or they can do with them what I do with so many others, when I have the need"—and this from a Père Duchêne whose political message was that the people owed complete obedience to the decrees of the National Assembly.[142] Only the satirical royalist journals like the *Actes des Apôtres* were equally obscene, and their dirty words, often incorporated in elegant verse, had a different function: they were intended to denigrate and outrage their targets, whereas the swearwords in the *Pères Duchêne* were used to give the illusion that they reflected the speech of the common people. Ironically, the pornographic royalist propaganda even inspired one *Père Duchêne* pamphlet urging *pères de famille* to protect their wives and children from obscene works.[143]

But the linguistic peculiarities of the *Père Duchêne* genre went beyond the constant employment of these two words. In all the pamphlet series, the title character expressed himself in high-flown bombast, full of colorful images. Jumel's Père Duchêne was given to imaginative oaths and ejaculations: "Oh, a thousand million elephants' trunks!" "A double million destroyed Bastilles!" "I swear to you on the wombs of a thousand pregnant women." Hébert's character was the most linguistically inventive: he had an entire vocabulary, most of which defies exact translation, that he tried to pass off as the slang of the common people but that in many cases seems to have been his own invention. He was particularly rich in imagery describing the work of the guillotine. The dread machine was the "vis à vis of Master Samson [the executioner]," and those who fell under it suffered a "raccourcissement" (shortening) or played "à la main chaude" (a children's game whose name Hébert adapted to mean execution).[144] The language of the *Pères Duchêne* has often been linked to the *poissard* tradition of satirical plays and pamphlets written in what was supposedly a rendition of the lower classes' speech, but in fact these journals eschewed the most common features of the *poissard* genre, such as phonetic spelling and the usage of the first-person singular pronoun with a plural verb form ("je parlons"), which stamped the *poissard* characters, even when they got the better of their social superiors, as uneducated.[145] The Pères Duchêne spoke a more dignified language, representing a common people who were in command of words and could make them serve their own purposes. They continued a prerevolutionary tradition of burlesque pamphleteering, in which profound truths were put in the mouths of characters from the lower classes, but they gave it a new, overtly political significance.[146]

Jacques-René Hébert was the most successful manipulator of the Père Duchêne formula, and the combination of his journalistic skill and his political importance eventually allowed him to capture the character for himself to the point where he became identified with his fictitious creation, just as Marat had made himself into the *Ami du Peuple*. The other early *Père Duchêne* pamphlet series died off by the end of 1791 or early 1792, as did the Jean Barts and the Mères Duchêne; Lemaire continued to use the name in his *Trompette du Père Duchêne*, but his publication was truly a "false *Duchêne*" in that he had never really followed the rules of the genre by building up the persona of his title character or writing in a burlesque fashion. This did not prevent him from being highly successful and influential. Until after 10 August 1792 Lemaire's paper seems to have been better known than Hébert's: he was one of the early campaigners for the abolition of the formal form of address *vous*, which became one of the most striking characteristics of the Revolution's radical phase,[147] and it was his *Père Duchêne* that inspired such provincial imitators as Besançon's "nephew of Père Duchêne." But he abandoned the genre altogether in June 1793, and during the most dramatic year of the Revolution, Hébert held the field alone, until his death returned the Père Duchêne to the public domain.

Hébert's success was due to his colorful writing, his sincere devotion to the rules of the genre, and his political views. He went farther than any of his rivals in building up the persona of his character, with his mustaches, his pipe, and his wife Jacqueline. For Hébert's rivals, particularly for Lemaire, the *Père Duchêne* machinery was often an evident hindrance to the delivery of a straightforward political harangue: Hébert never seemed to resent the necessity of accommodating himself to the requirements of his formula. After several years of grinding out three pamphlets a week, his work had become highly routinized: number after number followed the pattern of an opening "grande colère" denouncing some opponent, followed by a "grande joie," frequently occasioned by an execution, the whole topped off by some "bon avis aux braves Sans-culottes" apropos of some current political issue. But this predictability does not seem to have diminished Hébert's popularity. As in modern-day comic strips or television situation comedies, it was probably part of the *Père Duchêne's* appeal: the Père Duchêne could be counted on to make sense of the constantly changing revolutionary scene by putting its leading actors into familiar categories.

The political content of the *Père Duchêne* was considerably less original than its journalistic form. Hébert had started out as something of a moderate; in late 1790 he had been considerably less radical than some of his rivals, such as Jumel, who followed Marat closely and denounced Hébert's version as "aristocratic and dangerous."[148] By 1791, however, Hébert had swung considerably to the left, announcing that France's external enemies were less dangerous than the moderate factions at home. From attacking the constitutional-monarchist Feuillants in 1791, he passed to the campaign against the Girondins in 1792 and 1793. The Girondins revealed their estimate of the *Père Duchêne's* importance when they had Hébert arrested on 24 May 1793; he had his revenge a week later when the *sans-culotte* militia of the sections compelled the ouster of the leading Girondin deputies from the Convention and provided the occasion for a "grande joie . . . about the great revolution which just laid low the infamous clique of Brissotins and Girondins, who are going to *siffler la linotte* [Hébertese for imprisonment]."[149] And the silencing of their newspapers set the stage for the greatest blossoming of his own.

With the competition virtually silenced—Lemaire's *Trompette du Père Duchêne* ceased publication in June 1793 and Marat was assassinated in July—Hébert suddenly stood alone as the last of the great journalistic tribunes of the Revolution. Furthermore, the Montagnard-dominated government generously subsidized Hébert's publication. The army minister, Jean-Baptiste Bouchotte, was one of Hébert's supporters, and he ordered 4,000 copies of each issue for the troops; press runs of some particularly popular numbers reached 60,000–80,000 during this period.[150] It was in the second half of 1793 and the first months of 1794 that Hébert reached the peak of his influence. His paper contributed powerfully to the *sans-culotte journée* of 5 September 1793, which compelled a reluctant Convention to vote a general maximum on prices, to create the *armée revolutionnaire* to enforce it, and to step up the terror against opponents of the Revolution.[151] Hébert used this opportunity to propagate a doctrine compounded of populist appeals to the *sans-culottes*, vicious attacks on the fallen enemies of the Revolution, and a barely disguised bid for power in his own right. The Père Duchêne, who had always been the fictional embodiment of the common people, now claimed to be the advocate of a government that would devote itself to their interests. He praised the Montagnard constitution rushed through the Convention in late June 1793, assuring the public that "the *sans-culottes* will be satisfied with it, because this constitution, entirely based on liberty and equality, will make them independent of the rich and assure them work and enough to live on."[152] He supported the anticlerical campaign, the abolition of slavery, and a number of other measures taken by the Convention.[153] Indeed, one modern scholar has concluded that Hébert was nothing more than a clever propagandist for the Montagnards and that his populist language concealed a "bourgeois conception of democracy."[154]

As in the case of Marat, however, Hébert's positive program

paled in comparison with his vindictiveness toward those he considered the enemies of the Revolution. In contrast to Marat, whose most violent attacks were directed against targets who were still in power and who thus demonstrated some genuine courage, Hébert saved his most powerful thrusts for those victims who had just suffered their *raccourcissement*. He celebrated "the greatest of all the joys of Père Duchesne, after having seen with his own eyes the head of Veto female [Marie-Antoinette] separated from her *foutu* crane's neck," and he was equally nasty to the executed Girondin deputies, accusing them of cowardice in the presence of the guillotine.[155] Revolutionary France had introduced the guillotine as a humanitarian reform to carry out executions with a minimum of suffering, and the press of the Revolution tended to give antiseptic descriptions of the all-too-numerous public executions of 1793–94. Hébert put back into his descriptions of its victims the humiliation and cruelty that had been the lot of those put to death under the Old Regime. He was more closely in tune with the sentiments of the common people, who flocked to witness the guillotine in action, than were most of his fellow journalists. But this constant pandering to the blood lust of at least a sector of the *sans-culotterie* was not without its risks: Hébert's own execution was said to have drawn the greatest crowd ever to witness such a spectacle.[156]

Hébert ended up under the guillotine himself because he had employed his *Père Duchêne* in a campaign that menaced the Committee of Public Safety. In the wake of Marat's assassination, he claimed the martyred journalist's mantle and made a Marat-style call for the execution of up to three hundred unidentified "perfidious deputies of the people" in the Convention.[157] His paper called for the election of a new assembly to replace the Convention, and his *bon avis* to the *sans-culottes* was to "compose it this time only of real republicans." For good measure, he added that "the counterrevolution will be made in less than a month, if the Committee of Public Safety is left organized the way it is today."[158] He used the shortage of bread in the fall of 1793 as a weapon to incite the people against the government and generally endorsed the campaign of the so-called *enragés* against the Montagnard leaders until it became clear that Robespierre and his supporters were prepared to use force against these enemies on the left. The *Père Duchêne* thus espoused the interests of the common people of Paris—like every other paper published under this title during the Revolution, Hébert's was resolutely urban in its outlook—but it was also the overt tool of one man's political ambitions.

At the very end of 1793 and in early 1794, the *Père Duchêne* abandoned this campaign of agitation against the revolutionary government and sought to beat a retreat. A tone of worldweariness and discouragement invaded the discourse of the once indomitable *marchand des fourneaux*. He imagined that readers asked him, "What are you serving up for us with your old reflections that are as worn out as the reddish stubble that covers your peeling skull? Is someone greasing your palm to torment the *sans-culottes* and to terrify them with your sinister predictions?" And he expressed his dismay at observing "that the big fish always want to eat the little ones . . . and that three-quarters and a half of the two-legged animals think only of their own interest, and forget that of the fatherland."[159] On occasion, Hébert expressed the sense that he was no longer in direct contact with the *sans-culottes*. In one issue he had his character make a reference to Roman history and then pull himself up short for thus distancing himself from ordinary readers: "What a savant you are, they'll say to me, soon you'll be talking like a book. I agree, *foutre*, that I'm getting a little bit away from my furnaces."[160] Hébert's reputation suffered from Camille Desmoulins's revelations of the government subsidies his paper had received, and police reports show a certain disenchantment with his repetitious campaigns.[161] By March 1794 the Committee of Public Safety felt secure in moving against this weakened rival; the *Père Duchêne* and several of his political allies were arrested, given a show trial, and sent to the guillotine.

The execution of the Père Duchêne put an abrupt end to the

cocky, self-confident spokesman for the *sans-culottes*. The postthermidorian revivals of the *Père Duchêne* used the same *mise en scène* but they were never able to restore the spirit of the earlier versions. The disappearance of Hébert's paper truly signalled the end of the radical democratic phase of the Revolution. The triumphant Montagnard leaders denounced the entire genre of writing Hébert had represented. An article in the *Journal de la Montagne* condemned the use of popular language in the press as a holdover from the Old Regime, which "made a separate category of a more vulgar class of people, who spoke a more vulgar language, because the separating out of the more polished and cultivated people had left them in that condition. . . . Today, when equality has brought all men together, language should be the same for all."[162]

In their zeal to eliminate all visible evidence of divisions within the people, the victorious Montagnards sought to impose an abstract, universal public language and to do away with the distinctive style the *Père Duchêne* represented. Even though he was not himself *peuple*—like Robespierre, Hébert dressed elegantly at a time when many bourgeois revolutionaries had adopted the rough clothes of the *sans-culottes*—Hébert and the other *Père Duchêne* journalists had created an effective journalistic representation of the common people's intervention in politics. In the place of Marat's anonymous *peuple* expressing itself most effectively in the form of a violent mob, the *Père Duchêne* papers showed a flesh-and-blood individual attending section meetings, exchanging views with the nation's leaders, taking up arms, carrying out measures such as dechristianization, and exemplifying democratic citizenship. At a time when the Convention was employing classically trained artists to depict the people to itself in the form of a figure of Hercules,[163] an image drawn from the culture of the elite, the *Père Duchêne* authors offered a down-to-earth picture of the common man. Lusty, obscene, full of sound common sense, Père Duchêne was part of the real world of the 1790s, unlike Jacques-Louis David's Hercules.

In fact, the *Père Duchêne* formula gained such wide acceptance as the journalistic symbol of popular politics that even those who plotted Hébert's downfall had to adopt his techniques: they sponsored papers like Armand-Benoît-Joseph Guffroy's *Rougyff* to denounce him and Joseph Dusaulchoy's *Sappeur Sans-culotte* to try to capture his audience after his arrest.[164] In 1797, when the eminently bourgeois republicans of the Directory needed to appeal for popular support against the counterrevolutionary menace, they could think of nothing better than to revive the Père Duchêne, even if he was now forced to do violence to himself by delivering "bon avis" to the effect that the people should avoid creating "tumultuous scenes" and put its trust in "the paternal intentions of the government."[165]

The success of the Père Duchêne reflected his genuine roots in French popular culture. He drew not only on the figures of the prerevolutionary boulevard theaters, but also on a long tradition of cagy peasants and artisans who showed up their betters.[166] With his association with furnaces and fire and his uncanny ability to appear anywhere in the world and to assume any disguise, the Père Duchêne also amply justified his claim to be regarded as a "bon diable." In the *Père Duchêne* pamphlets, these borrowings from traditions of popular fantasy were mixed with realistic details from everyday life to create a convincing image of the common man who was active and successful in the political sphere. Unlike the high-flown speeches of Robespierre and Saint-Just, these small, crudely printed pamphlets succeeded in putting the revolutionary gospel into language the whole population could understand and appreciate and in bringing the *peuple* onto the political stage in a vivid, concrete way.

Historians have invested much effort into determining how widely read the *Ami du Peuple* and the *Père Duchêne* were and how closely they reflected the actual views of revolutionary France's common people. Neither of these questions can ever be answered precisely. There is abundant evidence that these papers did have a real popular following, but it is certain that there were never enough copies of any of them in circulation to have reached more than a minority of the population. It is clear that many of their readers were not from the lower classes, and it is also clear that there were always substantial groups among the lower classes, such as the counterrevolutionary peasants of the Vendée, who never identified themselves with Marat's or Hébert's radicalism. What is beyond question, however, is that this press forced the issue of democracy into the center of the revolutionary debate. The *sans-culottes* intervened in politics only episodically, in the great revolutionary journées, but the radical journalists who claimed to speak for them were heard every day. The liberal leaders of the National Assembly who tried to silence the *Ami du Peuple* in 1790 and 1791 and the Montagnard leaders who made the Père Duchêne the star of a show trial in 1794 both knew that they were at war with a newspaper as much as with a tangible social movement.

Marat and Hébert both demonstrated the indispensable role of words in creating a democratic consciousness. Their articles roused the people to an awareness of its power and its possibilities and roused the dominant elites to a recognition of the need to respond effectively to his popular force. At the same time, however, the journalists dramatized the dangers inherent in this democratic experiment. The violence of the Revolution was not the result of Hébert's or Marat's journalism, but both writers exploited and exaggerated it as a means of making their point. The reactions that these two very different forms of democratic journalism evoked, culminating in the violent deaths of both Marat and Hébert, demonstrated the power of these writers' words.

4. THE PRESS AND THE REVOLUTION

The End of the Revolutionary Press System

ALTHOUGH HUNDREDS OF ORATORS, STARTING IN 1789, saluted freedom of the press as one of the main accomplishments of the revolutionary movement, there was never a real consensus in favor of genuine freedom for political journalism in France. From the start of the Revolution, even those who called for the end of censorship voiced fears that unrestricted newspapers could undermine the construction of a stable political order. In his defense of press freedom in June 1789, Brissot explicitly admitted that it was necessary to have protections against "licence" and "libels"; he merely insisted that they be fixed laws rather than the arbitrary actions of the government. He specifically endorsed the English jurist William Blackstone's interpretation of freedom of the press as freedom from prior restraint on publishing, but not freedom from subsequent prosecution, and he insisted that the Estates-General should have the same power as the British Parliament to punish writers for breach of privilege, without their having the right of a jury trial.[1]

Article 11 of the Declaration of Rights approved by the National Assembly on 26 August 1789 combined the statement that "the free communication of thoughts and opinions is one of the most precious rights of man" with the reminder that anyone who exercised this freedom to "freely speak, write, and print" was "answerable for abuses of this liberty in cases determined by the law." This limited definition of press freedom was characteristic of the revolutionaries' tendency to define all liberties as existing within, not prior to, the law.[2] Even before the passage of the Declaration, the Paris municipal government established after the fall of the Bastille had asserted its right to regulate the distribution of newspapers, and successive revolutionary governments never wholly abandoned the harassment of journalists, publishers, and distributors. The freedom of the newspaper press at the start of the Revolution was protected less by positive legislation than by the National Assembly's inability to agree on the terms of an enforceable law. The Assembly first debated the issue as early as October 1789; in January 1790 the abbé Sieyès, one of the leading theorists of the revolutionary movement, introduced a detailed proposal along the lines of British practice. It would have banned anonymous publications and permitted the prosecution of seditious journalists if their words were followed by any public upheaval. Had it passed, freedom of the press would have been as threatened as it was after the passage of the Alien and Sedition Laws in the United States in 1798.[3]

Sieyès's proposal of January 1790 failed, but legislative concern about the abuse of press freedom continued, and several ad hoc prosecutions were undertaken even in the absence of a specific law justifying them. The increasing violence of revolutionary politics led even many journalists to call for stricter regulation. "Morality and public peace are the property of all. Every publication that tends to corrupt the first, or trouble the second, should be proscribed by the law, and its author pursued for the crime of *lèse-nation*," the *Journal des Clubs*, an unofficial organ of the Paris Jacobins, wrote in December 1790.[4] In August 1791, during the conservative "revision" of the constitution following the reinstatement of Louis XVI after his flight to Varennes, a press law was finally enacted, specifically permitting prosecutions for attacks on the Assembly as a whole and on individual members.[5] Only the growing disorder of revolutionary politics prevented its active use.

The outbreak of war in April 1792 made the publication of critical newspapers even more offensive to many of the deputies, and the Legislative Assembly voted to prosecute Marat and the abbé Royou in May 1792. But it was the overthrow of the monarchy on 10 August 1792 that led for the first time to truly effective measures against freedom of the press. The insurrectionary Paris Commune banned counterrevolutionary papers, forbade their distribution through the mail, and confiscated their presses for the benefit of journalists it favored. On 29 March 1793 the Convention decreed the death penalty for any public advocacy of the restoration of the monarchy or for incitement to murder or pillage.[6] Both the Girondin and the Montagnard factions that now struggled for control of the Convention were willing to violate press freedom to consolidate their power. In the provinces Montagnard deputies on mission banned hostile titles, including the leading Girondin papers; after the Montagnard victory on 2 June 1793, the Girondin press was liquidated, while the leaders of the federalist insurrections against the Convention naturally prevented the publication of hostile propaganda in the regions they controlled. Even without the benefit of a law authorizing such measures, the Jacobins imposed censorship on the surviving Paris papers. Robespierre, the main Montagnard leader, had already stated his view that "the interest of the Revolution may demand certain measures to repress a conspiracy founded on the freedom of the press."[7] Although the Committee of Public Safety stopped short of banning privately owned newspapers altogether—the Jacobins feared that granting government-directed newspapers a monopoly might pave the way for a dictatorship—it steadily expanded its definition of press offenses. In the spring of 1794 the former journalist Bertrand Barère, now the spokesman for the Committee, warned that the press should neither exaggerate nor underestimate the dangers facing the country; the numerous executions of journalists during the Terror forced the survivors to take his warning seriously, and there was little left for the press except to put out exactly what the revolutionary government told it to print.[8]

Not only did successive revolutionary governments take more severe measures against journalists and independently owned newspapers, they also took positive measures to get the kind of press they wanted. The supporters of the Revolution had initially reacted against the government-controlled journals of the Old Regime, but by 1792 the Interior Minister Roland had been granted 100,000 livres "for the printing and the distribution in the departments and the armies of all writings fit to enlighten minds about the criminal activities of the enemies of the state and the true causes of the problems that have for too long torn the country apart."[9] Roland was an associate of the Girondins, and Montagnard opponents like Robespierre vigorously denounced these "calumnies distributed everywhere at the nation's expense,"[10] but once their party had gained control of the Convention, the Montagnards adopted the same policy. The Committee of Public Safety and the ministry of the Interior founded the *Feuille du Salut publique* and a wallposter-journal, the *Sans-culotte observateur*, and gave money to a half-dozen other papers;[11] the war ministry underwrote distribution of Hébert's *Père Duchêne* to the troops.

This policy of promoting pro-government papers violated too many of the revolutionaries' avowed principles to be defended publicly: even at the height of the Terror, Convention deputies found it easy to denounce the danger that "the trustees of the public funds would be the masters of [public] opinion."[12] Like the suppression of opposition newspapers, however, it was a natural response to the crisis situation the revolutionary leaders found themselves in, particularly because an officially subsidized press had been a part of the nation's public life ever since Richelieu had helped Théophraste Renaudot start the *Gazette de France* in 1631. The great French historian of the Revolution, Alphonse Aulard, was correct in asserting that the Committee of Public Safety's press subventions were modest compared to those given out by several nineteenth-century regimes.[13] But the logic of the Committee's policy was clear: the total unity the embattled republic needed to survive required both the suppression of journalistic texts whose content might in any way suggest the existence of opposition or even apathy toward the regime and the active promotion of publications that would further government policy. Even moderate papers whose deviation from official policy was limited to articles about the public mood in Paris, thereby reminding readers that there was still a citizenry that could potentially think for itself, were a danger to the revolutionary government.[14]

The fall of Robespierre temporarily halted the evolution toward a thoroughly government-controlled press, but it certainly did not consolidate press freedom. A resurgent right-wing press flourished thanks to the pressure of public opinion and the divisions among the deputies in the thermidorian Convention, and the Constitution of 1795, which set up the Directory, did promise that "no one can be prevented from speaking, writing, printing and publishing his thoughts." But the new constitution not only repeated the 1789 declaration's reference to legal responsibility for publications, but also included a clause explicitly authorizing "provisional" restrictions on this and other freedoms "when circumstances make it necessary."[15] A law of 27 germinal IV, aimed at both royalists and "anarchists" nostalgic for the Terror, imposed the death penalty for any advocacy of changes in the 1795 constitution;[16] it furnished the basis for the execution of Gracchus Babeuf and his colleague Darthé in 1797. Robespierre's successors also continued the policy of using public funds to support loyal newspapers. Upon completion of the new constitution in 1795, the thermidorian Convention invested heavily in the creation of new newspapers to campaign for its acceptance; the new Directorial regime maintained these subsidies and gave free copies of these papers to the legislative deputies and to government officials throughout the country.[17] The establishment of the Directory's *Rédacteur* in December 1795 gave the executive branch of government its first avowedly official newspaper since the fall of the Old Regime.

The coup d'état of 18 fructidor V marked a major step toward

the final abolition of press freedom. The three republican Directors invoked the 1795 constitution's provision allowing temporary laws against the press; a law hurried through the rump
Councils after the coup gave them the power to ban offending
publications by decree. Preparations for the coup had included the
subsidizing of several new journals, and even more money flowed
to the press after 18 fructidor. But these subsidies were no longer
intended simply to facilitate the circulation of pro-republican
papers: they were part of a larger scheme to make the press
dependent on the government. The postfructidorian Directory
dribbled out small sums to various journalists, but at the same
time it imposed a stamp tax on newsprint, substantially raising
subscription prices and making it harder for publishers to cover
their costs. The government's favored journalists made no secret of
their hope that this law "will get rid of the three-quarters-and-
a-half of these scribblers who constantly try to steal each other's
subscribers."[18]

To bring the press even more effectively under control, the
Directory set up a secret office to prepare approved articles for
publication in the papers that took its money. This *Bureau politique*, active for nearly a year and a half in 1798 and 1799, also
reported on the conduct of the different papers and evaluated
requests for subsidies. Its chief, Vincent Barbet, imagined himself
as a veritable minister of propaganda and regularly offered his
superiors lengthy memoranda on the political situation.[19] Although Barbet never achieved his ambition to influence government policy, he did manage to replace the verve of self-appointed
editorialists with the artificial enthusiasm of officially prepared
propaganda. The *Bureau politique*'s work also served to discredit
the whole notion of an independent press. It manipulated papers
of varying political persuasions and staged faked debates among
them; in 1799 a neo-Jacobin journalist denounced the "horrible
machiavellianism" of this press policy, "which blew both hot and
cold, and employed the disgusting art of exciting party passions."[20] Readers could no longer tell if the opinions expressed in

the newspapers were sincere or just a carefully prepared simulacrum.

The *Bureau politique*'s activities were accompanied by intensified harassment of all newspapers that did not fall in line with the Directory's policies. The fructidor press law, originally used against the right-wing papers, was turned against neo-Jacobin titles less than three months later; it was applied as vigorously in the provinces as in Paris. The procedures used against refractory journalists became ever more arbitrary: in September 1797 the minister of police informed his agents that the constitutionally required formality of an arrest warrant could be disregarded where journalists were concerned, and an anonymous government memorandum recommended that the Directory simply dispense with specifying the offenses committed by the papers it banned, because this would lead to complicated debates about the evidence and the government would be forced to "lower itself to the humble role of commentator."[21] This harassment of the press was admittedly less severe than that of 1793–94; few of the journalists slated for arrest on 18 fructidor V were ever actually tracked down, and many of the papers banned during this period simply reappeared under new titles. But the Directory's police measures produced an atmosphere of insecurity that was distinctly unfavorable for the development of a free press.

The next-to-last of the coups d'état that punctuated the Directory's existence, the coup of 30 prairial VII (18 June 1799) in which the majority of the legislative Councils ousted four of the five Directors, introduced a last brief period of press freedom. The *Bureau politique* was abolished, and outspokenly royalist and neo-Jacobin newspapers reappeared. But the coalition of neo-Jacobins and conservative "men of 1789" who had engineered the prairial coup under the leadership of Sieyès, the one Director not dismissed in it, was inherently unstable. The upper hand belonged to Sieyès's group, and these men were no friends of the press. They were convinced that the only way to consolidate a republic in which property would be protected and the natural predominance of bourgeois elites would be respected was to make the government less dependent on public opinion.[22]

The intellectual spokesmen for the Directorial republicans had already prepared the way for systematic repression by formulating a thoroughgoing critique of the newspaper press as an inherently dangerous medium incompatible with stable government. Pierre Daunou—a leader of the Ideologue movement, a deputy, and a sometime journalist—argued that the Constitution's guarantees of press freedom did not apply to the newspaper press because it was incapable of treating issues of substance: one should not grant "impunity for Marat out of respect for Bacon and Montesquieu." The daily press could not represent the true convictions of the people; it was impossible for a country as large as France to have "a truly common opinion" on "particular new or complicated questions, on the personalities who succeed each other quickly in politics, on all the obscure incidents and hidden workings of a revolution."[23] Madame de Staël argued that newspapers necessarily had to lower themselves to the level of the mass audience they spoke to, and that they were used "to agitate with facts" rather than "to propagate ideas";[24] hence they did not deserve the protections given to serious discourse. Daunou and Madame de Staël were typical of the post-thermidorian republican elite: still seeing themselves as champions of the ideals of 1789, they had nonetheless lost faith in the possibility that France could be governed by open debate in which all citizens could participate.

This distrust of public political discussion prepared the way for legislation that would put an end to the revolutionary press system of competing partisan newspapers. Sieyès and his colleagues resumed banning newspapers several months before Napoleon took power. Recalling that the right-wing journalists whose papers had been suppressed in the fructidor coup were mostly still at large, the doomed Directory issued renewed warrants for their arrest; it lashed out at the neo-Jacobin press; and in a measure that truly symbolized the incompatibility between political stability and the ideals of 1789, the Directors even banned the *Ami des Lois*, the one paper that had been most faithful to the Constitution of 1795 since its establishment.[25] An anonymous bureaucratic memorandum dated four days before the Napoleonic coup d'état of 18 brumaire VIII lamented that such measures were not severe enough because there was nothing to prevent the creation of new titles to replace the banned ones. Its author recommended a simple policy: "Draw up a list of authorized journals, and permit no others to circulate."[26] The recommendation meant a return to a system of government-granted privileges like that of the Old Regime; all that was needed for its implementation was a government with the authority to enforce a measure that meant the repudiation of the basic principles of 1789.

When Napoleon Bonaparte, Sieyès, and their accomplices overthrew the Constitution of 1795 in the coup of 18 brumaire VIII (9 November 1799), they had only to follow the blueprint that their predecessors' bureaucracy had drawn up for them. On 27 nivôse VIII, two months after their seizure of power, the newly installed Consuls simply banned all newspapers in the capital other than thirteen specified titles; Napoleon's newly appointed prefects soon brought the provincial press into line. Compliance was not immediate: five years of experience with the Directory had persuaded many publishers that even the most stringent edicts would eventually prove to be dead letters, and unauthorized newspapers continued to appear for several years. But as the Napoleonic regime took root, the pressure on the press increased. Even the thirteen privileged papers suffered: some were soon suppressed, others were forced into shotgun weddings with old opponents that neutralized their political tendencies. Prior censorship was officially reinstituted in 1805; after 1807 other papers were forbidden to report news that had not appeared in the *Moniteur*, which the government had earlier taken over and turned into its official journal of record. In 1810 the number of printers was officially fixed and free entry into the trade forbidden, and a series of decrees in 1810 and 1811 limited the number of papers to four in Paris and one in each imperial *département*.[27] The Napoleonic regime had established a rationalized press system almost wholly under the government's control; the lively anarchy to which the Revolution had given birth was only a memory.

The Napoleonic period was not a wholly sterile one for the French press. Deprived of their political freedom, the newspapers turned to the cultural sphere they had neglected since 1789: theater reviews and critiques of books gained an increasingly prominent place in their columns, and the high-level magazine press, led by the revived *Mercure de France*, enjoyed a revival. Entrepreneurial initiative did not die out entirely: the Bertin brothers brought together the remains of the Directory's leading counterrevolutionary papers to create their *Journal des Débats*, the first great French paper of the nineteenth century, whose peak circulation during the Empire exceeded 23,000. In 1801 the *Journal des Débats* pioneered modern newspaper layout in France when it added a half-page *feuilleton* at the bottom of its regular printed page to accommodate literary and theater news: for the first time a French newspaper broke up its pages into distinct segments devoted to different topics. Rival papers quickly adopted this format, which was larger than that of the quarto papers of the Revolution, although still smaller than the folio page of the *Moniteur*, and the Parisian daily press never returned to the small formats of the revolutionary period. The Napoleonic press could boast of a number of distinguished writers: the *Débats*'s famous theater critic, Julien-Louis Geoffroy, a former writer for the *Ami du Roi*, earned as much as 25,000 livres a year for the articles in which he promoted a revival of classical literary taste, and the future liberal spokesman François Guizot began his career writing for the *Publiciste*.

Napoleon, who recognized the value of press propaganda—he had created his own newspapers to broadcast his successes during his early Italian campaigns in 1796 and 1797[28]—made much more effective use of the newspapers than his Bourbon predecessors did.[29] Not only did he fill them with articles extolling his achievements, but he was clever enough to let them give the impression that major decisions were still open to public debate. Thus he let the *Journal des Débats* publish the former member of the Committee of Public Safety Lazare Carnot's eloquent speech against the establishment of his hereditary Empire in 1804, thereby making it appear that his puppet legislature had freely accepted that measure.[30] In muted form the Napoleonic dailies kept alive the tradition of political partisanship in the press: with Napoleon's permission, the *Journal des Débats* represented the royalist current, while the *Publiciste*, a descendant of the *Gazette universelle* founded in 1789, spoke for moderate liberalism. When France became a constitutional and parliamentary monarchy in 1814, the journalists of the Napoleonic period were ready and able to create an appropriate press for it.

Whatever its merits, however, the Napoleonic press was quite different from the newspaper press that had flourished from 1789 to 1799. The experiment of an uninhibitedly partisan press, free to appeal to all classes of society and to challenge the authority of political institutions, went the way of such other aspects of the Revolution's political culture as freely elected assemblies, political clubs, and civic festivals. All were suppressed or emptied of any real content in the name of order and social stability. When the Napoleonic regime collapsed in 1814 and a constitutional monarchy with limited freedom for the press replaced it, journalists and politicians alike were careful not to allow the reappearance of the uncontrollable forms of the revolutionary press. The dominant nineteenth-century French newspapers were the large, well-capitalized enterprises of which the Old Regime publisher Panckoucke had dreamed in 1789, increasingly devoted to advertising as well as to news and polemic; when a cheap mass press established itself in the last third of the century, it purveyed sensationalism and entertainment, not the political radicalism and sense of political efficacy that the *Père Duchêne* had conveyed to the revolutionary *sans-culottes*. The Revolution of 1848 and the uprising of the Commune in 1871 saw brief revivals of famous titles like the *Ami du peuple* and the *Père Duchêne*, but for the most part, the revolutionary press seemed to have been an ephemeral product of that equally ephemeral phenomenon, the French Revolution itself.

The Press and the French Revolution: A Conclusion

Like the French Revolution, the newspapers founded during the 1790s had an impact even though few of them survived even for the duration of the revolutionary decade. As we have seen, the newspapers served as the Revolution's real "public space," its national forum for political debate. The press determined which of the words uttered in the Revolution's assemblies and clubs would be carried to the public; the journalists edited the debates to give them dramatic structure, and press commentary provided France's citizens with models to guide their reactions to their representatives' discourses. Press narratives made sense of the great crises of the Revolution and linked them together into an intelligible whole. The press represented the diverse groups that were mobilized in the struggle for political power; those groups that were effectively blocked from representation in the press, such as women and peasants,[31] were largely excluded from national politics. The press was vital to the functioning of all the other institutions of revolutionary culture. Deputies prepared their legislative initiatives by inspiring press campaigns; Jacobin clubs scheduled their meetings according to the arrival of the Paris newspapers and began their sessions with public readings; newspapers summoned the citizenry to the great festivals and reported their success afterward. And finally, it was the press that made the events of the revolutionary decade public and thus gave them legitimacy under the revolutionaries' own fundamental principles.

It is thus impossible to imagine the French Revolution without the press: the events of 1789 to 1799 could not have occurred as they did and taken on the meaning that they assumed without it.

Other media, such as the theater, caricatures, songs, and pamphlets, certainly helped spread the revolutionary message, but the special qualities of the periodical press—its ability to keep up with the speed of revolutionary events, its ability to reach an audience all across the country almost simultaneously, and its ability to carry messages both ways between that audience and the centers of power—made it uniquely important in the life of the Revolution. But if the press made the new politics of revolutionary France possible, the newspapers were also uniquely dangerous to the new political order the Revolution had proclaimed. François Furet has written of revolutionary language's tendency to undermine its own authority: "It strove for power yet denounced the corruption power inevitably entailed."[32] The press, too, subverted the new institutions it appeared to support.

Above all, the press sabotaged the revolutionary dream of national unity. As Bronislaw Baczko, among others, has argued, the men of the revolutionary decade never abandoned their deep-seated conviction, inherited from the experience of the Old Regime, that a stable polity was necessarily a united one. "The politicians and the ideologists of the revolutionary generation never reached the point of imagining or conceiving this political space as necessarily divided into competing political tendencies, as a place necessarily riven by conflicts and contradictions." But the corollary of this rejection of conflict was that each group saw its opponents as "elements harmful to the unity of the nation, and therefore alien to it," who needed to be eliminated by force if necessary.[33] Early revolutionary advocates of press freedom, such as Mirabeau and Brissot, had assumed that a free press would serve to unify public opinion: as Brissot had written in June 1789, through the newspapers the French people could "decide calmly and give their opinion" on public issues.[34] But both the politicians and the journalists were constantly revealing the scandal of disunity that pervaded revolutionary politics. The newspapers, driven by the necessity to compete in the marketplace, had an even greater tendency to denounce each other than the politicians had. They thus served to divide public opinion into hostile factions.

To compound the damage, the newspapers' denunciations of enemies served to unify and strengthen the political tendencies each paper represented, while widening the breaches with its enemies. The Revolution did not really see the birth of modern political parties with clear programs, cohesive parliamentary groups, and a defined hierarchy of leaders and supporters—the loose nationwide network of Jacobin clubs, held together by a vague sense of patriotism but deeply divided in its attitude toward crucial political questions, was far from resembling a modern party organization—but revolutionary France certainly had a press divided along partisan lines, and it was these papers that gave the politics of the revolutionary decade its party structure. Historians may continue to question whether there was a true Girondin "party" in the National Convention, in the sense of a cohesive group of deputies voting together on major issues,[35] but there is no doubt that there was a "Girondin" press, identifiable above all by its common campaigns against certain foes.

In the printed representations of politics provided by the press, all the untidy personal motives and inconsistencies of behavior that complicated parliamentary politics were stripped away, leaving only an ideological framework. Furthermore, the press included ideological currents that were not represented in the parliamentary system. It was not merely the radical democratic papers, such as the *Père Duchêne*, that succeeded in defining and mobilizing new political forces: organized political action on a national scale was new to all groups in French society in 1789. The imaginative counterrevolutionary editorialist De Rozoi, who launched a number of participatory schemes that demonstrated how a paper could direct its readers' actions, such as persuading hundreds of readers to take the perilous step of signing up as "hostages for the king" and having their names published in his paper after the flight to Varennes, was creating a new force of self-conscious royalists just as Hébert and his colleagues were conjuring up an altogether new movement of *sans-culottes*.[36]

For better and for worse, then, the press and the politics of the Revolution were coterminous. Pierre Rétat's assertion that "the birth of the [revolutionary] newspaper coincides with that of a new era"[37] applies not only to 1789 but to the entire revolutionary decade. France had experienced periods of internal upheaval before; during the sixteenth-century Wars of Religion, the country had even known ideological conflict fueled by printed propaganda. But it was the press that converted the conflicts of the late eighteenth century from struggles within the framework of a traditional set of institutions into an open debate on the nature of the proper institutions by which the country should be governed: in short, into a revolution. As the vehicle of the words and representations that made up revolutionary politics, the press was the great innovation that made the Revolution different from all earlier episodes in French history and thus opened the way to the modern political world.

Not only did the French press of the 1790s pave the way for the era of modern representative, partisan politics, but it was also a crucial milestone in the development of modern journalism. During the revolutionary decade, the urgent thirst for the latest news for the first time allowed the newspaper to elbow aside its aristocratic relative—the book—and make itself the dominant form of printed text, the most widely read, the most influential, the form in which the period's most original thought was expressed. To meet this demand for journalistic texts, the community of men of letters had to become more structured and professionalized than ever before, and the publishing industry was forced to adopt a completely new rhythm of work and to become more closely and directly tied to reader demand. The press tightened the bonds that linked the members of France's reading public: never before had they been so united in time and space. Thanks to newspapers, the diversified reading public that had grown up over the course of the eighteenth century became a nation of politically active citizens.

The newspaper press produced these changes although the newspaper titles of the revolutionary decade proved even more short-lived than many of the political institutions established in those years were. Compared to the famous publications whose names dot the history of the press—the *Gazette de Leyde*, which published continuously from 1677 to 1811, the London *Times*, founded in 1785 and still in existence, the French *Temps*, which lasted from 1861 to 1944—the revolutionary newspapers were truly ephemeral. Of the important revolutionary papers, Marat's *Ami du Peuple* and its continuations lasted less than four years, as did the *Révolutions de Paris*, Brissot's *Patriote françois*, and Hébert's *Père Duchêne*. Camille Desmoulins's *Révolutions de France et de Brabant* appeared for less than two years, as did the *Ami du Roi* and the *Actes des Apôtres*. Despite their short life-spans, the French newspapers of the revolutionary decade were of lasting importance in shaping the world's notion of what journalism could accomplish. They provided a unique demonstration of the power of the printed word on the threshold of an era in which the civilized world was to be flooded with printed texts. Historians remain uncertain whether the term *Fourth Estate* was first applied to the press during the revolutionary years, but it unquestionably derives from the French Revolution and aptly symbolizes the impact its newspapers made.

After 1800 the bureaucratic structures of the modern state, modern industry, and modern political parties worked to tame the power of the press. Not only did newspapers run up against more solid institutional structures, but the press itself became more institutionalized and less revolutionary. With more columns to fill and more copies to print, newspapers needed large teams of journalists and factory-sized printing plants. Even in the chaos of the Russian Revolution of 1917, the Bolsheviks' papers employed power-driven printing machinery and drew on networks of correspondents and distributors far larger than those the newsmen of the French Revolution had had access to. In 1919 *Isvestia* had a press run of 400,000—probably more than the combined circulation of the entire Paris press at the height of the French Revolution.[38] Even in revolutionary situations, it became harder for an unfettered, improvised press like that of the French Revolution to establish itself. In our modern era of global electronic communication, a media revolution would have to be worldwide in scope to achieve similar effects.

The French Revolution occurred at a unique moment, when the premodern era of hand-printing overlapped with the modern age of ideological politics. As a result, powerful individuals like Marat, the abbé Royou, and Hébert could create newspapers that were direct reflections of their personalities, but that were also able to exert real influence on the political world around them. It is this combination of journalistic individualism with modern mass politics that makes the French Revolution such a striking episode in the history of world journalism. Just as Napoleon was the last great general to command in person on the battlefield, the journalists of the Revolution were among the last of their profession to be able to deploy the columns of their words personally and to see them triumph. It is no accident that the most famous work of art stemming from the Revolution, Jacques-Louis David's portrait of the assassinated Marat, depicts a journalist with his pen in his hand: never before or since have political power and command of the printed word been so closely linked. So long as there are writers who aspire to guide the immediate course of events, the memory of the world-shaping journalism of the French Revolution will continue to exercise its fascination.

NOTES

INTRODUCTION

1. On the political culture of the Revolution, see Lynn Hunt, *Politics, Culture, and Class in the French Revolution* (Berkeley: University of California Press, 1984), and Colin Lucas, ed., *The Political Culture of the French Revolution* (Oxford: Pergamon Press, 1988).

2. Illustrations of these proposed devices are reproduced in Jacques Guilhaumou, "Zeitgenössische politische Lebensgeschichten aus der Französischen Revolution (1793–1794): Autobiographischer Akt und diskursives Ereignis," in *Die Französische Revolution als Bruch des gesellschaftlichen Bewusstseins*, ed. Rolf Reichardt and Eberhard Schmitt (Munich: R. Oldenbourg, 1988), 358–62.

3. Jean-Sylvain Bailly, proclamation of 13 August 1789, cited in Pierre Rétat, *Les journaux de 1789: Bibliographie critique* (Paris: Editions du Centre national de la recherche scientifique, 1989), 195.

4. Prospectus, *Journal logographique*, n.d. (late 1790).

5. The revolutionary media have been one of the leading areas of recent research on the French Revolution. For an introduction to the latest work in this field, see Robert Darnton and Daniel Roche, eds., *Revolution in Print: The Press in France, 1775–1800* (Berkeley: University of California Press, 1989), which surveys the major print media. A classic study of the Revolution's public festivals is Mona Ozouf, *Festivals and the French Revolution*, trans. Alan Sheridan (Cambridge, Mass.: Harvard University Press, 1988).

6. *Journal d'économic publique*, 30 bru. V (Dec. 1796).

7. Roederer provided a breakdown of newspaper subscriptions according to political tendency in the *Journal d'économic publique*, 30 flor. V (19 May 1797), although the figures were probably manufactured to demonstrate the popularity of the political viewpoint he himself supported.

8. Keith Baker, "Politics and Public Opinion under the Old Regime: Some Reflections," in *Press and Politics in Pre-Revolutionary France*, ed. Jack R.

Censer and Jeremy D. Popkin (Berkeley: University of California Press, 1987), 213.

9. "Those in high places only seem to tower over us because we are on our knees. Stand up!" On the importance of the concept of the "new man" in revolutionary political culture, see Mona Ozouf, "La Révolution française et l'idée de l'homme nouveau," in *Political Culture of the French Revolution*, ed. Lucas, 213–32.

10. On the Revolution as a conflict of claims to represent the will of the people and as a succession of efforts to proclaim the Revolution as finished, see François Furet, *Interpreting the French Revolution*. trans. Elborg Forster (New York: Cambridge University Press, 1981).

11. Pierre Rétat, "Forme et discours d'un journal révolutionnaire: les *Révolutions de Paris* en 1789," in *L'Instrument périodique*, Claude Labrosse and Pierre Rétat (Lyon: Presses Universitaires de Lyon, 1985), 162.

12. The most recent and most comprehensive works in this category are Jacques Godechot's section on "La presse française sous la Révolution et l'Empire," in *Histoire générale de la presse française*, ed. Claude Bellanger et al., vol. 1 (Paris: Presses Universitaires de France, 1969), and Hugh Gough, *The Newspaper Press in the French Revolution* (London: Routledge, 1988). For a selected bibliography on the history of the press in the French Revolution, see For Further Reading, below.

13. Thomas Carlyle, *The French Revolution* (New York: Random House, n.d.), 187.

14. Ibid., 186.

15. Alphonse Aulard, "La presse officieuse pendant la Terreur," *Études et Leçons sur la Révolution française*, 1er sér. (Paris: Alcan, 1893), 227–40; Albert Mathiez, "Le Bureau politique du Directoire," *Revue historique* 81 (1903): 52–76.

16. Among the prominent French historians in the tradition of Aulard, Mathiez, and Georges Lefebvre, one must make an exception for Jacques Godechot, who has both written about the press himself and encouraged a generation of younger French and American scholars to take it seriously as a subject.

17. Albert Soboul, *Les sans-culottes parisiens de l'An II* (Paris: Clavreuil, 1958), 174–75.

18. Jacques Guilhaumou, "'Moment actuel' et processus discursifs: le *Père Duchêne* d'Hébert et le *Publiciste de la République française* de Jacques Roux," *Bulletin du Centre d'analyse du discours de l'Université de Lille III* 2 (1975): 151. Guilhaumou, as the leading exponent of a computer-based linguistic approach to revolutionary language, challenged Soboul's assertion that Hébert's paper in any way represented *sans-culotte* ideas in this and another of his early articles, "L'idéologie du *Père Duchêne*, les forces adjuvantes (14 juillet–6 septembre 1793)," *Mouvement social* 85 (1973): 81–116. In his most recent publications, such as his article "L'Historien du discours et la

lexicometrie," *Histoire et Mesure* 1 (1986): 27–46, Guilhaumou seems to take a more nuanced view of Hébert's relations to the *sans-culotterie*.

19. Furet, *Interpreting the French Revolution*, 50.
20. Hunt, *Politics, Culture, and Class*, 25, 13, 56.
21. Rolf Reichardt, "Die städtische Revolution als politisch-kultureller Prozess," in *Die Französische Revolution*, ed. Rolf Reichardt (Frankfurt: Ploetz, 1988), 30.
22. Marc-Eli Blanchard, *St.-Just et Cie.—La Révolution et les mots* (Paris: Nizet, 1980), 55, 105.
23. Rétat, *"Révolutions de Paris,"* 142, 156–57.

CHAPTER 1

1. Isabelle de Charrière, "Attendez Revenez, ou les Delais Cruels," in vol. 7 of *Oeuvres completès* (Amsterdam: Van Orschoot, 1979–81), 115.
2. Figures from Jean Sgard, "Journale und Journalisten im Zeitalter der Aufklärung," in *Sozialgeschichte der Aufklärung in Frankreich*, ed. Hans-Ulrich Gumbrecht, Rolf Reichardt, and Thomas Schleich (Munich: Oldenbourg, 1981), 2: 32.
3. For a brief overview of the French domestic press before 1789, see Bellanger et al., *Histoire générale de la presse française*, vol. 1. See also Jean Sgard's excellent essay, "La Multiplication des périodiques," in *Histoire de l'Edition française*, ed. Roger Chartier et al. (Paris: Promodis, 1984), 2: 198–205. There is a review of the recent scholarly literature on the French press before the Revolution in the introduction to Censer and Popkin, eds., *Press and Politics in Pre-Revolutionary France*. Major publications issued since then include Nina R. Gelbart, *Feminine and Opposition Journalism in Old Regime France: The 'Journal des Dames'* (Berkeley: University of California Press, 1987); and Hans Bots, ed., *La Diffusion et la lecture des journaux de langue française sous l'ancien régime* (Amsterdam and Maarssen: APA-Holland University Press, 1988).
4. Suzanne Tucoo-Chala, *Charles-Joseph Panckoucke et la librairie française 1736–1798* (Pau: Marrimpouey, 1977), 243.
5. Jean Sgard, "Bilan du colloque," in *Diffusion et lecture*, ed. Bots, 279–82.
6. Tucoo-Chala, *Panckoucke*, 191–252.
7. On the prerevolutionary gazettes, see especially the contributions of Jeremy Popkin, Carroll Joynes, and Jack Censer in *Press and Politics in Pre-Revolutionary France*, ed. Censer and Popkin; and Jeremy D. Popkin, *News and Politics in the Age of Revolution: Jean Luzac's 'Gazette de Leyde,'* (Ithaca, N.Y.: Cornell University Press, 1989).
8. John Adams to President of Congress, 8 September 1783, in *The Revolutionary Diplomatic Correspondence of the United States*, ed. Francis Wharton (Washington, D.C.: Government Printing Office, 1889), 6: 682.
9. Jeremy D. Popkin, "The Prerevolutionary Origins of Political Journal-

ism," in *The Political Culture of the Old Regime*, ed. Keith Baker (Oxford: Pergamon, 1987), 211–16.

10. On Linguet's *Annales* and their impact, see Popkin, "Prerevolutionary Origins," 216–20; and Darline Gay Levy, *The Ideas and Careers of Simon-Nicolas-Henri Linguet* (Urbana: University of Illinois Press, 1980).

11. On the prerevolutionary pamphlets, see Ralph M. Greenlaw, "Pamphlet Literature in France during the Period of the Aristocratic Revolt (1787–1788)," *Journal of Modern History* 29 (1957): 349–54; and Jeremy D. Popkin and Dale Van Kley, "The Pre-Revolutionary Debate," in *The French Revolution Research Collection*, ed. Colin Lucas (Oxford: Pergamon), forthcoming.

12. Figures communicated by Ralph M. Greenlaw as a result of research subsequent to his 1957 article (see note 11, above).

13. Jeremy D. Popkin, "The *Gazette de Leyde* and French Politics under Louis XVI," in *Press and Politics*, ed. Censer and Popkin, 112–13.

14. It is not certain that Volney's paper was subsidized, but its successor, Michel Mangourit's *Hérault de la Nation*, published from January to June 1789 and also aimed at Brittany, definitely was.

15. Documents in Archives nationales (Paris), V(1) 549. Documents in the Archives nationales (Paris) are subsequently identified by AN. For a detailed account of the breakdown of pre-revolutionary regulations and the emergence of a new press in the spring and summer of 1789, see the stimulating work of Claude Labrosse and Pierre Rétat, *Naissance du journal révolutionnaire 1789* (Lyon: Presses Universitaires de Lyon, 1989), 9–51.

16. On the *cahiers*, see Alma Söderhjelm, *Le Régime de la presse pendant la Révolution française* (Helsinki and Paris: Welter, 1900–1901), I: 59–64. On the English tradition of press law, see Leonard Levy, *Emergence of a Free Press* (New York: Oxford University Press, 1985).

17. AN, V(1) 549, no. 731 (17 May 1789).

18. Comte de Mirabeau, prospectus to *Etats-Généraux* (Le Jay, publisher); Jacques-Pierre Brissot, *Mémoire aux Etats-Généraux: Sur la nécessité de rendre dès ce moment la presse libre, et surtout pour les journaux politiques* (Paris, 1789), 10.

19. J. Bénétruy, *L'Atelier de Mirabeau* (Geneva: Jullien, 1962), 184.

20. Brissot, *Mémoire aux Etats-Généraux*, 10, 52–53.

21. On these deputy-correspondents, see Edna Hines Lemay, "Ecouter et renseigner: le journalisme du député-constituant, 1789–1791," in *La Révolution du Journal, 1789–1794*, ed. Pierre Rétat and Jean Sgard (Lyon: Presses Universitaires de Lyon), forthcoming.

22. *Gazette de Leyde*, 7 July 1789; *Courrier d'Avignon*, 4 July 1789.

23. Jacques Beffroy de Reigny, *Supplément nécessaire au Précis exact de la prise de la Bastille, avec des Anecdotes curieuses sur le même sujet* (Paris, 24 July 1789), 1.

24. Rétat, *"Révolutions de Paris,"* 141–42.

25. Labrosse and Rétat, *Naissance du journal*, 19–25. Twenty-four of these first

appeared in July 1789, the peak month for new titles; twenty were launched in August and nineteen in October.

26. Hugh Gough, "Continuité ou rupture? Les transformations structurelles de la presse provinciale 1789–1799," *Annales historiques de la Révolution française* 273 (1988): 247–53.

27. *Journal de Lyon,* 31 December 1789.

CHAPTER 2

1. Details of Madame Vaufleury's establishment are taken from the prospectus for the Cabinet Littéraire National, au Palais-Royal, in the Newberry Library, French Revolution Collection, Case FRC 1591.

2. Paris figures from "Tableau des Journaux rédigés et publiés à Paris et dont les rédacteurs ou propriétaires ont fait leurs déclarations," in AN, F7 3448B; provincial figures from police surveys in AN, F7 3448B and F 7 3451.

3. Gough, *Newspaper Press,* 65–67.

4. Ferréol Beaugeard, in *Journal de Marseille,* 15 May 1797. On Beaugeard and his journal, see René Gérard, *Un journal de province sous la Révolution. Le 'Journal de Marseille' de Ferréol Beaugeard (1781–1797)* (Paris: Société des Etudes robespierristes, 1964).

5. Albert Soboul, "Sentiments religieux et cultes populaires pendant la Révolution: Saintes patriotes et martyrs de la liberté," *Annales historiques de la Révolution française* 148 (1957): 193–213; Richard Cobb, "Marat comparé à Jésus," *Annales historiques de la Révolution française* 161 (1960): 312–14.

6. Figures for 1784 from Robert Darnton, "The Facts of Literary Life in Eighteenth-Century France," in *Political Culture,* ed. Baker, 269.

7. Figures from Sgard, "Journale und Journalisten," *Sozialgeschichte der Aufklärung in Frankreich,* ed. Gumbrecht, Reichardt, and Schleich, 2: 28.

8. Marc Martin, "Journalistes parisiens et notoriété (vers 1830–1870): Pour une histoire sociale du journalisme," *Revue historique* 539 (1981): 44.

9. *Journal de la République française,* 14 January 1793.

10. Jeremy D. Popkin, "From Dutch Republican to French Monarchist: Antoine-Marie Cerisier, 1749–1828," in *Tijdschrift voor Geschiedenis* (1989), forthcoming.

11. Elizabeth Eisenstein, "The Tribune of the People: A New Demagogic Species," in *Studies on Voltaire and the Eighteenth Century,* forthcoming.

12. Cited in Bellanger et al., *Histoire générale de la presse française,* 1: 453–54.

13. On Bonneville and his circle, see Gary Kates, *The 'Cercle social,' the Girondins, and the French Revolution* (Princeton: Princeton University Press, 1985).

14. *Ami du Roi,* 1 June 1790.

15. William J. Murray, *The Right-Wing Press in the French Revolution: 1789–1792* (London: Royal Historical Society, 1986), 31–34.
16. *Ami du Roi* [Royou edition], "Avis" bound in with vol. 1, Harvard College Library copy.
17. Charles Lacretelle, *Dix Années d'épreuves pendant la Révolution*, (Paris: Allouard, 1842), 29–31.
18. *Révolutions de Paris*, 1–8 May 1790.
19. Louis Jacob, *Hébert. Le Père Duchesne chef des sans-culottes*. (Paris: Gallimard, 1960), 37–40.
20. Figures for Lacretelle in Lacretelle, *Dix années*, 57; for Desmoulins and Loustallot in Jean-Paul Bertaud, *Camille et Lucile Desmoulins* (Paris: Presses de la Renaissance, 1986), 90; for Mallet du Pan, Frances Acomb, *Mallet du Pan* (Durham, N.C.: Duke University Press, 1973), 230–31.
21. Contract in AN, F 7 4281, d. 23.
22. *Révolutions de France et de Brabant*, no. 27.
23. *Ami du Roi* [Royou edition], "Avis" bound in with vol. 1, Harvard College Library copy.
24. *Censeur des Journaux*, 25 flor. V (14 May 1797). Gallais plagiarized this passage from an article in Linguet's *Annales politiques* of 1777.
25. On payments to royalist journalists in the Directory period, see Jeremy D. Popkin, *The Right-Wing Press in France, 1792–1800* (Chapel Hill: University of North Carolina Press, 1980), 30–31.
26. Ernest Labadie, *La Presse Bordelaise pendant la Révolution* (Bordeaux: Cadoret, 1910), 278–79.
27. *Echo des Pyrénées*, 25 July 1793; *Courrier d'Avignon*, 28 June 1790.
28. Cited in A. Aulard, ed., *La société des Jacobins*, (Paris: Cerf, 1891–98), 4: 528 (debate of 30 November 1792).
29. Popkin, *Right-Wing Press*, 90.
30. Popkin, *Right-Wing Press*, 30.
31. See the classic portrait of this proletarianized literary underworld in Robert Darnton, "The High Enlightenment and the Low-Life of Literature," in *The Literary Underground of the Old Regime*, ed. Darnton (Cambridge, Mass.: Harvard University Press, 1982), 1–40.
32. Marie Jeanne Phlipon Roland de la Platière, *Mémoires de Madame Roland*, ed. C. A. Dauban (Paris: Plon, 1864), 230.
33. Benjamin Constant, *Des réactions politiques* (Paris, 1797), 42.
34. *Gazette française*, 17 niv. III.
35. Police report on public opinion, 31 January 1794, cited in Pierre Caron, ed., *Paris pendant la terreur* (Paris: Klincksieck, 1910–58), 3: 244.
36. *Censeur des journaux*, 18 niv. V.
37. *Ami du Peuple*, 25 January 1791.
38. *Courier de Versailles à Paris, et de Paris à Versailles*, no. 2, n.d. (early July 1789).

39. Etienne Dumont, *Recollections of Mirabeau, and of the Two First Legislative Assemblies of France* (London: E. Bull, 1832), 102–4.
40. *Echo des Pyrénées,* 24 May 1793.
41. Marc Martin, "L'Information de guerre dans la presse parisienne de 1792 à 1800. L'Exemple du Moniteur Universel," in *Voies nouvelles pour l'histoire de la Révolution française* (Paris: Bibliothèque nationale, 1979), 225, 229.
42. *Journal de Perlet,* 5 vent. V (23 February 1797).
43. *Aux voleurs, aux voleurs,* no. 10 (1790).
44. Carla Hesse, "Economic Upheavals in Publishing," in *Revolution in Print,* ed. Darnton and Roche, 69–97.
45. Bernard Vouillot, "La Révolution et l'empire: une nouvelle réglementation," in *Histoire de l'édition française,* ed. Roger Chartier, Henri-Jean Martin, and Jean-Pierre Vivet (Paris: Promodis, 1983–85), 2: 532.
46. M. S. Boulard, *Le Manuel de l'Imprimeur* (Paris: Boulard, 1791), 81–84, 91–92.
47. A. J. Dugour, in *Eclair,* 2 January 1797.
48. Proposed merger contract (never implemented), in AN, F 7 3445.
49. Charles-Joseph Panckoucke, "Sur les journaux anglais," *Mercure de France,* 30 January 1790.
50. Bankruptcy dossier, 10 February 1804, in Archives départementales de la Seine (Paris), D 11 U(3) 24, d. 1638.
51. AN, F 18 25, "Notes sur les imprimeurs ci-après désignés."
52. On Duplain's efforts, see André Fribourg, "Le Club des Jacobins en 1790, d'aprés de nouveaux documents," in *Révolution française* 58 (1910): 507–54. Duplain's prerevolutionary publishing career is recounted in Robert Darnton, *The Business of Enlightenment* (Cambridge, Mass.: Harvard University Press, 1979).
53. AN, F 7 4694.
54. On Caillot's work for Royou, see Harvey Chisick, "Pamphlets and Journalism in the Early French Revolution," *French Historical Studies* 15 (1988): 630.
55. Caillot letters in AN, F 7 3446.
56. Jeremy D. Popkin, "Joseph Fiévée, imprimeur, écrivain, journaliste: une carrière dans le monde du livre pendant la Révolution," in *Livre et Révolution,* ed. Frédéric Barbier (Paris: Aux Amateurs de livres, 1989), 63–74.
57. On the explosive growth of administrative printing, see Pierre Casselle, "Printers and Municipal Politics," in *Revolution in Print,* ed. Darnton and Roche, 98–106.
58. Robert Darnton, "L'Imprimerie de Panckoucke en l'an II," in *Revue française d'histoire du livre* 9 (1979): 365. Not all these presses were used for Panckoucke's periodicals: many were employed in producing books such as his mammoth *Encyclopédie methodique.*

59. On the official printing shops, see Auguste Bernard, *Notice historique sur l'imprimerie nationale* (Paris: Dumoulin and Bordier, 1848), 67–79. By the end of the Napoleonic period the *Imprimerie nationale* had grown to two hundred presses.

60. Boulard, *Manuel*, 68, 73.

61. Charles-Joseph Panckoucke, "Sur l'état actuel de l'imprimerie," *Mercure de France*, 6 March 1790; *Ami du Peuple* (counterfeit edition by Guignot), 5 March 1790.

62. Philippe Minard, "Agitation in the Work Force," in *Revolution in Print*, ed. Darnton and Roche, 120.

63. Police report, 13 December 1795, cited in Alphonse Aulard, ed., *Paris pendant la réaction thermidorienne et sous le Directoire* (Paris: Cerf, 1898), 2: 502; *Courrier républicain*, 10 December 1795, cited in ibid., 2: 486; *Courrier républicain*, 10 ther. IV.

64. Van Nussel, publisher of *Diurnal*, to Minister of Police, 6 bru. VI, in AN, F 7 3448B.

65. *Ami du Peuple*, 23 November 1790.

66. *Courrier extraordinaire*, 16 June 1792.

67. Gérard Walter, *Hébert et le 'Père Duchesne'* (Paris: Janin, 1946), 343–44. On the colporteurs during the Revolution, see *Colporteur la Révolution*, Lise Andries, ed. (Montreuil: Bibliothèque Robert-Desnos, 1989).

68. *Ami du Peuple*, 25 December 1789.

69. Caillot correspondence in AN, F 7 3446; *Journal de la Montagne* registers in AN, T 1495 A and B.

70. Murray, *Right-Wing Press*, 79–80.

71. AN, F 7 3445.

72. Letter to *Gazette française*, in AN, F 7 6239B.

73. Correspondence of *Précurseur*, in AN, F 7 6239A, plaq. 1.

74. Rétat, "*Révolutions de Paris*," 173–80.

75. Murray, *Right-Wing Press*, 35.

76. *Ami du Peuple*, 18 May 1790, 18 June 1790.

77. Contract of 13 flor. V, in AN, F 7 3448B.

78. *Véridique*, 17 and 23 ger. IV.

79. *Rôdeur*, 19 ger. IV.

80. Letter of Beyerlé, 7 mess. IV, in AN, BB 16 708; report of Cochon, minister of police, in AN, AF III, dr. 165, pp. 79–80.

81. *Ami du Roi* [Royou edition], 19 November 1790.

82. Report of police commissioners, section Théâtre-français, 9 March 1793, in Bibliothèque de la Ville de Paris, ms. 749, p. 100. On these attacks, see A. M. Boursier, "L'émeute parisienne du 10 mars 1793," *Annales historiques de la Révolution française* 208 (1972): 204–30.

83. *Vedette, ou Journal du département du Doubs*, 29 June 1792, 24 Aug. 1792.

84. Interrogation, 7 flor. II, in AN, F 7 4694.

85. Labadie, *Presse Bordelaise*, 278–79.

86. Charles-Frédéric Perlet, letter to Police Minister Fouché, 13 ger. VIII, in AN, F 7 3452. Perlet put his financial losses as a result of 18 fructidor at over 40,000 livres.

87. Jean-Pierre Gallais, in *Censeur*, 18 fruc. III (5 September 1795).

88. Gilles Feyel, "Les frais d'impression et de diffusion de la presse parisienne entre 1789 et 1792," in Rétat and Sgard, eds., *Revolution du Journal*.

89. Jean-Paul Bertaud, *Les Amis du Roi*, (Paris: Perrin, 1984) 55. These figures agree with estimates made from the more fragmentary records from papers in the Directory period (Popkin, *Right-Wing Press*, 193 n. 27).

90. *Courrier extraordinaire*, 2 May 1792. On publishers' pricing policies, see Labrosse and Rétat, *Naissance du Journal*, 64–68.

91. For an analogous argument about the relationship between the growth of consumerism and the rise of mass politics in late eighteenth century England, see John Brewer, "The Commercialization of Politics," in *The Birth of a Consumer Society*, ed. Neil McKendrick, John Brewer, and J. H. Plumb (Bloomington: Indiana University Press, 1982), 197–262.

92. François Furet and Jacques Ozouf, *Lire et écrire* (Paris: Editions de Minuit, 1977), 1: 60. A number of deficiencies in Maggiolo's data make it difficult to give a meaningful figure for literacy at the national level.

93. Jean Quéniairt, *Culture et société urbaines dans la France de l'Ouest au XVIIIᵉ siècle* (Paris: Klincksieck, 1978).

94. Daniel Roche, *Le Peuple de Paris* (Paris: Aubier Montaigne, 1981), 204–41.

95. Johann Heinrich Campe, *Briefe aus Paris zur Zeit dur Revolution geschrieben* (1790; reprint, Hildesheim: Gerstenberg, 1977), 51.

96. *Le Patriotisme du véritable Père Duchesne, ou l'Abolition de tous les faux Pères Duchesne;* on rhe *Sentinelle,* a wallposter-journal of 1792, see Marcel Dorigny, "La *Sentinelle* de J. B. Louvet, un organe officieux du ministère girondin en 1792," in *Révolution du Journal,* ed. Rétat and Sgard. Of course, a journal given away free or published as a wallposter had to be subsidized by some interested party or other.

97. Roger Chartier, and Daniel Roche, in "Les livres ont-ils fait la Révolution?" *Livre et Révolution,* ed. Frédéric Barbier, 15–20.

98. Jean Boutier, "Les révoltes paysannes en Aquitaine (décembre 1789–mars 1790," *Annales E.S.C.* 34 (1979): 767.

99. Report of 23 September 1793, cited in Caron, ed. *Paris pendant la terreur* 1: 175.

100. Louis André, "La papeterie et les approvisionnements en papier sous la Révolution," in paper given at the colloquium "Livre et Révolution," Bibliothèque nationale (Paris), 1987.

101. Cited in Gough, *Newspaper Press,* 212.

102. For a discussion of the sources of this figure and other estimates from the period, see Popkin, *Right-Wing Press,* 195–96.

103. Cited in Jeremy Black, *The English Press in the Eighteenth Century* (Philadelphia: University of Pennsylvania Press, 1986), 105.

104. Figures for 1802 from André Cabanis, *La presse sous le consulat et l'empire (1799–1814)* (Paris: Société des Etudes robespierristes, 1975), 320; for 1836 and 1846 from J. P. Aguet, "Le Tirage des quotidiens de Paris sous la Monarchie de Juillet," *Revue suisse d'histoire* 10 (1960): 237–38.

105. Archives de la Préfecture de Police (Paris), A/A 244, d. 472.

106. See the figures in Popkin, *Right-Wing Press*, 177–79. Evidence from press numbers in surviving copies confirms the publisher's claim that the *Journal de Perlet* used four presses in 1794, which would have given it the capacity to produce between 9,000 and 12,000 copies per day; a letter from the Dutch emigré P. A. Dumont-Pigalle states that the *Gazette universelle* had 10,000–11,000 subscriptions in 1792 (Dumont-Pigalle to Johan Valckenaer, 21 August 1792, in Leiden University Library, ms. BPL 1031 [I]).

107. *Journal de Perlet*, 19 mess. III; Friedrich Johann Meyer, *Fragmente aus Paris im IV*ten *Jahr der Französische Republik* (Hamburg: Bohn, 1797), 1: 114.

108. Jean-Paul Marat, *Appel à la nation* (Paris: Marat, 1790), 44.

109. Bertaud, *Amis du Roi*, 53.

110. *Indispensable*, 6 vend. VIII.

111. Gilles Feyel, "Les conditions d'imprimerie," in *Révolution du journal*, ed. Rétat and Sgard.

112. *Echo des Pyrénées*, 24 May 1793.

113. Pierre-Louis Roederer notes in AN, 29 AP 91, pp. 118–19. He gave no basis for his estimates of this multiplier effect.

114. The Baron de Barante, a prominent nineteenth-century politician born in 1782, has left an interesting testimony on the age at which children began reading the papers during the Revolution. He asserts that he and his ten-year-old classmates paid no attention to the events of 10 August 1792: "we didn't know what it was about; . . . it is true that we didn't read a paper." But when the revolutionary government closed down his school the following year and he had to continue his studies at home, with fewer distractions, he would "read the paper before doing my homework" (Baron de Barante, *Souvenirs*, ed. Claude de Barante [Paris: Calmann Lévy, 1890], 1: 7, 10).

115. Vassier, letter to *Gazette française*, 20 ther. V, in AN, F 7 6239B.

116. Harvey Chisick, "The Public of a Conservative Daily of the Early Revolution: The Subscribers to the *Ami du Roi* of the abbé Royou," paper given at colloquium on "Presse d'élite, presse populaire et propagande pendant la Révolution française," Haifa University, 1988; Laurence Coudart, "Les lecteurs de la *Gazette de Paris*," in *Les résistances à la Révolution*, ed. François Lebrun and Roger Dupuy (Paris: Imago, 1987), 211–21.

117. Melvin Edelstein, *La Feuille villageoise: Communication et modernisation dans*

les régions rurales pendant la Révolution (Paris: Bibliothèque nationale, 1977), 74.

118. M. Dupont-Constant, *Essai sur l'Institut philanthropique* (Paris, 1823), 58.

119. Police reports in AN, F 7 3448B and 3451.

120. Marquis de Ferrières, *Correspondance inédite (1789, 1790, 1791)*, ed. Henri Carré (Paris: Armand Colin, 1932), 266.

121. Julien to Frasans, editor of the *Annales universelles*, 19 July 1797, in AN, F 7 3445.

122. Typical *avis* are in the *Courrier universel de Husson*, 24 flor. III, and *Courrier républicain*, 16 ther. III.

123. Aulard, *La société des Jacobins* 3: 130–31 (15 September 1791); report of 23 January 1794 cited in Caron, *Paris pendant la terreur*, 3: 104.

124. Letters in AN, F 7 4591, plaq. 5, no. 24, and F 7 3445.

125. Aulard, *La société des Jacobins*, 3: 322 (session of 17 January 1792); Michael Kennedy, *The Jacobin Clubs in the French Revolution: The First Years* (Princeton: Princeton University Press, 1982), 58–59; and Michael Kennedy, *The Jacobin Clubs in the French Revolution: The Middle Years* (Princeton: Princeton University Press, 1988), 177.

126. Robespierre, speech to Jacobins, 12 December 1792, in Aulard, *La société des Jacobins*, 4: 577.

127. P. C. L. Baudin des Ardennes, *Eclaircissements sur l'article 355 de la Constitution, et sur la liberté de la presse* (Paris: Imprimerie nationale, 1796), 20.

128. Ferrières, *Correspondance inédite*, letters of 29 June 1790 (224–25) and 8 June 1790 (198).

129. Ibid., letters of 14 June 1790 (203–4); 30 June 1791 (377–78); 24 June 1791 (371).

130. Ibid., letter of 8 June 1790 (198).

131. Bonnet-St. Priest to *Gazette française*, in AN, F 7 3446.

132. *Moniteur*, 17 May 1790, advertisement for a newspaper distributor in Lyon.

133. Binding was not very expensive: in 1791 one Montpellier reader paid 1.2 livres for the binding of two months' copies of his paper. This added 20 percent to the cost of his annual subscription (Ms. note on flyleaf, vol. 1, *Mémorial politique et littéraire*, in Newberry Library French Revolution Collection).

134. Jeremy D. Popkin, "The Book Trades in Western Europe during the Revolutionary Era," *Papers of the Bibliographical Society of America* 78 (1984): 424–27.

135. Prospectuses, *Cabinet Littéraire National* and *Chambre patriotique et littéraire*, in Newberry Library French Revolution Collection.

136. Soboul, *Sans-culottes*, 672.

137. Georges Lesage, ed., *Episodes de la Révolution à Caen, racontés par un*

bourgeois et un Homme du peuple (Caen: ?, 1926), 18. I would like to thank
Paul Hanson for furnishing me with this citation.

138. Auguste Quesnot, "Les Dieppois et la presse périodique à la fin du XVIIIe
siècle," *Annales historiques de la Révolution française* (1938): 54–66.

139. Kennedy, *Jacobin Clubs: First Years,* 53–56; Kennedy, *Jacobin Clubs:
Middle Years,* 3; John A. Lynn, *The Bayonets of the Republic* (Urbana:
University of Illinois Press, 1984), 130.

140. Pierre Paganel, *Essai historique et critique sur la Révolution française* (Paris:
Panckoucke, 1815) 2: 259.

141. *Ami du Peuple,* 3 January 1791.

142. Resolution of the Société des Amis de la Constitution, Vire, concerning
royalist papers of De Rozoi and Mallet du Pan, in *Journal des Amis de la
Constitution,* 18 January 1791.

CHAPTER 3

1. Furet, *Interpreting the French Revolution*, 49, 73.
2. Stanley Morison, *The English Newspaper* (Cambridge: Cambridge University Press, 1932), 184–85.
3. *Journal de Perlet*, 28 December 1792.
4. Prospectus, *Journal Logographique*, n.d. (1790).
5. List in Léonard Gallois, *Histoire des journaux et des journalistes de la Révolution française (1789–1796)* (Paris: Société de l'industrie fraternelle, 1845), 1: 164, attributed to *Actes des Apôtres*, but I have not been able to find the original in that journal. Nevertheless, the titles on the list which can be identified were all appearing in the fall of 1790, and very few papers known to have been publishing at that time are omitted. Of sixty-four papers listed, forty were octavos, fourteen were quartos, one used the folio format, and nine cannot be identified.
6. *Journal de Perlet*, 22 mess. III.
7. Labrosse and Rétat, *Naissance du journal*, 35.
8. *Journal de Perlet*, 28 December 1792.
9. Labrosse and Rétat, *Naissance du journal*, 34.
10. *Journal de Perlet*, 28 December 1792.
11. For an analysis of the content of one paper's engravings, see Jack R. Censer, "The Political Engravings of the *Révolutions de France et de Brabant*, 1789 to 1791," *Eighteenth-Century Life* 5 (1979): 105–24.
12. Labrosse and Rétat, *Naissance du journal*, 40.
13. Rijklof Michael van Goens, in *Ouderwetse Nederlandsche Patriot*, 1 September 1781.
14. Peter D. G. Thomas, "The Beginnings of Parliamentary Reporting in Newspapers, 1768–1774," *English Historical Review* 74 (1959): 623–36.
15. *Courier du Bas-Rhin*, 29 June 1788.
16. Jacob Friedrich von Bielfeld, *Institutions politiques*, 2d ed. (Leiden: Lucht-

mans, 1767–72), 2: 369. Bielfeld's book was a standard manual for diplomats.

17. Filippo Mazzei to King Stanislas-August of Poland, 3 July 1789, in Filippo Mazzei, *Lettres de Filippe Mazzei et du roi Stanislas-Auguste de Pologne* (Rome: Istituto Storico Italiano, 1982), 1: 306.

18. Prospectus, *Journal logographique,* n.d. (late 1790).

19. *Moniteur,* 24 November 1789 (first issue).

20. *Moniteur,* 1 December 1789.

21. *Moniteur,* 7 December 1789.

22. Cited in David I. Kulstein, "The Ideas of Charles-Joseph Panckoucke, Publisher of the *Moniteur universel,* on the French Revolution," *French Historical Studies* 4 (1966): 317.

23. *Journal des Amis de la Constitution,* 21 November 1790.

24. Prospectus, *Recueil des Décrets de L'Assemblée nationale . . . ,* in *Affiches, Annonces et Avis divers du département de l'Yonne,* 16–30 June 1791.

25. "Avis" to "Discours preliminaire," n.d. (October 1789), in *Journal des Décrets de l'Assemblée nationale, pour les Habitans des Campagnes,* vol. 1.

26. *Feuille villageoise,* 7 April 1791.

27. Ibid., 20 December 1792.

28. Edelstein, *La Feuille villageoise,* 68.

29. *Patriote françois,* 28 July 1789.

30. Ibid., 1 August 1789.

31. Ibid., 5 September 1789.

32. *Chronique de Paris,* 18 November 1791.

33. Ibid., 19 November 1791.

34. See Pierre Rétat, "Partis et factions en 1789: émergence des désignants politiques," *Mots* 16 (1988): 69–89.

35. *Journal de Perlet,* 17 December 1792.

36. On the new threats to this form of liberal journalism posed by industrialization and the rise of modern mass politics, see Habermas, *Strukturwandel der Oeffentlichkeit,* (Berlin: Luchterhand, 1962), chaps. 5 and 6

37. *Publiciste parisien,* 12 September 1789.

38. *Ami du Peuple,* 22 November 1789, 3 May 1792.

39. *Patriote françois,* 2 August 1790; *Chronique de Paris,* 27 January 1791.

40. *Ami du Roi,* 1 June 1790.

41. Ibid., 8 September 1790.

42. *Ami du Roi* [Royou edition], 1 September 1790.

43. *Actes des Apôtres,* vol. 6, nos. 166–67.

44. *Journal général de la Cour et de la Ville,* 1 June 1791; *Sottises de la semaine,* no. 11.

45. Hugh Gough, "The Provincial Jacobin Club Press during the French Revolution," *European History Quarterly* 16 (1986): 54–55.

46. On the background to the creation of the *Journal de la Montagne,* see Hugh Gough, "Les Jacobins et la presse: le 'Journal de la Montagne' (juin 1793–

brumaire an III)," in *Girondins et Jacobins*, ed. Albert Soboul (Paris: Société des Etudes robespierristes, 1980), 269–96.

47. *Journal de la Montagne*, 11 June 1793, 12 September 1793 (reports on Jacobins).

48. Ibid., 30 vent. II.

49. Ibid., 12 ger. II.

50. Aulard, *La société des Jacobins*, 4: 642 (4 January 1793).

51. *Feuille du Jour*, 6 ther. VII (24 July 1799).

52. *Europe politique*, 17 prair. V (5 June 1797).

53. *Gazette universelle*, 1 Dec. 1789; *Trompette du Père Duchêne*, no. 18.

54. *Quotidienne*, 7 flor. V (26 April 1797).

55. *Lettres bougrement patriotiques du véritable Père Duchêne*, no. 18.

56. *Ami du Peuple*, 25 April 1792; *Patriote françois*, 2 August 1790.

57. *Finissez-donc, Cher pere. Entreveu de Hyacinthe la begueule, poissarde et marchande de bagatelles, du Marché de la Place-Maubert, avec le roi, la reine et les principaux de l'état*, no. 1, n.d. (probably early 1790).

58. *Vedette* (Besançon), 19 July 1793.

59. Cited in Michel Vovelle, ed., *Marat: Textes choisis* (Paris: Editions sociales, 1975), 108.

60. *Journal de Perlet*, 21 February 1793.

61. On the modern media's dependence on sensational events, see Pierre Nora, "Le retour de l'événement," in *Faire de l'histoire*, ed. Jacques Le Goff and Pierre Nora (Paris: Gallimard, 1974), 1: 210–27. Claude Labrosse has offered a challenging analysis of the revolutionary press's literary structuring of events in Labrosse and Rétat, *Naissance du Journal*, 87–148.

62. Popkin, *News and Politics*, 83–87.

63. Pierre Rétat, "Les gazettes: de l'événement à l'histoire," *Etudes sur la presse* 3 (1978): 28.

64. Keith Baker, "Revolution," in *Political Culture of the French Revolution*, ed. Lucas, 43.

65. *Gazette de Leyde*, 21 July 1789.

66. Rétat, "*Révolutions de Paris*," 147.

67. Jean Sgard, *Les trente récits de la Journée des Tuiles* (Grenoble: Presses universitaires de Grenoble, 1988), 70–71.

68. *Gazette de Leyde*, 21 and 24 July 1789 (reports from Paris, from 13 to 17 July).

69. *Courrier d'Avignon*, 22 July 1789.

70. Hans-Jürgen Lüsebrink and Rolf Reichardt, "La prise de la Bastille comme 'événement total': Jalons pour une théorie historique de l'événement à l'époque moderne," in *L'événement* (Colloque d'Aix-en-Provence, 1983) (Marseille: Jean Laffitte, 1986), 92–94. The short-lived periodical was the *Supplément au Point du Jour*.

71. *Courier de Versailles à Paris*, 15 July 1789; *Lettres du Comte de Mirabeau à ses commettants*, no. 19, 9–24 July 1789.

72. *Observateur du Midi*, 26 and 29 September 1792, 2 October 1792. On the historical preface to Panckoucke's *Moniteur*, see Suzanne Tucoo-Chala, "Un *Moniteur universel* idéal: le supplément historique de l'an IV," in *Studies on Voltaire and the Eighteenth Century* (1990), forthcoming.

73. Bertrand Barère, speech of 22 prair. II, in *Moniteur*, 23 prair. II.

74. *Hamburg Correspondent*, 21 August 1792 (dated Paris, 13 August).

75. *Publiciste*, 25 ther. VII; *Journal des Hommes libres*, 27 ther. VII.

76. For the concept of journalistic "strategic rituals" in the presentation of news reports, see Gaye Tuchman, "Objectivity as a Strategic Ritual: An Examination of Newsmen's Notions of Objectivity," *American Journal of Sociology* 77 (1972): 660–79.

77. *Moniteur universel*, 22 June 1791.

78. *Geschichte der gegenwärtigen Zeit*, 26 June 1791; *Annales patriotiques*, 22 June 1791; *Journal de Perlet*, 22 June 1791.

79. *Journal général de la Cour et de la Ville* [*Petit Gautier*], 23 and 24 June 1791.

80. Murray, *Right-wing Press*, 122.

81. *Journal général de la Cour et de la Ville*, 27 June 1791.

82. *Chronique de Paris*, 4 Sept. 1792. Unlike most of the patriot papers, the *Chronique* did subsequently publish articles critical of the killings, such as an excerpt from Jourgniac de Saint-Méard's eyewitness account (*Chronique de Paris*, 1 November 1792).

83. *Journal de Perlet*, 8 September 1792; *Moniteur*, 6 September 1792; *Journal de la Vienne*, 17 September 1792.

84. Prospectus, *Quotidienne*, 23 September 1792.

85. Pierre Caron, *Les massacres de Septembre* (Paris: Maison du livre français, 1935), 150.

86. *Feuille du Matin*, 27 November 1792.

87. *Chronique de Paris*, 11 August 1792; *Journal de Perlet*, 16 August 1792.

88. Gough, *Newspaper Press*, 233. For examples of historians' evaluations of the press's impact on specific events, see Caron, *Massacres de Septembre*, 469; Soboul, *Sans-culottes*, 160, 174; Suzanne Petersen, *Lebensmittelfrage und revolutionäre Politik in Paris 1792–1793* (Munich: Oldenbourg, 1979), and the biographies of Marat by Gottschalk, Walter, and Massin cited in For Further Reading.

89. *Trompette du Père Duchêne*, 16, 26, and 28 July, 8 and 12 August 1792.

90. For this notion of scripting, see Keith Baker, "A Script for a French Revolution: The Political Consciousness of the abbé Mably," *Eighteenth-Century Studies* 14 (1981): 235–63.

91. *Annales patriotiques*, 12 August 1792.

92. Colin Lucas, "The Crowd and Politics," in *Political Culture of the French Revolution*, ed. Lucas, 257–85.

93. *Moniteur*, 31 July 1792; *Journal de Perlet*, 5 August 1792.

94. Bertaud, *Amis du Roi,* 243–45.
95. Jean Massin, *Marat* (Paris: Club français du livre, 1969), 202.
96. *Trompette du Père Duchêne,* 12 August 1792 (the paper did not appear on 11 August).
97. *Feuille villageoise,* 28 July 1791; Jacob, *Hébert,* 83.
98. *Annales patriotiques,* 10 and 20 July 1791.
99. *Gazette universelle,* 17 July 1791.
100. Cited in Jacob, *Hébert,* 75.
101. *Sentinelle,* 5 ger. V; *Ami des Lois,* 23 flor. V.
102. *Thé,* 3 ther. V; *Historien,* 24 ther. V.
103. *Europe politique,* 4 fruc. V.
104. Soboul, *Sans-culottes,* 588.
105. Figures from George Rudé, *The Crowd in the French Revolution* (New York: Oxford University Press, 1959), 76, 104, 123.
106. Edelstein, *La Feuille villageoise,* 211, 213.
107. *Ami du Peuple,* 3 October 1790.
108. Ibid., 6 August 1790.
109. Ibid., 22 September 1790.
110. Ibid., 14 September 1789.
111. Ibid., 18 November 1789.
112. Ibid., 7 January 1790.
113. Ibid., 17 September 1790.
114. Ibid., 16 December 1790.
115. Ibid., 25 July 1790.
116. Ibid., 13 June 1790.
117. Ibid., 14 June 1790.
118. Ibid., 10 December 1790.
119. Roughly translated: scoundrel, coward, traitor, infamous, atrocious, horrible, terrifying, criminal, knave.
120. *Ami du Peuple,* 22 November 1789.
121. Ibid., 7 November 1790.
122. Ibid., 7 January 1790.
123. On this religious aspect of Marat, see Massin, *Marat,* 5–6.
124. *Ami du Peuple,* 9 February 1791.
125. Ibid., 22 December 1790.
126. Jacques-René Hébert, *Petits Carêmes de l'abbé Maury, ou Sermons prêchés dans l'assemblée des enragés* (Paris, 1790).
127. Olivier Coquard, "La correspondance dans les journaux de Marat," *Annales historiques de la Révolution française,* 267 (1987): 64.
128. Robert M. Isherwood, *Farce and Fantasy: Popular Entertainment in Eighteenth-Century Paris* (New York: Oxford University Press, 1986), 177–78.
129. Antoine-François Lemaire, *Reclamation du Père Duchesne, contre un Libelle, intitulé: Arrivée du Père Duchêne, a Rouen.*

130. Anonymous, *Le Patriotisme du véritable Père Duchesne, ou l'Abolition de tous les faux Pères Duchesne* (probably from late 1791).

131. F. Braesch, *Le Père Duchesne d'Hébert* (Paris: Sirey, 1938), 42.

132. *Je m'en fouts*, no. 3.

133. On the role of publishers in promoting the genre, see Ouzi Helyada, "Presse populaire et diffusion des rumeurs à Paris: 1789–1791," in *Studies on Voltaire and the Eighteenth Century,* forthcoming. On Hébert's debut as a regular author of *Père Duchêne* pamphlets, see Jacob, *Hébert,* 46.

134. Hunt, *Politics, Culture, and Class,* 93–94. The representations of the Père Duchêne in revolutionary prints and caricatures deserve a study in their own right. Other artists did not copy the quasi-realistic image used in Jumel's and Hébert's paper, instead depicting Duchêne variously as a rotund, rather comic figure or even as a dog snapping at the heels of the counterrevolutionaries.

135. *Sixième Entretien, entre le père Duchêne, et Jean Bart.*

136. Walter, *Hébert,* 11–17.

137. The royalist Père Duchêne appeared in *Sixième Entretien, entre le père Duchêne, et Jean Bart.* The ultrareactionary *Actes des Apôtres* once offered a "Dialogue between the Père Duchêne, the Mère Duchêne and the abbé Duchêne, their son," in which the mother denounced her husband as "a lousy drunken dog" and the son was a priest opposed to the Civil Constitution of the Clergy (*Actes des Apôtres,* vol. 10, no. 254). The counterrevolutionary *Mère Duchesne,* by the abbé Buée, was published by the royalist printer Crapart in 1791–92. On this subgenre of the *Père Duchêne* literature, see Ouzi Helyada, "La Mère Duchesne: Masques populaires et guerre pamphlétaire 1789–1791," *Annales historiques de la Révolution française* 271 (1988): 1–16.

138. *Père Duchêne* [Hébert], 1st ser. (1790), nos. 26 and 28.

139. On the *parade,* see Jacques Guilhaumou, "Les mille langues du Père Duchêne," *Dix-huitième siècle* 18 (1986): 143–54.

140. *Père Duchêne* [abbé Jumel], no. 45.

141. See the discussion in Ferdinand Brunot, *Histoire de la langue française des origines à 1900* (Paris: Armand Colin, 1927), 10 (1): 181.

142. Prospectus, *Journal du Père Duchesne.*

143. *Remontrances bougrement patriotiques du véritable père Duchesne.*

144. See the "Lexique de la langue d'Hébert," in Walter, *Hébert,* 359–99.

145. On the *poissard* genre, see Pierre Frantz, "Travestis poissards," *Revue des Science humaines* 190 (1983): 7–20; on the usage "je parlons," see Alexander Hull, "The First Person Plural Form: *Je Parlons,*" *French Review* 62 (1988): 242–48.

146. On the development of prerevolutionary art criticism attributed to ordinary men and women, see Bernadette Fort, "Voice of the Public: The Carnivalization of Salon Art in Prerevolutionary Pamphlets," *Eighteenth-Century Studies* 22 (1989): 368–94.

147. *Lettres bougrement patriotiques du véritable Père Duchêne*, no. 17. The elimination of the distinction between *tu* and *vous* was not a spontaneous expression of revolutionary egalitarianism: philosophes such as Voltaire and Montesquieu had suggested it. Louise de Kéralio, a woman journalist, was apparently the first revolutionary writer to propose the idea, in December 1790 (Brunot, *Histoire*, 9[2]: 689–90).

148. *Père Duchêne* [abbé Jumel], no. 14 bis.

149. *Père Duchêne* [Hébert], no. 242. "Siffler la linotte" was one of Hébert's terms for incarceration. On Hébert's role in the *journée* of 31 May 1793, see Jacob, *Hébert*, 152–61.

150. Jacques Mallet du Pan, *Memoirs and Correspondence of Mallet du Pan*, ed. A. Sayous (London: Bentley, 1852), 2: 511.

151. Jacob, *Hébert*, 197–207.

152. *Père Duchêne* [Hébert], no. 249.

153. Ibid., no. 347.

154. Jacques Guilhaumou, "L'Idéologie du *Père Duchêne*, les forces adjuvantes (14 juillet–6 septembre 1793)," *Mouvement social* 85 (1973): 115.

155. *Père Duchêne* [Hébert], nos. 299 and 296.

156. Jacob, *Hébert*, 353.

157. *Père Duchêne* [Hébert], no. 264.

158. Ibid., no. 269.

159. Ibid., nos. 317 and 318.

160. Ibid., no. 317.

161. Caron, *Paris pendant la terreur*, 2: 282–83 (10 January 1794), and 3: 294 (31 January 1794).

162. *Journal de la Montagne*, 18 plu. II.

163. Lynn Hunt, *Politics, Culture and Class*, 95–107.

164. Jacob, *Hébert*, 257, 339.

165. *Père Duchêne* [Coesnon-Pellerin], no. 43.

166. See Robert Darnton's comments on French folk literature in *The Great Cat Massacre* (New York: Vintage, 1984), 61–65.

CHAPTER 4

1. Brissot, *Mémoire aux Etats-Généraux*, 15–17, 53. On Blackstone's definition of press freedom, see Levy, *Emergence of a Free Press*, 12–13.

2. Gerd van den Heuvel, *Der Freiheitsbegriff der Französische Revolution* (Göttingen: Vandenhoeck and Ruprecht, 1988), 100–103, 108.

3. Söderhjelm, *Régime de la presse*, 1: 114–26. On the evolution of British press law in the eighteenth century, see Levy, *Emergence of a Free Press*.

4. *Journal des Clubs*, 17–24 December 1790.

5. Söderhjelm, *Régime de la presse*, 1: 146–48.

6. Ibid., 1: 221–22, 247.

7. Speech to Convention, 19 April 1793, in *Oeuvres de Maximilien Robespierre*,

ed. Marc Bouloiseau and Albert Soboul (Paris: Société des Etudes robespierristes, 1938–58), 9: 452.

8. Bertrand Barère, speech to Convention, 22 prair. II, published in *Moniteur*, 23 prair. II.

9. Cited in Claude Perroud, "Roland et la presse subventionnée," *Révolution française* 62 (1912): 318.

10. Robespierre, *Lettres à ses commettans*, in *Oeuvres*, 5: 77 (23 November 1792).

11. Pierre Caron, "Les publications officieuses du ministère de l'intérieur en 1793 et 1794," *Revue d'histoire moderne et contemporaine* 14 (1910): 7, 15, 25–27.

12. Bourdon de l'Oise, speech to Convention, 23 vent. II, cited in Caron, "Publications officieuses," 23.

13. Aulard, "La presse officieuse pendant la Terreur," 227–28.

14. Jacques Guilhaumou, "Les journaux parisiens dans les luttes révolutionnaires de 1793: presse d'opinion, presse de salut public et presse pamphlétaire," in *Révolution du Journal*, ed. Rétat and Sgard.

15. Articles 353 and 355 of Constitution of 1795, in Jacques Godechot, *Les Constitutions de la France depuis 1789* (Paris: Garnier, 1970).

16. Söderhjelm, *Régime de la presse*, 2: 77.

17. Jeremy Popkin, "Les journaux républicains, 1795–1799," *Revue d'histoire moderne et contemporaine* 34 (1984): 145–48.

18. *Ami des Lois*, 29 fruc. V.

19. Laurence W. Stoll, "The *Bureau politique* and the Management of the Popular Press" (Ph.D. diss., University of Wisconsin, 1975), 59–63, 80–81, 84.

20. *Ami de la liberté*, 20 fruc. VII.

21. AN, Minister of Police, circular letter of 7 vend. VI, in F 7 3448B, dr. 3589B; anonymous "Rapport sur les journaux" in AN, AF III, 45, no. 250.

22. For a convincing exposition of the process by which the postthermidorian republicans moved to limit the expression of public opinion in order to consolidate what they saw as the essential achievements of the Revolution, see Werner Giesselmann, *Die brumairianische Elite* (Stuttgart: Klett, 1977), 298–300.

23. Pierre Daunou, *Rapport fait par Daunou au nom d'une commission spéciale, sur la répression des délits de la presse* (Paris: Imprimerie nationale, 1796), 4, 15.

24. Germaine de Staël, *Des circonstances actuelles qui peuvent terminer la Révolution, et des principes qui doivent fonder la République en France*, ed. J. Vienot (Paris: Fischbacher, 1906), 35. On the Directory-era debate about the press, see Jeremy D. Popkin, "The Newspaper Press in French Political Thought, 1789–99," in *Studies in Eighteenth-Century Culture* 10 (1981), 113–33.

25. Jeremy D. Popkin, "The Directory and the Republican Press: the Case of the *Ami des Lois*," in *History of European Ideas* 10 (1989), 429–42.

26. "Minute sur journaux," 14 bru. VIII, in AN, F 7 3452.
27. On the press in the Napoleonic period, see André Cabanis, *La presse sous le Consulat et l'Empire (1799–1815)* (Paris: Société des Etudes robespierristes, 1975).
28. Marc Martin, *Les origines de la presse militaire en France à la fin de l'ancien régime et sous la Révolution* (Vincennes: Ministère de la Défense, 1975), 342–53.
29. See Robert Holtman, *Napoleonic Propaganda* (Baton Rouge: Louisiana State University Press, 1950).
30. *Journal des Débats*, 2 May 1804.
31. There were several efforts during the Revolution to create periodicals either written by or addressed to women, but the only one that lasted for more than a few issues was the *Journal des Dames et des Modes*, an apolitical fashion magazine founded in 1797. Evelyne Sullerot, *Histoire de la presse féminine en France, des origines à 1848* (Paris: Armand Colin, 1966), 43–66, 87.
32. Furet, *Interpreting the French Revolution*, 49.
33. Bronislaw Baczko, "The New Symbolism: Presentation," in *Political Culture of the French Revolution*, ed. Lucas, 95–96.
34. Brissot, *Mémoire aux Etats-Généraux*, 10.
35. For a recent review of this controversy and a renewed attempt to resolve it (without reference to the press), see Michael S. Lewis-Beck, Anne Hildreth, and Alan B. Spitzer, "Was There a Girondin Faction in the National Convention, 1792–1793?" *French Historical Studies* 15 (1988): 519–36.
36. Murray, *Right-Wing Press*, 126–27.
37. Rétat, *"Révolutions de Paris,"* 142.
38. Cited in Peter Kenez, "Lenin and the Freedom of the Press," in *Bolshevik Culture*, ed. Abbott Gleason, Peter Kenez, and Richard Stites (Bloomington: Indiana University Press, 1985), 143.

FOR FURTHER READING

The basic materials for the study of the press during the French Revolution are the newspapers themselves. The largest collection by far of original revolutionary newspapers is that of the Bibliothèque nationale in Paris. Volume 5 of André Martin and Gerard Walter's *Catalogue de l'histoire de la Révolution française* lists the library's holdings and constitutes an invaluable guide for the identification of papers in other collections as well. The Bibliothèque nationale's holdings are far from exhaustive, however. Titles or issues missing from its holdings must often be sought in other Paris libraries, such as the Bibliothèque de l'Arsenal, the Bibliothèque historique de la Ville de Paris, and the newspaper collection of the Archives nationales. In the English-speaking world, there are large collections at the British Library, the Newberry Library in Chicago, the New York Public Library, and the Harvard College (Widener) Library.

In recent years an increasing number of newspapers from the revolutionary period have been reproduced in facsimile editions or on microfilm and microfiche. The Association pour la conservation et la réproduction photographique de presse, located at the Bibliothèque nationale, can supply microfilms of two hundred titles. Various publishers have put out reprints of such important papers as the *Ami du Peuple*, the *Révolutions de France et de Brabant*, and Hébert's *Père Duchêne*. The *French Revolution Research Collection and Videodisk*, in preparation by Pergamon Press, will include an important selection of newspapers from the period.

There is no comprehensive guide to archival documents concerning the press. Relevant items can be found in several of the revolutionary-era series in the Archives nationales (Paris), particularly F 7, F 18, AF III, and BB 16 and BB 18, but there is undoubtedly much material in other series as well. Other archival materials are scattered: some can be found in the Archives départementales de la Seine, in the Archives de la Préfecture de Police, the manuscript collections of the major French libraries, and various departmental archives and libraries.

Apart from the Martin and Walter catalogue, mentioned earlier, there are two other basic guides to the press of the period, both of which have retained some utility because they give capsule descriptions of the papers as well as bibliographic data: Eugène Hatin, *Bibliographie historique et critique de la presse périodique française* (Paris: Didot, 1866), still the only printed inventory of the provincial press, and Maurice Tourneux, *Bibliographie de l'histoire de Paris pendant la Révolution française*, 5 vols. (Paris: Imprimerie nouvelle, 1894). The Institut français de presse is currently compiling a bibliography of the provincial press that will, when completed, finally replace Hatin's work in this area. Pierre Rétat, *Les journaux de 1789. Bibliographie critique* (Paris: CNRS, 1988), gives a detailed description of the papers published in 1789 (including those founded earlier). Ouzi Elyada, *Presse populaire et feuilles volantes de la Révolution à Paris: 1789–1792* (Paris: Société des Etudes robespierristes, 1989) is a critical bibliography of the *Père Duchêne* publications and related papers.

The earliest attempt at a general history of the press during the Revolution, Léonard Gallois, *Histoire des Journaux et des Journalistes de la Révolution française*, 2 vols. (Paris: Société de l'Industrie fraternelle, 1845), shows the link between the revolutionary journalists and nineteenth-century radicalism, but it is factually unreliable. The relevant volumes of Eugène Hatin's classic *Histoire politique et littéraire de la presse en France*, published in 1859–61, on the other hand, still have some real value thanks to Hatin's encyclopedic knowledge of the various papers. The other older general histories of the press have been superseded by Jacques Godechot's survey of "La presse française sous la Révolution et l'Empire" in volume 1 of Claude Bellanger et al., *Histoire générale de la presse française* (1969), which synthesizes the scholarly literature as of the mid-1960s and includes a good bibliography. Hugh Gough, *The Newspaper Press in the French Revolution* (1988), follows the same essentially chronological and political pattern as Godechot, but adds considerably to our knowledge of the provincial papers and includes an up-to-date bibliography.

Most of the major journalists of the revolutionary period have been the subject of one or more biographies, although too often studies of figures who were both journalists and political leaders give short shrift to the former aspect of their subjects' careers. Among the more interesting biographic studies from the point of view of journalism history are Jean-Paul Bertaud, *Camille et Lucile Desmoulins* (1986); Eloise Ellery, *Brissot de Warville: A Study in the History of the French Revolution* (1915; reprint 1970); Louis R. Gottschalk, *Jean Paul Marat: A Study in Radicalism* (1927; reprint 1967); Louis Jacob, *Hébert: Le Père Duchesne chef des sans-culottes* (1960); Jacques Janssens, *Camille Desmoulins: Le premier républicain de France* (1973); Hélène Maspéro-Clerc, *Un journaliste contre-révolutionnaire: Jean-Gabriel Peltier* (1973); Jean Massin, *Marat* (1960); R. B. Rose, *Gracchus Babeuf: The First Revolutionary Communist* (1978); Gérard Walter, *Hébert et le 'Père Duchesne'* (1946), and the same author's *Marat* (1933; reprint 1960). The one major biography of a Revolutionary-era newspaper publisher is Suzanne Tucoo-Chala, *Charles-Joseph Panckoucke et l'imprimerie française* (1977). The memoirs of writers who were journalists during the period generally skip the details of the newspaper business; the major exception is Charles Lacretelle, *Dix années d'épreuves pendant la Révolution* (1842).

The past two decades have seen a number of major studies of the period's newspapers, primarily from an institutional and political perspective. Particularly useful are those monographs that take in a number of related papers, such as Jean-Paul Bertaud, *Les Amis du Roi* (1984); Jack R. Censer, *Prelude to Power: The Parisian Radical Press, 1789–91* (1976); Gary Kates, *The 'Cercle social,' the Girondins, and the French Revolution* (1985); William J. Murray, *The Right-Wing Press in the French Revolution: 1789–92* (1986); and Jeremy D. Popkin, *The Right-Wing Press in France, 1792–1800* (1980), and on a specialized sector of the press, Marc Martin, *Les origines de la presse militaire en France à la fin de l'ancien régime et sous la Révolution* (1975). There is a brief treatment of periodicals for women in Evelyne Sullerot, *Histoire de la presse féminine en France, des origines à 1848* (1966). Monographs on individual papers include Melvin Edelstein, *La Feuille villageoise: Communication et modernisation dans les régions rurales pendant la Révolution* (1977); Max Fajn, *The 'Journal des Hommes libres de tous les pays,' 1792–1800* (1976); René Gérard, *Un journal de province sous la Révolution. Le 'Journal de Marseille' de Ferréol Beaugeard (1781–1797)* (1964); and Joanna Kitchen, *Un Journal 'Philosophique': La Décade* (1965). On the legal status of the press there is the old but solid work of Alma Söderhjelm, *Le Régime de la presse pendant la Révolution française*, 2 vols. (1900–1901). The Napoleonic press regime is described in André Cabanis, *La presse sous le Consulat et l'Empire* (1975).

Studies of the press during the French Revolution are just beginning to reflect the impact of the new historiographical interest in the French Revolution as a cultural, rather than a political or institutional, event. Robert Darnton and Daniel Roche, eds., *Revolution in Print: The Press in France, 1775–1800* (1989), includes essays on a variety of print media during the Revolution. Claude Labrosse and Pierre Rétat, *Naissance du Journal révolutionnaire, 1789* (1989), offers a stimulating and original interpretation of the journals of the early Revolution as literary texts. The volume on *La Mort de Marat*, edited by Jean-Claude Bonnet (1986), contains a number of suggestive essays illuminating Marat's journalistic work. The articles of Jacques Guilhaumou, widely scattered in a number of French journals and volumes of conference proceedings, exemplify a quantitative and language-centered approach to the study of the press. Jack R. Censer, "The Political Engravings of the *Révolutions de France et de Brabant*, 1789 to 1791," *Eighteenth-Century Life* 5 (1979): 105–24, is a unique look at the use of illustrations in the press. When published, the proceedings of the two major international colloquia on the press and the French Revolution held at Haifa in May 1988 (to appear in 1990 in the journal *Studies on Voltaire and the Eighteenth Century*) and at Vizille in June–July 1988 (to be published in 1989 under the title *La Révolution du journal, 1789–1794*) will provide overviews of the variety of ways in which historians and other scholars are now approaching this subject. *History of European Ideas* 10 (1989), no. 4, is a special issue devoted to the history of the revolutionary press.

Index

Library of Congress Cataloging-in-Publication Data
Popkin, Jeremy D., 1948–
Revolutionary news: the press in France, 1789–1799/Jeremy D. Popkin.
p. cm.—(Bicentennial reflections on the French Revolution)
ISBN 0-8223-0984-X.—ISBN 0-8223-0997-1 (pbk.)
1. Journalism—France—History—18th century. 2. French
newspapers—History—18th century. 3. Revolutionary literature—
Publishing—France—History—18th century. 4. Press and politics—
France—History—18th century. 5. France—History—Revolution,
1789–1799. I. Title. II. Series.
PN5176.P59 1990
074'.09'033—dc20   89-28511